BROOKLANDS
BOOKS

FORD
AUTOMOBILES
1949-1959

Compiled by
R.M. Clarke

ISBN 1 870642 767

Distributed by
Brooklands Book Distribution Ltd.
'Holmerise', Seven Hills Road,
Cobham, Surrey, England
Printed in Hong Kong

CONTENTS

ACKNOWLEDGEMENTS

Brooklands Books publish source books. There is nothing original within their covers and their purpose is to make available to today's owners the road tests and other technical stories that were printed about a marque when it was in production.

Amongst our 350 titles are three others on 50's Fords. One covering the Fairlanes another reporting on the original 2-seater Thunderbird and finally one on the larger Thunderbird introduced in 1958.

The fifties have become an important period for motor enthusiasts and should you doubt this, visit one of the great automobile get-togethers at Carlisle or Hershey and see how well they are represented.

We are guided in our choice of subjects by popular demand and recently have produced 50's titles on Cadillac, Buick, Packard, Studebaker and Chevrolet, and have currently at the printers 'Oldsmobile Automobiles 1955-1963'.

Our books are printed in small numbers as works of reference for those that indulge in the hobby of automobile collecting and restoration. We exist firstly because there is a need by owners for this information and secondly because the publishers of the world's leading automotive journals generously assist us by allowing us to include their copyright articles in our series. We are indebted in this instance to the management of Auto Age, Auto Sport Review, Car Life, Motor, Motor Life, Motor Trend, Road & Track, Science and Mechanics and Speed Age for their ongoing support.

R.M. Clarke

The FORD Six-cylinder Tudor Sedan

A Popular-priced American Automobile with Outstanding Performance and Behaviour on the Road

GENUINE enthusiasm is an emotion rarely aroused in those whose regular duty it is to conduct road tests of new cars, since, apparently, no vehicle yet built combines all the virtues displayed separately by different models. Enthusiasm was certainly aroused recently, however, in two members of our staff whose pleasure it was to spend several days covering a substantial and varied mileage in the latest " Forty Niner " six-cylinder Ford.

The test car was taken over as representing the lowest price group of full-sized American automobiles, and was put at our disposal by the Ford Motor Co. (Belgium) S.A. It was a car which had been assembled at Antwerp from American components, using local upholstery materials, and with a slightly increased number of spot welds in the body structure provided as a concession to the atrocious road surfaces encountered in parts of Belgium. A regular production model loaned at short notice, it carried none of the optional de luxe equipment available with these cars except for an interior heater.

Love at First Sight

First impressions of the car, interesting, if not always lasting, in this instance were very favourable. Immediately on taking the wheel in the midst of Brussels traffic, it was evident that the driving position was good, the controls responsive to a light touch, and the engine smoothly willing. Growing familiarity with the car, so far from revealing flies in the ointment, steadily increased our respect for a simple but very soundly engineered automobile.

Unfamiliar in Britain, the current U.S.-built Ford, in its 3.9-litre V-8 and 3.7-litre six-cylinder alternative forms, is apparently of orthodox modern layout. Specification features include a side-valve engine mounted well forward, I.F.S. by wishbones and coil springs, a three-piece steering track rod, box section chassis frame, open propeller shaft, and semi-elliptic springs linked to a hypoid rear axle. Body lines are relatively bluff, with the short bonnet matched by a capacious luggage locker. The recipe is sound and fashionable, but depends for its success on proper planning of details.

As has been mentioned, the driving position is good, with everything placed really conveniently. The bench seat is of comfortable height and shape for long journeys, and from it the driver has very satisfactory visibility over the short bonnet with its clearly defined spine. There is generous width for three people to occupy the front seat, and armrests are provided on each side at just the right height for comfort; cloth upholstery may not facilitate sliding into the seat, but does steady the driver and passenger on winding roads.

The twin-spoke steering wheel

AN AMERICAN IN BELGIUM.—Stopped near Comblain au Pont, on a winding road through the Ardennes, the 1949 Ford shows its characteristic recognition features. Six- and eight-cylinder models are distinguished by numerals on the "bullet" motif.

MADE TO MEASURE.—Seat, armrest, wheel and pedals in correct relative positions, accessible controls for gears on the right and starter on the left, and clearly visible instruments, are points which make the Ford attractive to keen drivers.

is of unusual section, giving very comfortable hand-holds on either the rim or the thick spokes. Geared at four-and-a-half turns of the wheel from one extreme to the other of a generous range of travel, the steering needs appreciable movements on corners, but extreme lightness and the correct placing of the wheel result in this being no noticeable disadvantage. The effort required for steering is at all times extremely light, and no road-wheel reaction is felt on bumpy surfaces, yet there is a quite adequate amount of self-centring action.

The steering column mounted gear lever exactly matches the steering, in that it is well placed and while its travel is appreciable it operates smoothly with but the pressure of a single finger. Synchromesh mechanism effectively facilitates engagement of second and

encounter wet roads during our test, occasional unforeseen patches of ice on winding Ardennes roads held no terrors.

It may be noted from our data that, empty, the car carries 58 per cent. of its weight upon the front wheels, and only 42 per cent. on the driving wheels. Such a distribution of weight is widely acknowledged as excellent for stability on straight roads, but has not hitherto been associated with notable controllability on corners—the evolution of a car of such all-round merit reflects great credit on the reorganized Ford engineering department.

Body Details

Perfection, alas, is not in any one car, and low selling prices cannot be attained without certain sacrifices. A few details must be criticized, such as doors which require to be slammed very firmly before they shut properly and which lack good hand-holds for this purpose. Trafficators on the test car were controlled by a rather remote facia switch, with no self-cancelling device, interior lighting comprised but a single lamp on one door pillar, and the sealed-beam head lamps as usual set a night speed limit of about 60 m.p.h. Instrument lighting was excellently clear and non-dazzling, invisible light causing green figures and red pointers to glow luminous: the speedometer, deeply recessed in a dial before the driver, is, incidentally, almost invisible to passengers.

The five-seater body of the test car was of two-door type, with four windows which wound down completely out of sight. Simply but not displeasingly finished with cloth and grey painted metalwork, it seats three in front, gives ample space for two passengers in the rear seat, and has a vast luggage locker.

This latest American design of Ford represents a complete departure from the previous practice of its manufacturers. It is a more complex car than its predecessors, as is evident from study of a lubrication chart, but seen on the assembly line its detail excellence is evident and it is backed by a service organization whose efficiency is proverbial. Judged by its all-round performance on the road, the " Forty Niner " model is certainly an amazing example of how excellent a modern low-priced automobile can be.

Ford Road Test—Contd.

third gears and, like the single dry-plate clutch, escapes notice by being inconspicuously efficient.

Brakes are light in action, especially at moderate car speeds, without being in any sense fierce. Equally, they give confidence by their ability to check the car from high cruising speeds without causing instability, although emergency braking with the car lightly loaded induces locking of the rear wheels. It is a surprising yet true fact that the only control on the whole car requiring real effort for its operation is the button actuating a single rather unmelodious horn.

Concerning performance, the figures carefully observed and recorded on the data page speak for themselves so clearly that little need be said concerning them. For a car which, in its country or origin, is classed as cheap to accelerate from rest to 50 m.p.h. in under 11 seconds, and attain a genuine speed of 90 m.p.h., is indeed excellent. This high performance, further, is combined with a fuel consumption which certainly cannot be regarded as extravagant.

Fast Cruising

How performance is obtained cannot be expressed in terms of cold figures, but is indeed an important matter. The six-cylinder Ford engine is notably smooth and docile, idling iconspicuously when the car is at rest, pulling smoothly down to extremely low speeds in top gear, yet never becoming fussy on the open road.

At low speeds, a minor flat-spot was evident in the carburation of the test car if the throttle was snapped fully open, and the published figures show that top gear acceleration is best at 30 m.p.h. and above: the engine of the test car was running very cool, and some blanking of the radiator might have eliminated this hesitation. Even with it, however, the urge at low speeds was outstandingly good, and made town driving almost entirely a top gear matter. Outside town it is difficult to name an ideal cruising speed, so effortless was the Ford at all times, but a genuine 75 m.p.h. is a comfortable everyday pace, leaving plenty of speed in reserve for occasions when it is necessary to hurry.

Apart from the silent willingness of the engine, the low level of wind noise inside the car is greatly appreciated on the open road. Much of our test mileage was over rough cobblestone surfaces, when the total freedom from squeaks or rattles of any kind was also very noteworthy, although at 80 m.p.h. cruising speeds on such roads rear-seat passengers felt and heard some vibration of the metal floor below their feet.

Initial impressions of the suspension characteristics gained in town were of just that softness popularly associated with U.S. designs, the car paying singularly little attention to bumps encountered at low speeds. On the open road the car retains almost precisely the same smooth, absolutely level riding characteristics: there is only a very restrained rise and fall of the complete car over the worst surfaces, clever design having apparently evolved a springing system which requires very little damping to give high-speed stability.

Cornering qualities cannot be said to have suffered in the quest for riding comfort. Splayed rear shock absorbers, and an anti-roll torsion bar linking the front springs, have effectively checked any unpleasant traces of sway, roll or other undesirable characteristics.

Cornering ability is inseparable from general handling qualities, and it is these which give the Ford much of its charm. Mechanically, the steering mechanism is not by any means rigid, yet the driver can at all times place the car just where he wants it—not merely on open corners, but also when traffic conditions call for a sudden change of course. Cobbled or bumpy surfaces, steep cambers, fast or slow corners, all proved unable to disturb the balance of the car, and although we did not

Make: Ford **Type:** 6-Cyl. "Forty Niner" Tudor Sedan

Makers: The Ford Motor Company, Dearborn, Michigan, U.S.A.

(Test car submitted by The Ford Motor Company (Belgium), S.A., Antwerp.)

Dimensions and Seating

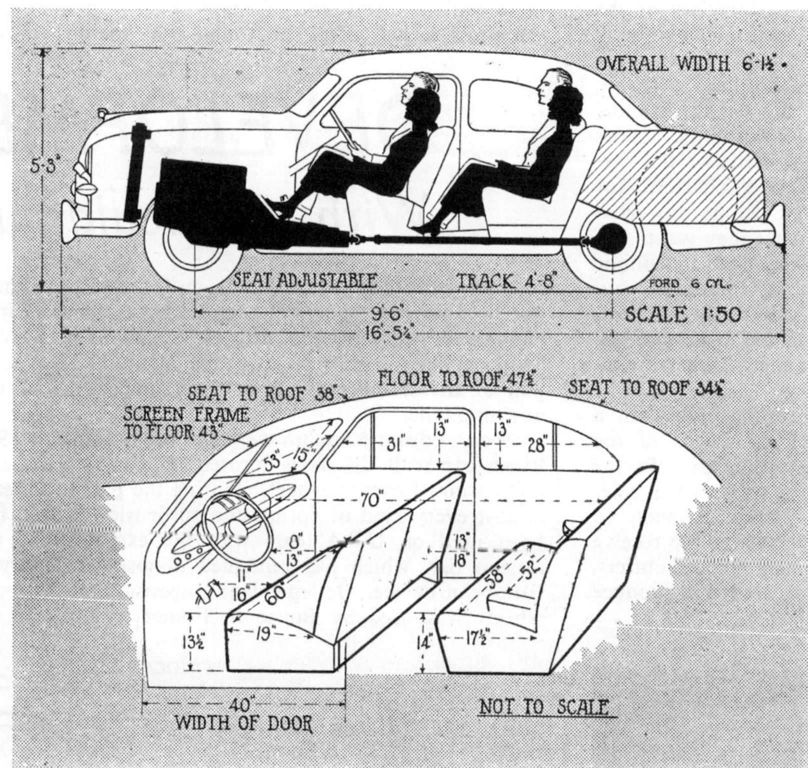

In Brief

Price : Ex - works Detroit, $1,425.50. Equivalent at £1 = $4.03, £353.

Capacity .. .. 3,700 c.c.

Road weight unladen 27½ cwt.

Front/rear weight distribution 58/42

Laden weight as tested 31 cwt.

Fuel consumption 18.4 m.p.g.

Maximum speed .. 90.2 m.p.h.

Maximum speed on 1 in 20 gradient .. .. 77 m.p.h.

Maximum top gear gradient 1 in 8½

Acceleration, 10-30 on top 9.4 secs.

0-50 through gears 10.6 secs.

Gearing : 21.6 m.p.h. in top at 1,000 r.p.m. 73.5 m.p.h. at 2,500 ft. per minute piston speed.

Specification

Engine

Cylinders	6
Bore	.. 83.8 mm.
Stroke	.. 111.8 mm.
Cubic capacity ..	.. 3,700 c.c.
Piston area	51.4 sq. ins.
Valves	.. side
Compression ratio	.. 6.8
Max. power	.. 95 b.h.p.
at	3,300 r.p.m
B.h.p. per sq. in. piston area	.. 1.85
Piston speed at max. b.h.p.	2,420 ft./min.
Carburetter	Downdraught
Ignition	.. 6-volt coil
Sparking plugs 14 mm.	Ford 7 RA-12405
Fuel pump	.. Mechanical

Transmission

Clutch	Single dry plate
Top gear ..	..3.73 (optional 3.54 or 4.10)
2nd gear	5.99
1st gear	10.5
Propeller shaft	Open Tubular (needle roller universals)
Final drive	Hypoid bevel

Chassis

Brakes	Hydraulic
Brake drum diameter	.. 10 ins.
Friction lining area	176 sq. ins.
Suspension	Coil and wishbone I.F.S., half-elliptic rear
Tyres	..6.00 x 16
Steering gear	Worm and roller

Performance factors (at laden weight as tested)

Piston area, sq. ins. per ton	33.1
Brake lining area, sq. ins. per ton ..	113.5
Litres per ton-mile	3,320

Test Conditions

Cool, slight cross-wind, dry concrete surface. Belgium pump petrol.

Test Data

ACCELERATION TIMES on Two Upper Ratios

	Top	2nd
10-30 m.p.h.	9.4 secs.	5.4 secs.
20-40 m.p.h.	8.7 secs.	5.3 secs.
30-50 m.p.h.	8.8 secs.	6.0 secs.
40-60 m.p.h.	9.4 secs.	—
50-70 m.p.h.	13.1 secs.	—
60-80 m.p.h.	21.1 secs.	—

ACCELERATION TIMES Through Gears

0-30 m.p.h.	4.8 secs.
0-40 m.p.h.	7.7 secs.
0-50 m.p.h.	10.6 secs.
0-60 m.p.h.	16.0 secs.
0-70 m.p.h.	23.6 secs.
0-80 m.p.h.	36.8 secs.
Standing quarter-mile ..	20.2 secs.

BRAKES at 30 m.p.h.

0.30 g (= 100 ft. stopping distance) with 25 lb. pedal pressure.

0.81 g (= 37 ft. stopping distance) with 50 lb. pedal pressure.

0.96 g (= 31½ ft. stopping distance) with 60 lb. pedal pressure.

FUEL CONSUMPTION

Overall consumption for 191 miles, driven hard, 10.4 gallons, equals 18.4 m.p.g.

27.5 m.p.g. at constant 30 m.p.h.

25.5 m.p.g. at constant 40 m.p.h.

23.0 m.p.g. at constant 50 m.p.h.

20.5 m.p.g. at constant 60 m.p.h.

17.5 m.p.g. at constant 70 m.p.h.

14.0 m.p.g. at constant 80 m.p.h.

HILL CLIMBING

Max. top gear speed on 1 in 20, 77 m.p.h.

Max. top gear speed on 1 in 15, 71 m.p.h.

Max. top gear speed on 1 in 10, 57 m.p.h.

Max. gradient climbable on top gear, 1 in 8½ (Tapley 260 lb. per ton).

Max. gradient climbable on 2nd gear, 1 in 5¼ (Tapley 425 lb. per ton).

MAXIMUM SPEEDS

Flying Quarter-mile

Mean of four opposite runs .. 90.2 m.p.h.

Best time equals .. .. 90.9 m.p.h.

Speed in Gears

Max. speed in 2nd gear .. 65 m.p.h.

Max. speed in 1st gear .. 39 m.p.h.

STEERING

Left- and right-hand lock .. 41 ft.

4¼ turns of steering wheel, lock to lock.

Maintenance

Fuel tank: 14 gallons. **Sump:** 6¾ pints, S.A.E., 20 Summer, S.A.E. 10 Winter. **Gearbox:** 3½ pints, S.A.E. 80 E.P. gear oil. **Rear axle:** 3 pints, S.A.E. 90 Hypoid gear oil. **Radiator:** 27 pints. **Chassis lubrication:** By grease gun to 26 points every 1,000 miles. **Ignition timing:** T.D.C. static (1/6 mark on vibration damper). **Spark plug gap:** 0.030 in. **Contact breaker gap:** 0.024 in. to 0.026 in. **Front wheel toe-in:** $\frac{1}{16}$ in. to $\frac{1}{8}$ in. **Camber angle:** $-\frac{1}{4}°$ to $+\frac{3}{4}°$. **Caster angle:** Zero to $-\frac{3}{4}°$. **King pin inclination:** 5°. **Tyre pressures:** Front, 28 lb., rear, 25 lb. **Battery:** 6-volt, 100 amp-hour. **Generator:** 6-volt, 30 amp.-hour. **Lamp bulbs:** Parking, number plate, interior and luggage boot, 3 candle power; tail/stop lamps, 3/21 candle power. Headlamps, sealed beam-type units.

Ref. U.S./37/49

AMERICAN engineers are fortunate in having access to one of the finest collections of historical motor cars ever assembled; these are housed in the Edison Museum at Dearborn and have been preserved by a remarkable act of foresight by the late Henry Ford. He chose only vehicles which embody significant engineering or styling features and, extending as they do over many decades, this collection forms, as it were, a panorama in which we can see how motor-cars have been affected by social and economic factors which have together determined the needs of the car-buying public. The word " need " is emphasized, for too many have learned, too late, that people buy what they need but by no means always what they want.

For example, it is often said to-day that the public want " a light dependable car without trimmings," but automobile manufacturers have not arbitrarily increased the size and cost of their products in the face of public resistance. Quite simply they have met an overwhelming need for bigger cars.

Most large manufacturing organizations maintain a number of channels through which the needs of the customer are made known to the producers. In the case of the Ford Motor Company, we have a sales organization in constant touch with the customers, we take heed of the opinion of their agents, and we receive valuable opinions from the component manufacturers. who supply us with many of the parts needed to produce cars in large quantities.

We have, of course, our own market research specialists and we also receive thousands of letters each year written to us by Ford users. The automobile designer must be guided by the information gained in these various ways and if many earlier designs are examined it will often be found that the reason for

DEVELOPMENT
With Particular Refer

commercial failure resided not in technical weakness but because ideas good in themselves came too early, too late or were insufficiently developed to meet contemporary need. In most cases the energy and imagination of the technician outran the requirements of the buying public.

In our Edison Museum we have, for example, a 1910 Brush car with the axles located by radius rods, and coil springs for each wheel. During the past fifty years almost every kind of spring and suspension system has been used on U.S.A. cars with the exception of the torsion bar, which has remained almost exclusively a European device. Independent suspension to the front wheels was used by Bollee in France as far back as

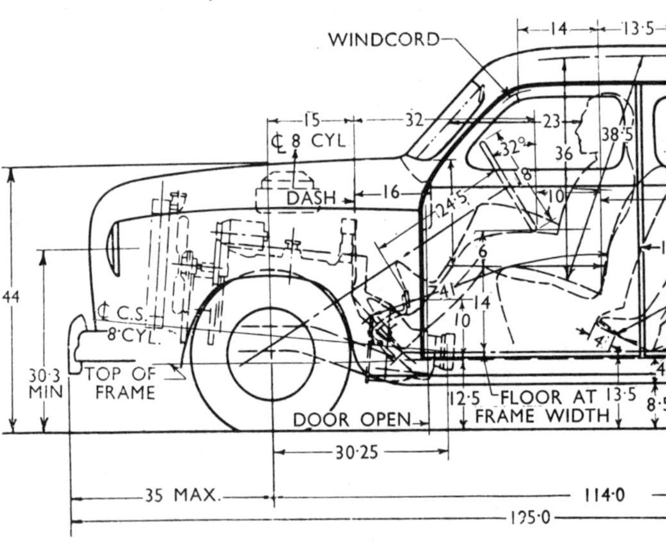

1898, and great interest was aroused in America by the Italian Lancia car in 1922. The I.F.S., however, was not adopted by U.S.A. constructors until 1934 and the delay is to be explained by the lack of real need, for until this time motorists used their cars for comparatively short journeys, and women did not usually drive.

Since then there has been an ever mounting need for a better ride, which can only be provided by independent suspension to the front wheels.

Another interesting piece of history is to be seen in the steering-column-mounted gear lever used on the 1898 model Benz. This arrangement was used by many other European companies and by the George N. Pierce

FINAL CHOICE.—The centre picture shows the production model Ford, whilst above and below are models of slightly modified versions which were runners up for this honour.

Company on their Great Arrow car made in 1904. With the increase from one to two indirect gears and the greater range of motion required in the lever, the advent of the unit construction engine and gearbox, and the transfer from right-hand to left-hand steering, the central gear lever became so much more attractive from a simplicity and cost viewpoint that it became universal.

Recently, however, public need for greater space in the front compartment has sent the lever back to the steering column, where it will remain as long as manual gear changing remains with us.

We see, however, from the museum specimen of the 1909 Carter car, that an infinitely variable gear (in this case by friction faces) was featured 40 years ago, and,

and DESIGN:

ce to the 1949 Ford

in another model built in the same year, Schact used a rear-mounted horizontally opposed engine.

Coming to more recent times, the Museum has an example of a car produced jointly by Pierce-Arrow and the Aluminum Corporation of America to the designs of the late L. H. Pomeroy. This car had a wheelbase of 11 ft. 1 in., and a 4-litre power unit, but weighed only 27 cwt. complete with a large and roomy saloon body. Of this weight 85 per cent. was in light metal, and 10 cars were built, several of which ran

In planning and conceiving any engineering programme a definite series of objectives or ground rules must be established so that all concerned are working for the same results—and as a team.

The new Ford cars were designed to achieve the following objectives:—

(1) A car of the same general package size or overall dimensions as the previous model, appreciating that the Ford car must maintain its position in its price class.

(2) Completely new styling of the most advanced design.

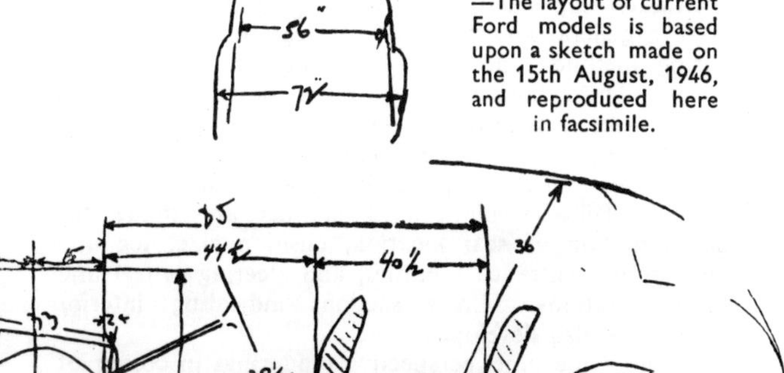

DESIGNER'S DOODLE.—The layout of current Ford models is based upon a sketch made on the 15th August, 1946, and reproduced here in facsimile.

(3) A roomier, wider interior, taking full advantage of the car width.

(4) Providing the most advantageous ride and general car handling.

(5) A lower car without sacrificing ease of entrance to either front or rear seats.

(6) Reduction in car weight due to more efficient design and use of materials, with resulting advantages in car performance and from a manufacturing standpoint.

(7) Better visibility.

(8) Adequate engine capacity with improved gasoline economy.

With the above broad fundamentals in mind a rough sketch of the car was made which indicated basic requirements as to seating arrangement, adequate leg and head room, and other basic dimensions. Although this may look like a mere "doodle," it was actually the first step in creating the new Ford. It is dated August 15, 1946, and actually the variation between these basic dimensions and the final car was not more than ½ in.

This sketch was, in turn, reflected in a one-tenth scale drawing (September 27), this drawing being the basic data around which the styling was developed. It was then the function of the styling department to assist the engineers in creating a practical, advanced design that would appeal to the buying public.

There are certain factors that the stylists must bear in mind when approaching an automobile styling problem. First is the area reserved for passengers, as outlined in the sketch; the stylist must not compromise this for the sole purpose of styling. Second, the stylists must consider the feasibility of their designs from the

ENGINEERING INTERPRETATION.—It is interesting to compare this fully dimensioned chassis and body drawing of the 1949 Ford car, with the first preliminary sketch. The striking similarity shows how the experienced engineer can picture in his mind the final product.

over 100,000 miles with little trouble. But despite this technical success there remains to-day a far greater need for lower cost than for lighter weight, and as a result steel has remained our principal material.

In designing the new Ford car we were free to draw upon any acceptable ideas that have been pioneered by previous engineers, because it was designed as a completely new car with no strings attached to the use of any units used by our previous models.

We were, therefore, able to design a car as we thought it should be, bearing in mind that Ford cars, by virtue of their cost and volume, must be adaptable to all sections of this country and, virtually, the entire world.

manufacturing standpoint. Consequently, stylists must have a general knowledge of fabrication and manufacturing methods and must keep them in mind at all times. Third, cost of the proposed design, in relation to the price class of the automobile, is vitally important.

With the above three factors in mind, a Styling Department functions, generally speaking, as follows:—

Exact full-size blackboard layouts are made for determination of seat location, cushion size, leg and head room, entrance facilities, and steering wheel and pedal locations. Cross sections indicating interior widths are also developed.

At the same time, perspective renderings in colour of various types of styling are being made for discussion and selection of the styling trend. Many hundreds of sketches are made not only on overall car styling but also on various details. Of these, probably the greater proportion are discarded, due to various reasons, for the styling must be developed around the basic requirements of the car as a passenger-carrying vehicle and not as an artist's dream.

Modelling the Future

When the general styling trend as proposed by the Engineering Department is approved by the management, three-eighths size clay models are fabricated. The three-eighths scale is advantageous in that it is large enough for smaller detail and small enough so that changes can be made more quickly than in full size.

Following agreement of the general styling exemplified by the three-eighths size models, full-size clay models are next in order. Before any actual modelling is started, an undersize wood slat body structure is made on to which the clay can be packed to make the full-size model.

The full-size clay model progresses through the rough and finishing stages in close relationship with the body development group, which at this same time is determining contours, sections, etc. A " bridge " is used during the finishing stages of the model so that the completed job represents an actually scaled model. As the model is completed the bright work is covered with a metal foil to represent as nearly as possible the plated units.

In addition, it is sometimes desirable to have a quick look at the general appearance of the car. A body shell is built out of plaster and strengthened on the inside with layers of plaster-soaked burlap. This shell is mounted on a regular chassis, making it easier to move about and more permanent than the clay models. When smoothed, painted and trimmed, the car is difficult to distinguish from a real one.

In the new Ford, two full-size clay models were developed, each conforming to the basic and styling trend, but differing in detail of treatment. An illustration of these two full-sized clay models, with the production car in the centre, shows the difference between them and the final one, particularly in the tail lamp treatment. This change was suggested by Mr. Henry Ford II, who was a splendid critic during the programme.

On final approval of the styling, templates, drafts, etc., are furnished to the Body Engineering Department for complete design and release of body and sheet metal units. Some 1,800 templates were made in developing the contours of the die models from the body drafts and 15,000 drawing releases were made by Engineering to Manufacturing on the 1949 car.

The chassis design programme started at the same time as the styling programme, and in the case of the 1949 Ford was materially ahead of the body programme so that completed chassis were run under 1947 reworked bodies. The first 1949 chassis with reworked bodies were completed in early March of 1947 and considerable experience was gained with these cars between that time and July, at which time the 1949 hand-made bodies were available. Approximately 1,000,000 miles of testing were put on these cars up to the time of their complete release for production—at our test track at Dearborn and in different parts of the United States and Canada. This included extensive testing at our test section at Phœnix, Arizona, and each of our experimentally built cars cost 25 to 50 times as much as a production built unit.

We might now discuss a few of the design features of the new Ford car and some of the principles involved. In securing maximum seating width it was, of course, necessary to get the rear seat ahead of the rear-wheel housing. Therefore, the seating was moved forward

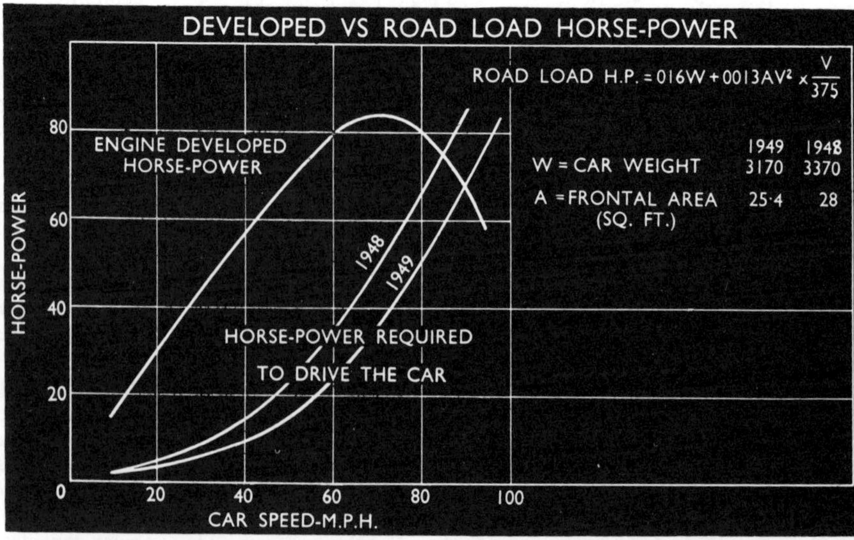

	1949	1948
W = CAR WEIGHT	3170	3370
A = FRONTAL AREA (SQ. FT.)	25·4	28

REDUCING DRAG.—Despite greater interior accommodation the 1949 car has 9½ per cent. less frontal area, and this has, inter alia, raised the maximum speed from 84 to 90 m.p.h.

5 ins. on the chassis. This is what the Sales Department calls our "midship" ride. It also necessitated the forward positioning of the engine. An illustration demonstrates the basic differences in the body and chassis relationship of the 1948 and of the new Ford.

In repositioning the body and engine in the chassis, the proportion of weight on the front end was naturally increased. This necessitated an extensive brake-development programme. It was obvious that the front brakes must do a proportionately greater share of the braking effort. The weight transfer on any stop must also be considered in the ultimate brake size, but other factors, such as feel, fade and lining life, are of equal importance in the development programme.

The frame and body are designed and integrated to each other, so that they function as a unit to provide the best possible conditions as to beam loading and torsional rigidity. A box-section frame was selected for two basic reasons: it gives maximum torsional strength and also allows a lower car, due to its minimum cross-sectional depth.

Strength and Lightness

Body and frame-deflection checks are accurately determined both in beam and torsion. Torsional rigidity is determined by holding various point of the car and checking frame deflections. The 1949 car frame proved to be much more rigid than the 1948 unit. This increased rigidity has been determined to be approximately 60 per cent. A similar test on the body and frame as a unit is also made.

It might be of interest at this point to discuss briefly the weight of the 1949 Ford. At its inception it was agreed that, with sufficient care and attention to design detail, a reduction in weight of the car as a whole, was possible, with no sacrifice of durability or riding characteristics.

Approximately 120 lb. reduction in weight was made in the body and frame. This was accomplished by a more intelligent use of materials without a reduction in the gauges of the steel used. Also, as previously shown, the strength of the frame and body unit was increased. The balance of a total decrease of 200 lb. was in the remainder of the chassis units.

The performance of a car must be in the best possible balance between fuel economy and accelerating ability. Due to the decreased power required to drive the new Ford, and improved engine performance, we have been able to improve our m.p.g. and maintain adequate performance ability.

Reduction in power to drive the car is a function of wind and rolling resistance of the car as a whole, and a chart illustrating the power requirements at the rear wheels of the 1948 and 1949 Fords indicates this reduction. The power output of the engine is shown and the point of intersection is the theoretical top speed of the car. With reduced power requirements of the car, the fuel economy and performance of the car have been improved, as shown in another set of curves.

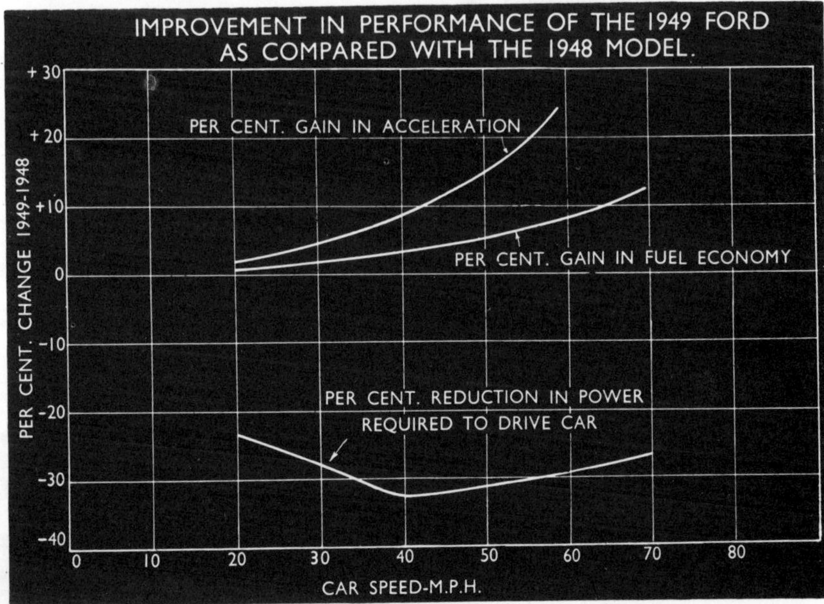

IMPORTANT GAINS.—The effect of lower drag and less weight on those important aspects of performance, acceleration and fuel economy, are shown in these curves.

The overdrive unit now available on the 1949 Ford is interesting from a performance and fuel-economy standpoint. With a standard three-speed transmission, the axle ratio is a compromise between acceleration and fuel economy. With the overdrive unit, an additional ratio is available, and therefore a higher overall ratio is possible, which provides improved acceleration in third gear, and with the reduction in the overdrive unit, fourth gear provides reduced engine speed for improved fuel economy.

New Line

I have touched on only a few of the design features of the new Ford. The roof line has been lowered approximately 4 ins., this having been accomplished without any sacrifice of headroom or entrance facilities. New independent front suspension and Hotchkiss rear drive, in conjunction with a new steering layout, give us a car which we believe handles well under all conditions and a ride that gives the impression of the car being much heavier than it is. The six-cylinder engine is entirely new, and both the six and eight have been much improved from a service accessibility standpoint.

To complete our engineering story, as you know, we also developed and produced the new Mercury, which is an entirely new car with no resemblance to the Ford, and also the new Lincoln and Cosmopolitan, the latter cars being powered with a new 337-cubic-in. V8 engine developing 152 h.p.

This complete line of new cars, in conjunction with new trucks, tractors and buses, was developed almost simultaneously, and Mr. Henry Ford II, President of our company, has pointed out that seldom, if ever, has any large industrial organization in the automotive field undertaken at one time so great and revolutionary a change as that which the Ford Motor Co. carried out in 1947 and 1948. The result was not simply a series of new models, but an entirely new line of post-war cars and commercial vehicles, and we have had to invest £25,000,000 in new tools to build them.

*(The six-cylinder version of the latest American Ford was Road-tested in "The Motor" on April 6, 1949.
—Ed.)*

MOTOR TRIALS

Ford with Fordomatic is a top performer

by *Walter A. Woron*

PHOTOS BY THOMAS J. MEDLEY

IF YOU'RE familiar with the power and acceleration of Ford products, you were probably as credulous as I was by the announcement that the Ford automatic transmission was to be used on cars without increasing the engine power output. You no doubt thought, "The '51 Ford can't possibly go as good now as it *did*." If you're of this belief, then you're in for a surprise. And if you're not a "leadfoot" now, you probably will be after driving the Fordomatic.

The test of the '51 Ford was necessarily shrouded in secrecy: only our research staff and the Ford Motor Company was aware it was taking place. Since the '51 Fords had not yet had their first public showing in dealers' windows, it was necessary (at the Ford Motor Company's Long Beach plant) to do a thorough job with paper and masking tape to hide the car's identity. Considerable co-operation was necessary for the motor trials to be run off smoothly.

Fortunately, even though the car was practically new, it had sufficient mileage on it for an exhaustive test because it had been used for test purposes by the company.

Detailed Test Report

TRANSMISSION: In the opinion of your editor and your technical editor, Don Francisco, the Fordomatic transmission is the best automatic transmission we have tested to date. Although we both prefer conventional gearshifts (because we believe you can better use maximum engine efficiency in this manner) we both made the comment that if automatics continue to improve as they have, they'll eventually win us over. The Fordomatic has a smooth shift (having only one shift in DRIVE) and the engine does not rev up excessively before the car begins to move. For normal acceleration, engine rpm gradually builds up to around 1400 rpm, and shifts to third gear (in DRIVE) around 2000 rpm. In DRIVE range, with only the one shift up or down, the shifting does not wear on your nerves. DRIVE range is used for most conditions (traffic, cruising, easy grades, etc.); it has two ratios, intermediate and high. Intermediate (automatic) is used for hard pulls (shifts itself at 20 mph), normal acceleration (automatic), and added acceleration (additional throttle pressure for shift). Low has one ratio for acceleration (see "Acceleration"), two for deceleration (in a hand shift to LOW, transmission goes to intermediate, then into low ratio). We tested the car in sand and found that by rocking the car, using LOW and REVERSE, you can get out without trouble.

ACCELERATION: The acceleration of the '51 Ford with Fordomatic doesn't exactly pin you to your seat, but it has more-than-average speed up and down the scale. In a test against a '50 Ford with conventional transmission and 4.10:1 rear axle, the two

LEAVING the Ford Motor Co. plant in Long Beach, Calif., for the secretive road test, the '51 Ford can be distinguished by its general lines, but changes are not visible due to the masking job

cars stayed practically even for 0-60 mph and for standing start ¼-mile. The acceleration trials were made with Mobilgas Special and employed two different methods: using DRIVE range only, and starting in LOW and shifting to DRIVE at 40-42 mph (see Table of Performance). Out of curiosity, we made some runs directly against the speedometer and confirmed our belief: because of speedometer error, it is possible to get a reading from three to four seconds faster than the *actual* time. Our tests are made against a *calibrated electric speedometer*, correct to less than one-half of one per cent at 100 mph.

TOP SPEED: There is a slight amount of wind wander with the '51 Ford at very high speeds, but not enough for you to have to apply constant correction. The top speed of the particular Ford tested was slightly higher (about two mph) than a '50 Ford tested recently for top speed. A major improvement is the elimination of driveshaft "throb," arrived at by raising the rear of the engine 1½ ins. so that the U-joint operates at 1½-2 degrees, instead of 4-6 degrees.

FUEL CONSUMPTION: Although fuel consumption averages obtained with the '51 Fordomatic were not quite as good as those on a 1950 Ford V-8 test car, the overall average (not counting acceleration and top speed runs) was still quite high—18.28 mpg. The consumption increases slightly in heavy traffic and at high speeds (see Table of Performance), as with all automatics.

BEHIND THE WHEEL: One major improvement has been made in regard to the '51 Ford front seat. As the seat is adjusted fore-and-aft, the seatback pivots at the lower end, bringing the top closer to your shoulders or moves it away, as the case may be. One common complaint that is still evident, however, is that the right side of the seat doesn't hold well in its track. Vision is good in all directions, although the left windshield post could be moved back further to provide better vision. With the new instrument panel controls are as easy, or easier, to reach than before. The panel boasts safety features in the recessed knobs (individually lighted) and a speedometer pointer with a glowing ring that encircles the numerals to emphasize your speed. Legroom and headroom is good in both seats, unless you're more-than-average size.

STEERING: When it comes to controllability of new cars, the Ford is hard to beat. On long, open stretches, or over curving, climbing grades, the car is extremely easy to handle. Body sway is at a minimum; one corner taken at around 80 mph proved this point to me. There is a slight amount of road shock going over sharp dips and railroad tracks, but never enough to be perturbing.

RIDE: Whether you're behind the wheel, or riding as a passenger, you're generally comfortable in the Ford. The only slight objection in this category would be the amount of wind noise (with windwings open) above 60 mph, which makes conversation a little difficult without raising your voice. Although the ride is somewhat "softer," it hasn't appreciably affected control. Reason for the changed ride: a control valve in the tubular shock absorbers (to adjust the cushioning effect), a tension-type rear spring suspension and a softer front spring rate.

A WOMAN'S VIEWPOINT: When I turned the car over to my wife to drive, she

AFTER reaching a secluded spot along the coast, we took this and other photos showing changes

had these remarks to say: "This is the lazy way to drive. I'd like to take off on a trip right now." (We did, about 20 miles.) "It's so relaxing to drive and the seat is just about perfect—it supports your back so well. Looks certainly isn't everything, but I'd say the '51 Ford is better-than-average in this department. Features that I particularly like about this car are the changed grille, the new dashboard, the upholstery, the easy-lift trunk lid and the way the car handles."

Appearance and Mechanics

My first impression of the '51 Ford, appearance-wise, was that it was too liberally sprinkled with chrome. (Much of the added chrome could have been deleted and would not have been missed, although manufacturers in the past have relied somewhat on chrome for identification change purposes;

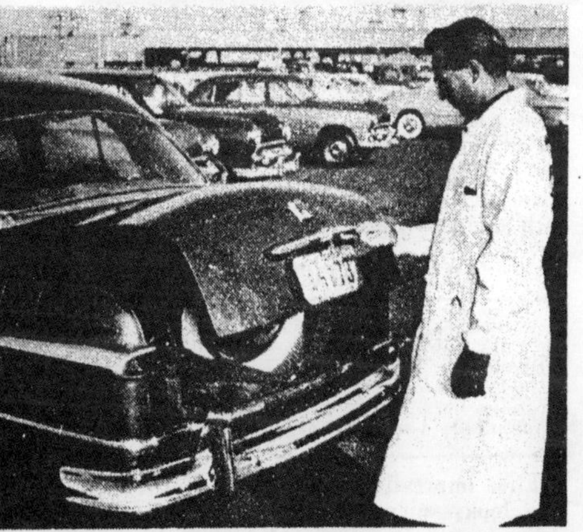

MT EDITOR shows how easy it is to lift counter-balanced trunk lid by raising it with one finger

POINTING out the strap to which lower shackle is attached, and new method of rear springing

then, again, many persons like lots of chrome.) Basically, body styling is the same, with changes being the "two-spinner" grille, a lowered hood, restyled parking lights, larger chrome headlight rims and redesigned tail lights. Something on the '51 Ford which '49 and '50 Ford owners would appreciate having on their cars is the counter-balanced trunk lid, with springs to assist in raising and holding the lid in position. (It's now a "one-finger lift.") The chassis side rails have been additionally strengthened, being boxed in almost to the rear.

In some respects, the interior appointments of the '51 Ford are not quite up to the usual high Ford standards (evident in the substitution of leatherette with plastic in several instances and the use of a different head lining material), but in others there appears to be used even better materials (upholstery, for one) than previously. This could be an indication that wartime shortages in some lines are being felt more critically than the general public realizes.

STABILITY of new Ford shown on hairpin curve. Although ride is "softer," controllability is good

Engine changes in the '51 Ford add to the overall efficiency, but have not increased the horsepower output. The changes are: addition of valve rotators, a chrome-flashed top compression ring, waterproof ignition system, and a larger capacity fuel pump.

Trend Trials Number

Last month MOTOR TREND inaugurated a system of rating cars which we believe will help a person decide between two cars that he may be considering for purchase. We term this system of rating, "Trend Trials Number," a figure arrived at through totaling the cost per bhp (how must it costs for the power of an automobile), the fuel cost per year (based on the overall fuel consumption average obtained on the Motor Trial) and the normal maintenance cost. For the purposes of standardization, normal maintenance is based on the same items for each car, the replacement and labor costs providing the variance (ref: *Motor's Flat Rate Manual*). The total cost is added up and then divided by 10 (to give an easier number to work with)—*the lower the number, the better the value*.

The 1951 Ford with Fordomatic has been given a Trend Trials No. 22.1, a more-than-satisfactory rating, considering the sales competition this car has in the $1450-1700 class.

In buying a new car, there are many points to consider; some of these are: its cost, its economy of operation, its all-around performance, its dependability, its lines (styling), its ease of maintenance, and its trade-in value. Since the '51 Ford can meet all of these qualifications with an above-par rating, we feel that it is a good buy. And for the person who prefers an automatic transmission, the Fordomatic is just about tops.

<hr>

GENERAL SPECIFICATIONS

ENGINE

Type	L-head, in-line V-8
Bore and Stroke	3 3/16x3 3/4
Stroke/Bore Ratio	1.18:1
Cubic Inch Displacement	239.4
Maximum Bhp	100 @ 3600 rpm
Bhp/Cubic Inch	.418
Max. Torque (Bare Engine)	181 @ 2000 rpm
Compression Ratio	6.8:1

DRIVE SYSTEM

Transmission — Conventional three - speed; Ratios: Low—2.819:1, Second—1.604:1, Third—1:1, Overdrive—.7:1, Reverse—3.625:1 Fordomatic Ratios: Low—2.44:1, Intermediate—1.48:1, High—1:1, Reverse—2.0:1

Rear Axle—Semi-floating Hypoid; Ratios: 3.73:1 (Standard), 4.10:1 (Overdrive)*, 3.31:1 (Fordomatic)**

DIMENSIONS

Wheelbase	114 ins.
Overall Length	196 ft. 8 ins.
Overall Height	63 ft. 2 ins.
Overall Width	72 ft. 9 ins.
Road clearance	7.9 ins.
Tread (Front and Rear)	56 ins.
Turning Radius	20 1/2 ft.

Weight (Test Car)	3300 lbs.
Weight/Bhp Ratio	33:1
Weight/Road Hp Ratio	55.9:1
Weight Distribution (Front to Rear)	57.4/42.6%

* Optional equipment—$96.90
** Optional equipment—$160. (approx.)

TABLE OF PERFORMANCE

(For explanation of any figures or conditions in the following table, see copy under the particular heading.)

DYNAMOMETER TEST

1800 rpm (full load) 34 mph	44 road hp
2000 rpm (full load) 44.5 mph	48.5 road hp
2500 rpm (full load) 60 mph	58 road hp
2950 rpm (full load) 72 mph	59 road hp (max.)

ACCELERATION TRIALS (SECONDS)

Standing start 1/4-mile	:21.89 (D)*; :21.19 (L-D)**
0-30 mph through gears	:06.54 (D); :05.45 (L)
0-60 mph through gears	:18.91 (D); :17.82 (L-D)
10-30 mph in high	:18.74 (D)
30-60 mph in high	:13.34 (D)

* Shift using DRIVE range only.
** Shift using LOW range, then shifting to DRIVE.

TOP SPEED (MPH)

Fastest one-way run	88.50
Average of four runs	87.25

DECELERATION TEST (SECONDS)

From 60 to 30 mph	:25.41
From 45 to 20 mph	:26.16
From 30 to 10 mph	:32.29

BRAKE CHECK

Stopping distance at 30 mph	35'3"
Stopping distance at 45 mph	92'0"
Stopping distance at 60 mph	182'3"

FUEL CONSUMPTION (MPG)

At a steady 30 mph	24.69
At a steady 45 mph	20.00
At a steady 60 mph	18.44
Through light traffic	19.75
Through medium traffic	15.63
Through heavy traffic	11.17

SPEEDOMETER CHECK

At 30 mph indicated 32 mph	6.6% error
At 45 mph indicated 49 mph	8.9% error
At 60 mph indicated 66 mph	10.0% error

ROAD and TRACK ROAD TEST A-2-52

Ford Customline

SPECIFICATIONS

	six	eight
Arrangement & no. of cyl.	6 in line	V-8
Valve Arrangement	ohv	L-head
Compression Ratio	7:1	7.2:1
Horsepower	101 at 3500 rpm	110 at 3800 rpm
Bore & Stroke	3.58 x 3.6	3.187 x 3.75
Displacement	215 cu in.	239 cu in.
Transmission	3 speed standard	Ford-O-Matic torque converter
Weight as Tested	3210 lb.	3390 lb.
Overall Length	197.8 in.	197.8 in.
Overall Width	73 9/10 in.	73 9/10 in.
Number of Seats	3 front 3 rear	3 front 3 rear
Price, del. L.A.	$2026.00	$2285.00

FUEL CONSUMPTION

(6-cylinder)

At a steady	Miles Per Gallon
30	32
40	26
50	25
60	21

SPEEDOMETER

Speedometer	Actual Speed six	eight
30	27.7	33.2
40	37.0	42.5
50	44.7	50.0
60	54.0	59.0
70	62.5	69.2

PERFORMANCE

	six	eight
Flying 1/4 mile ave.	83.2	83.3
Standing 1/4 mile	21.8	22.2
Fastest One Way	88.3	85.0

Personal impressions, prejudices, and individual traits play a large part in road tests conducted by the press. Performance figures and physical dimensions are precise factors . . . opinions are subject to human multi-division. **Every** car, no matter how ugly or poorly built, has its rabid proponents.

Road and Track's Road Tests have been conducted as a four-man project—the report rendered was usually a majority opinion, but expressed by a single writer. The inevitable deadlock with neither side willing to give in.

As a result, a new type of Road Test presentation has been devised . . . each member of the crew reports individually. To give you a key to the automotive personality of each tester, there appears a brief "car-biography" at the beginning of each report. Choose up sides and let the fun begin!

OLIVER BILLINGSLEY'S REPORT

Oliver's Automotive Biography
Have owned: Saxon 19??, Fordson, '23 T. Ford, '29, '30, '31, '34, '37, '41 and '42 Fords, '31, '33 and '34 American Austins, '39 Bantam, '44 Ford Jeep, '45 Studebaker Weasel, '49 Renault, '50 Morris Minor, '51 MG TD Mk II. I like small foreign cars. Would like to have: Aston-Martin, Jaguar XK-120, Ferrari, or Lancia Gran Turismo. Also a Morris Minor or new Austin 7.

You know how old-time Ford fans are . .

When the Model A replaced the "T", they mourned the demise of the planetary transmission and other simplified construction. Then came the V-8 and anguished wails were heard over the more complicated engine. And 1949, gone was individuality—they said. So . . . 1952 and they snort, "Never thought Ford would go "jet-and-rocket-happy".

Well, guess I am one of these "traditionalists" because that's just the way I've felt every time Ford makes a change. Somehow, Ford always seemed right just the way it was. Wanted to explain this as I probably was prejudiced when the '52 Ford arrived,

In the first place, I don't like the current "false front" reeket ship design seheel . . .

triple spinners, high fenders, and the stamped-metal script "Crestline" ornaments give me a pain . . . So that's off my chest!

I do like the wonderful picture-window visibility, the very practical nylon headliner, and the reduced amount of chrome. As usual, the Ford instrument panel is both attractive and practical . . . a joy for night driving. Foreign car manufacturers would do well to follow this fine example. Turn indicators, hardware, and upholstery are all excellent. The suspended brake and clutch petals are very nice altho somewhat high for a man . . . evidently located for French heels and cowboy boots. The horn right is too close to the rim . . . irritating and dangerous.

Altho the Fordomatic is smooth as glass, it has that sqwishie feeling typical of automatic drive. You are sure the clutch is slipping, but after the first few feet, you're going as fast as others so it must be o.k.

On the open road, the Ford performs very well. Considerable sidewind effect is noticed. It does fine on curves until they become "turns" . . . then one must take it slow to keep up with the "steering wheel revs". Credit must be given for a very comfortable ride and general ease of operation.

The new overhead valve six shows a great amount of careful engineering . . . "square" bore and stroke, short rockers, integral oil filter, adequate quench area, and very neat arrangement of service fittings.

Having owned a 1942 Ford six, I was anxious to see how the new six performed. My '42 shook like a nervous groom while idling and bucked like a Brahma bull at low speeds. The new six idles even smoother than the eight and will run smoothly at 7 mph, High gear starts produced only a slight ping, Thru gears, it would wind up fast and seemed to have more on-the-ball than the V-8 Ford or the reeently tested Plymeuth.

Perhaps it was a difference in wheel alignment between the cars tested, but it must be reported that the Six handled better on the turns than did the Eight.

For the average American family, Ford has produced a car which will please their taste and satisfy their demands. The Six with standard transmission is my choice . . .

BILL BREHAUT'S REPORT

Bill's Automotive Biography
Cars owned include '37 DeSoto, '39 Plymouth, '40 Ford, '46 Ford 8, '37 Cord, '39 DeSoto, '49 Ford 6, '51 Henry J 6. Likes foreign cars. Would want MG but has family and needs 4-seater. Favorite car: Lancia.

First impressions of the new Ford: Don't like looks—nice interior—good get-away in drive range—low range doesn't seem much better—visibility sensational—hood seems a little longer than the '51—ride seems better at high speeds than low speeds.

The '52 Ford, as I see it, is a compromise car—the designers have gone "all out" for a comfortable ride and that "big car feel."

There is no question about the improved ride of the new Ford. It seems to ride as well as any of the higher priced cars which, apparently, is one of the objectives Ford has been aiming at with this new model. In fact, if the nameplate read Mercury instead of Ford, I don't think many people would recognize the car as a Ford. To the old-time Ford fans, who liked Fords because of their light weight and sparkling performance, even at a sacrifice in finish and comfort, this car will be a great disappointment.

There is no question about which of these groups is the most numerous . . . it's the latter—and for this reason I predict that the new Ford will be a roaring success even tho I would rather see Ford produce something more like their British Consul and Zephyr.

Unfortunately, these cars wouldn't sell as well as the '52 Customline with Fordomatic.

The compromise mentioned earlier means that the manufacturer has had to sacrifice performance fo. good ride, has had to increase weight to add quality. Thus, the '52 Ford is one of the slowest, least economical and poorest handling Fords built in recent years. However, it has the highest quality construction and the best ride of any car Ford has ever built. More horsepower will solve the performance problem (where's the ohv V-8?) but to help the handling problem is difficult . . . your wife would probably hate you if you did change it.

I liked the new instrument panel and the curved windshield, also the heating and ventilating system. The Fordomatic torque converter, plus transmission, operates very smoothly and is ideal for traffic driving. On the open road, acceleration from 50 and up is pretty sluggish. The position indicator of the drive unit would be easier to operate at night if illuminated.

The speedometer of the Ford was the most conservative of any car I have ever driven, being actually slow at top speed (see chart).

The '52 is the quietest Ford ever built . . . in my opinion, just as quiet as the most expensive American cars. Careful soundproofing, rubber mounting, and solid construction combine to make this silence possible.

Enroute to the test area, Bill Quinn drove the ohv Ford Six while I followed in a new V-8. Watching the Ford from my vantage point, I was surprised by the lack of roll on corners. Bill was really throwing it into the turns hard and it seemed to handle well. A little later, when I tried the car myself, I thought it handled and drove better than the V-8 . . . probably because of less weight up front and the "lower-geared" rear end combined with 3-speed manual transmission. The performance figures seem to bear out my feeling that the Fordomatic on the 110 hp eight just about cancels the increase of horsepower over the standard transmission 101 hp six. Personally, I'd rather have the six than the eight, tho I would try out the standard transmission eight before deciding.

BILL QUINN'S REPORT

> **Bill's Automotive Biography**
> Cars owned: '51 Jaguar XK-120, '48 Cadillac, '41 Buick plus 1937-39-42-46-47-51 Fords. Thinks for sheer pleasure you couldn't improve on the Jag (in its price class). Likes a high power/weight ratio. Goal is Ferrari America plus Ford for everyday use.

My first reaction to the new Ford was one of disappointment. With an all-new body for 1952, it is felt, by many (myself included), that much more could have been done. A direct comparison with my own '51 Ford shows that, in many respects, the '51 has a slight edge on the '52. The 1952 has the added burden of extra weight.

Bob Menaffee was on hand to greet us when we arrived at the modern showrooms of Montrose Ford (Montrose, California).

With only 4 miles on the odometer, we took it rather easy for the first few days of the test. After a very short break-in period, the car was given the all-out phase.

. . . it was still very stiff and tight. The steering wheel had very poor return action which proved awkward on turns. However, my '51 was like that for 5000 miles, so, no doubt, the test car would free up after a few thousand miles. On the other hand, the '52 Ford has a sharper turning radius, a great improvement for parking and maneuvering in narrow quarters. Visibility is greatly improved by the addition of many square inches to windshield and window area. This results, however, in a somewhat higher and boxier appearance.

On the road to the test area the Ford invoked favorable comment with its effortless high speed cruising ability . . . attained without the aid of an optimistic speedometer. At top speed the Ford holds the road well, altho slight irregularities in the road surface are magnified by rather mushy suspension. The 1952 Ford seems ideally suited for the average American conception of reliable low-cost motoring. However, we can't help remembering the first Ford V-8's with their terrific power/weight ratio. Year by year (Ford is not alone in this), Ford builds them a little bigger and heavier.

Actually, I was much more impressed by the 6 cylinder Ford than I was with the Fordomatic 8. Much better acceleration plus practically the same top speed added up to better all 'round performance. The mileage figures were particularly impressive. . . . 32 mpg at a constant 30 mph should assures the buyer of at least 20 mpg.

I would definitely say that of the two Fords, the 6 with standard transmission would be my choice.

BOB DEARBORN REPORTS

> **Bob's Automotive Biography**
> Cars owned: '26 Model T Ford, '28 Model A, '32 Buick Six, '33 Cadillac, '34 Buick, '34 Ford, '36 Ford, '38 Ford, '39 Ford, '41 Ford, '48 Plymouth, '48 Chrysler, '48 Austin A-40, '49 Austin A-40, '50 MG TD, '52 Riley Sedan. Ideal: new Rolls sedan and a Frazer-Nash sports. Now driving Riley sedan for sports plus passenger space.

In glancing back over notes made while checking out the '52 Ford, I see that I have jotted: "an overall, darn good car." And this, I know, will come as a dash of cold water to my sports-car-partial friends.

Let me state, then, that American cars are *still* not my choice. They don't have the variety of design or the "built-in fun" to be found in the European product. Still, I must confess that the Ford people have accomplished what they set out to do, and that is to present the public with a roomy, quality car, in the low range.

Let's italicize "*low price*" and then put quotes around it—the better to point up the fact that the cheapest Ford now available on the West Coast will cost you a fraction under $2,000, license and tax paid. And the same upward flight of prices holds true for all the other "low price" cars. In fact, cheap cars don't exist anymore. They're just a fond memory.

The car *Road and Track* tested had (for me) more of a quality feel than any Ford I remember, plus some engineering which benefits the driver. I cranked the car into some rather severe corners and it seemed to sit very flat as it came around. Ford has paid some attention to the steering which you will find improves the handling qualities.

I dislike automatic transmissions. It's a matter of principle with me. So, I am not a fair judge of Fordomatic. Tho this mechanism was as smooth as any I've tried, I came away from it wishing Detroit had spent more time developing a smooth and easy clutch and braking system. If they had, maybe the public wouldn't be demanding (and getting) automatic transmissions with their power losses and added weight.

While on this subject, a word should be given to the new suspended-type clutch and brake pedals. Similar to those on the British Ford Consul and Zephyr, they're wonderful. However, I would like them even better if they had a much shorter "throw."

Some like V-8s, some like 6s. I'll not take a stand on either side, but I defy you to drive both and then decide on the V-8. Actually, if I didn't know what was under the hood, I would choose the 6 as the smoother.

The American six-passenger sedan is a clumsy, awkward car. I have about as much use for it as for a covered wagon. But as American cars go, I conclude my report as I started it. The Ford is "overall . . . a darn good car."

Violent cornering tactics produced a surprisingly small amount of roll.

A sharp dip at 37 mph brought both front wheels off the ground.

Two '52 Fords

ROAD TESTS BY . . .

MT RESEARCH FINDS THE AVERAGE BUYER CAN FLIP A COIN TO CHOOSE BETWEEN THE SIX AND THE V-8

BY WALT WORON

W HICH FORD shall I buy?" is the big question facing millions of Ford fanciers in '52. "Which Ford is the better buy?" was, therefore, the issue that prompted MOTOR TREND Research to test both the six and eight-cylinder versions. We bent over backwards to detect the tiniest performance variations between these two cars. The differences turned out to be astonishingly slight, so the answer to "which Ford?" cannot be made on the basis of performance figures at all.

As we see it, this is what happened. In 1932 the Ford Motor Company introduced the V-8—an extremely advanced engine design for its time and a whole lot of performance for a very low price. The skill with which that simple design was executed is honored by the fact that, although not radically revised for 20 years, the Ford V-8 continues to be one of the most reliable and one of the most popular powerplants manufactured in the world today.

PHOTOS BY ERIC RICKMAN

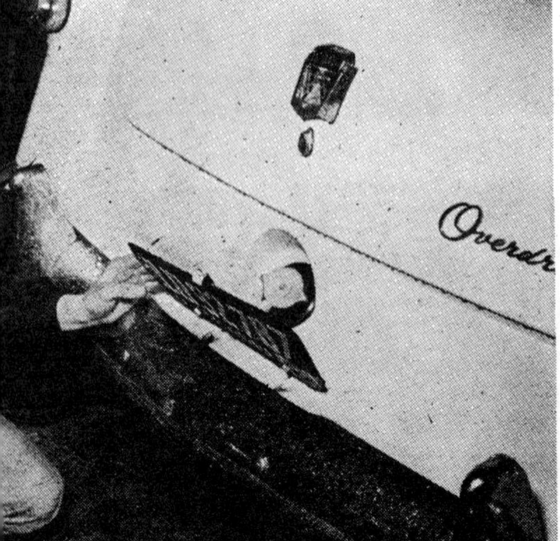

Ford stylists cleaned up the fender lines this year by moving the gas filler cap and covering it with rear license plate

However, no one knows better than its makers just what the limitations of this engine are. Obviously, they feel that it has been developed to the practical limit and therefore they have introduced an entirely new engine—the Six. But it will be a long time before the millions of Ford V-8 fans will all swing to a six-cylinder engine; so Ford has very sagely made its '52 cars available with either the old or the new powerplant.

The Six is a new engine in every sense. Its design shows the influence of many progressive, modern theories, while the Eight remains a classic of pre-war practices aimed at producing a fairly high-performance engine at low cost. The Eight has *been* developed; the Six is *to be* developed. One is the engine of the future, the other is that of the past. As they both stand today, performance is equal, and you have to decide upon one of these alternatives, if you're going to buy a Ford—"I can stick with the V-8 which has been tried and proved reliable by tens of millions of owners, but which still isn't a top-efficiency engine," *or* "I'll assume that Ford has really taken all the important bugs out of the Six and I'll take my stand with the more modern, easier-to-work-on, more efficient unit."

How They Compare

The Six proved itself to be a slightly faster car in acceleration; it did 0-60 mph in just about one second less than the V-8. Top speed for both cars can be regarded as identical. The V-8 gets better gasoline mileage at low speeds but the Six is more economical at high speeds. In average fuel consumption, the V-8 actually turns out to be the more economical car but the difference is too slight to be a factor. Using our test figures as a basis, we find that the cost of gasoline for the two cars for 10,000 miles of operation would only differ by $4. Both engines are smooth and quiet in operation but the ohv Six should be cheaper to maintain because it's so easy to work on.

How They Handle

This year Ford has new steering that requires five full turns to get the wheels from lock to lock. This makes for slow enough steering, but it is augmented by a sort of slackness in the steering gear that adds up to somewhat less control than we consider to be the desirable minimum. This "sloppiness" in the steering is reflected in overall road behavior. While the springing of the car is really quite good and there is practically no body roll during high-speed cornering, the steering comes along and upsets the car's stability in a way that can be very disturbing and actually unsafe.

Ford's brakes are among the best we've ever tested. Remarkably enough, there was *no* tendency of the brakes to fade, even during the severest punishment. Too, with all four wheels locked up tight at 60 mph, the Six came to a fast stop in a *perfectly straight line*. That doesn't happen too often! The Six was equipped with stock tires with the now generally used wavy tread pattern; the V-8 happened to be equipped with some fancy whitewall rubber using parallel grooves for a tread pattern with no transverse grooving at all. These tires were fine in braking tests at 30 and at 45 mph. But at 60 mph even slight brake pedal pressure would send the car well on its way to full loss of control.

Two similar relationships were brought home dramatically here: Good suspension can be spoiled by stability-robbing,

loose steering, and good brakes can be spoiled by the wrong tire tread pattern.

We should repeat that the '52 Ford, equipped with the sort of tires specified for the car, has brakes of the very first quality. Like all Bendix servo units, they lock right now and there's a strong tendency to pitch passengers forward even when stopping at only five mph. Another strong point in Ford's favor, however, is that—even though Hotchkiss drive is used—there is none of the rear-axle, trac-tion-breaking bounce that so often takes place when the brakes are slammed on hard in cars with the Hotchkiss layout.

During our top-speed runs we found that the cars handled well, except for the already-mentioned lack of anything like precision control in the steering. Both cars took a good long time in which to get up to top speed, were definitely slow on pickup in the upper rpm range.

The '52 Ford has a somewhat stiffer ride, more solid-feeling suspension than last year's model. It's good, feels firm and stable on the straightaway and in turns. The stock shock absorbers, however, do not give the best control of rebound over dips and "wavy" surfaces.

How They're Finished

Of course, both the Six and the V-8 are identical in appearance except for chrome identification marks. The interior
(Continued on next page)

Convertible interior, similar to rest of line, is noteworthy because of large, bracket-mounted brake pedal. Instrument-panel design is excellent—no knobs on the passenger's side

Rear-end new for '52 is a legitimate boast for Ford. Square bustle-back is all ready, stylewise, to receive a rear-mounted spare. Taillights have popular, customized "jet" look

FORD SIX SPECIFICATIONS

PERFORMANCE
CLAYTON CHASSIS DYNAMOMETER TEST
(FULL LOAD)

RPM	MPH	ROAD HP
1200	24.0	28.5
2000	49.5	47.0
....	66.0 (maximum)	63.0

Per cent of advertised hp delivered to driving wheels—62.4

ACCELERATION TRIALS (SECONDS)

Standing start ¼ mile	:21.27
0-30 mph	:05.74
0-60 mph	:19.45
10-60 mph in high	:24.40
30-60 mph in high	:15.34

TOP SPEED (MPH)

Fastest one-way run	93.16*
Average of four runs (two ways)	86.28

* With tail wind of approximately 10 mph

FUEL CONSUMPTION (MPG)*

	CONV	OD
Steady 30 mph	18.7	23.0
Steady 45 mph	17.7	22.2
Steady 60 mph	16.0	19.1
Approximate average in traffic	15.3	19.3

* "Regular" Mobilgas used.

BRAKE CHECK

Stopping distance at	
30 mph	35 ft. 3 ins.
45 mph	81 ft. 2 ins.
60 mph	165 ft. 6 ins.

SPEEDOMETER CHECK

Actual	Indicated	% error
30	30	0.0
45	47	4.4
60	63	5.0

Odometer correction factor for 100 miles 98.6

GENERAL SPECIFICATIONS
ENGINE

Type	OHV
Bore and stroke	3.56 x 3.60
Stroke/bore ratio	1.01:1
Compression ratio	7.0:1
Displacement	215.3 cu. ins.
Advertised bhp	101 @ 3500 rpm
Piston travel @ max. bhp	2566 ft. per min.
Bhp per cu. in.	.469
Maximum torque	185 lbs. ft. @ 1500 ± rpm

DRIVE SYSTEM
Same as 1952 Ford V-8

DIMENSIONS

Wheelbase	115 ins.
Tread	Front—58, Rear—56 ins.
Wheelbase/tread ratio	2.01:1
Overall width	73.9 ins.
Overall length	197.8 ins.
Overall height	62.3 ins.
Turning radius	20 ± ft.
Turns, lock to lock	5
Weight (test car)	3370 lbs.
Weight/bhp ratio	33.4:1
Weight/road hp ratio	53.5:1
Weight distribution (front to rear)	56.1/43.9

OPERATING COST PER MILE ANALYSIS

1. Cost of gasoline	$128.20
2. Cost of insurance	$112.50
3. First year's depreciation	$113.00
4. Maintenance:	
a. Two new tires	$ 39.60
b. Brake reline	$ 17.70
c. Major tune-up	$ 11.90
d. New front fender	$ 27.50
e. Renew rear bumper	$ 21.40

FIRST YEAR COST OF OPERATION IN CENTS PER MILE $.047

---

finish of the two sedans we tested was fine. All the trim—both metal and fabric—fitted nicely, as it was intended to do. The single-stitched upholstery was very good-looking and the headlining neat and rich. The instrument panel uses the grouping of instruments around the steering column and there are *no* projections from the panel on the passenger's side, an important safety feature.

Exterior finish of our Fords was spotty. In the case of some body panels, the paint seemed to have been well rubbed down, while elsewhere there were large areas of "orange-peel"—that dimpled texture that un-rubbed paint from a

New Ford ohv six-cylinder engine produces 101 bhp. Compact design aids maintenance. Note redesigned oil filter

---

FORD V-8 SPECIFICATIONS

PERFORMANCE
CLAYTON CHASSIS DYNAMOMETER TEST
(FULL LOAD)

RPM	MPH	ROAD HP
1200	26.0	30.0
2000	42.0	52.0
....	62.0 (maximum)	64.0

Per cent of advertised hp delivered to driving wheels—58.2

ACCELERATION TRIALS (SECONDS)

Standing start ¼ mile	:21.35
0-30 mph	:05.69
0-60 mph	:20.47
10-60 mph in high	:26.93
30-60 mph in high	:17.00

TOP SPEED (MPH)

Fastest one-way run	93.36*
Average of four runs	86.70

* With tail wind of approximately 10 mph.

FUEL CONSUMPTION (MPG)*

	CONV	OD
Steady 30 mph	20.5	24.9
Steady 45 mph	17.7	23.8
Steady 60 mph	14.9	18.7
Approximate average in traffic	15.0	18.8

* "Regular" Mobilgas used.

BRAKE CHECK

Stopping distance at	
30 mph	39 ft. 0 ins.
45 mph	85 ft. 5 ins.
60 mph*	— ft. — ins.

* Test impossible due to skidding: unsafe tire tread pattern.

SPEEDOMETER CHECK

Actual	Indicated	% error
30	31	3.3
45	47	4.4
60	63	5.0

Odometer correction factor for 100 miles 103.3

GENERAL SPECIFICATIONS
ENGINE

Type	L-Head V-8
Bore and stroke	3.187 x 3.75
Stroke/bore ratio	1.18:1
Compression ratio	7.2:1
Displacement	239.4 cu. ins.
Advertised bhp	110 @ 3800 rpm
Piston travel @ max. bhp	2375 ft. per min.
Bhp per cu. in.	.459
Maximum torque	194 lbs. ft. @ 2000 ± rpm

DRIVE SYSTEM

Transmission: Three-speed synchro-mesh with overdrive. Ratios:

First—2.779	Second—1.614
Third—1.000	Overdrive—0.700 Reverse—3.635

Rear axle:
Semi-floating, Hotchkiss drive, hypoid gears. Ratios: Standard*—3.90, with Overdrive—4.10, Optionals— 3.15, 3.31.
* Standard for sedans and coupes.

DIMENSIONS

Wheelbase	115 ins.
Tread	Front—58, Rear—56 ins.
Wheelbase/tread ratio	2.01:1
Overall width	73.9 ins.
Overall length	197.8 ins.
Overall height	62.3 ins.
Turning radius	20 ± ft.
Turns, lock to lock	5
Weight (test car)	3530 lbs.
Weight/bhp ratio	32.1:1
Weight/road hp ratio	55.2:1
Weight distribution (front to rear)	56.4/43.6

OPERATING COST PER MILE ANALYSIS

1. Cost of gasoline	$124.38
2. Cost of insurance	$121.50
3. First year's depreciation	$124.00
4. Maintenance:	
a. Two new tires	$ 39.60
b. Brake reline	$ 17.70
c. Major tune-up	$ 11.90
d. Renew front fender	$ 27.50
e. Renew rear bumper	$ 21.40

FIRST YEAR COST OF OPERATION IN CENTS PER MILE $.049

INTERIOR SAFETY CHECK CHART

QUESTION	YES	NO
1. Blind spot at left windshield post at a minimum?		X
2. Vision to right rear satisfactory?	X	
3. Positive lock to prevent doors from being opened from inside?		X
4. Does adjustable front seat lock securely in place?	X	
5. Minimum of projections on dashboard face?		X
6. Is emergency brake an emergency brake and is it accessible to both driver and passenger?		X
7. Are cigarette lighter and ash tray both located conveniently for driver?	X	
8. Is rear vision mirror positioned so as not to cause blind spot for driver?		X
TOTAL FOR FORD SIX AND V-8		50.0

spray gun always has. At the bottom rear extremity of each rear fender there were indications that the sheet metal had torn during the stamping process. The area of injury had been leaded over, but not very smoothly. The door frame areas were immaculate and most body panels were well fitted. If you're going to buy a Ford, do as you should when selecting any car: examine several specimens of the make and model you want and select the one which seems most well assembled. There can be quite a bit of variation between supposedly identical cars.

Comfort and Safety

The seating position in the '52 Ford sedans is fine for all passengers: you sit high, have plenty of head and leg room, and the large windows give an excellent view in all directions. The steering wheel angle is good, left windshield pillar could stand to be located a bit farther aft, rear-view mirror is definitely hung too low and gets in the way of vision to the right front. Fords used to be rather drafty cars to ride in at speed, with a window or two down. This has been corrected and the amount of wind noise present at any given speed seems to have been reduced; also, very little road noise is picked up by the body. The rear doors are cut back to a point where they overlap a good portion of the rear seat, and this makes for really unusual ease of exit and entry. With the sun fairly high in the sky, reflections from the top of the instrument panel, chromed horn contact ring, plus secondary reflections off of windshield can be very bothersome. But then, on the credit side, there's a lock on the front seat adjustment that seems to be highly positive—a terribly important safety feature.

The New Engine

Naturally, the big Ford news of the year is its six-cylinder engine. We're revealing no secrets when we say that the possibilities of this power unit have scarcely been tapped. As our performance figures demonstrate more eloquently than words, the Six has been set up to match the performance of the V-8 with remarkable accuracy. But the Six is the engine to watch—the engine that can and will go places in the years ahead.

When MOTOR TREND Research called at Ford's Southern California plant to take delivery of the two test cars, one of the new six-cylinder engines was torn down for us and many of its important features explained. Here are some of the interesting things we noted:

First of all, the new powerplant is rugged. Its camshaft is one of the largest in diameter that we've ever seen in any engine. The nodular iron crankshaft is mounted higher in the crankcase than is the shaft in any of the other new ohv engines. This contributes to the rigidity of the crankshaft support, as do its very massive main bearing bulkheads.

The four-main-bearing lower end looks like one of the most sturdily-built in the industry. Still, the engine has been so laid out that seven main bearings can be used at any time that higher compression ratios come along to demand extra stiffness.

The connecting rod and piston assembly is marked by the same designed-in compactness and strength. The rods are very short and are of a good, wide H-section; the pistons are of heavy aluminum with steel reinforcement in the wrist pin bearing areas. We could go on and on giving illustrations that all point to one conclusion: the Ford Six engine's carefully designed-in ruggedness puts it in a good position to carry on the "world's workhorse" tradition of the Model T, the Model A, and the Ford V-8.

In the new power unit, Ford engineers have turned their attention more than ever before to lubrication. A full-

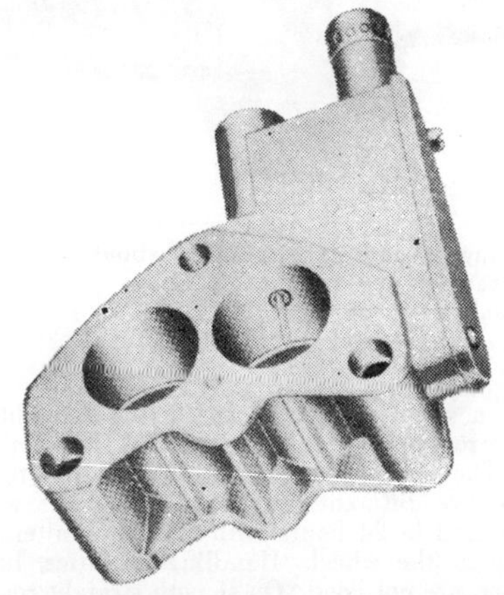

Novel accessory is engine governor. It can be set for any maximum speed

flow oil filtering system is standard equipment, meaning that every drop of oil is filtered before it is used, rather than just a small percentage of the oil, as in the case of the more commonplace by-pass system. A neat lubrication detail that appeals to us greatly is the provision of a jet in each connecting rod which sprays an oil mist against the load side of the cylinders. Topping off this good, full-pressure lubricating system is a method of metering oil to low-pressure parts by means of simple flat spots on rotating shafts. Every time the flat spot comes around, lining up with its corresponding oil passage, a carefully predetermined amount of oil is metered by. This does away with more "cloggable" metering jets and is in keeping with that efficient, direct simplicity that has always been an earmark of Ford engine design.

The top side of the ohv engine is as clean and straightforward as the lower end. Intake and exhaust manifolds are both located on the same side of the engine. Perfect alignment of the intake ports with the manifold is assured by the use of aligning rings which fit machined portions of both the mating parts. The exhaust manifold uses a gasket-less, machined fit to the block which permits the manifold to creep as it expands from heat, without any tendency to distort the block.

Ford engines have long been the favorites of soup-up enthusiasts and one naturally wonders, "What are the souping possibilities of the new Six?" They're mighty good. In the first place, the ohv layout will permit higher compression ratios than the old L-head arrangement could ever hope to. Dual carburetion will be very easy and so will be the installation of a high-efficiency exhaust system. Enlarging and polishing of *both* intake and exhaust ports will be easy and 1⅞-in. valves can be installed with no strain. Except for the fabrication of aluminum heads, the Six will be an easier, cheaper engine to hop up than the V-8 ever was.

Ford Accessories

A completely new line of custom accessories has been brought out by the Ford Motor Company to match the 1952

Stem-wind clock is a precision-built timepiece and is moderately priced

styling. Several interesting additions are on the list, including speed governor, turn indicators, an illuminated vanity mirror, and an engine-compartment light.

Two radios are available, a seven-tube Custom and a five-tube Deluxe. Of the two clocks offered, the less expensive springwound model is the more attractive. Simply styled rubber floor mats are available in matching colors for the front floors.

Wheel disks, wheel trim rings, and rear fender skirts will help dress up the 1952 models as will the deluxe hood ornament

Redesigned hood ornament is chrome-plated, will appeal to new car buyer

and the rocker-panel trim strip along the bottom of the body.

A hand-brake signal light is almost a must nowadays because of more efficient emergency braking equipment. Ford's Magic Air System is a combination heater, defroster, and air-conditioner with the controls contained in an attractive dash-mounted panel.

—**Walt Woron**

48,000 MILES
IN A
1949 FORD

by John R. Bond

Despite my intense enthusiasm for sports cars, a new 1949 Ford V-8 Custom club coupe was purchased by the writer late in 1948. The car was intended for normal everyday use, for contemplated long trips, and to use as a "sort-of" test car during construction of a sports car based on a similar chassis.

The car was revised slightly: a dual exhaust system with two stock mufflers was installed immediately, because I would not drive any V-8 with a single muffler. At 5000 miles the heads were milled and redomed to give 8.0 to 1 compression ratio. Since the axle ratio ordered was the standard 3.73 to 1 (the best ratio available for ultimate maximum speed), the extra 10 or 15 bhp gives a low speed performance at least equal to the 4.10 axle. The standing quarter mile has been clocked at 19.62 seconds, the standing half-mile at approximately 32.5 seconds. Top speed is substantially 90 mph.

While on the subject of performance, the speedometer-error should be mentioned. To clock a measured mile in 60.0 seconds, the needle must be kept at 67-68, to go 70 actual mph requires 80 on the indicator, and at 90 the needle goes an inch past the top calibration mark of 100 mph! In addition, the odometer is 3 to 4% optimistic, depending on tire pressure.

Fuel consumption varies from 16.0 to 19.6 miles per gallon. Two trips to the East Coast at an honest cruising speed of 70 mph most of the time gave 18.3 miles per gallon. From this data it is apparent that the slight modifications made give results equal to or better than an overdrive equipped car at a saving of $96 in original cost of the extra gearbox.

Oil consumption was, and still is, remarkably good. In 1949, on a 9000 mile trip, exactly 3 quarts of #20 oil were used — counting amount low at changes, etc. In 1950, with 42,000 miles registered, the trip to Watkins Glen resulted in only one quart of #30 oil consumed per 1000 miles.

No work has been done on engine, clutch, transmission, or rear end in 48,000 miles except the usual preventive maintenance, adjustments, and tuneups. The excellent economy on fuel and oil has been offset somewhat by fairly high maintenance costs, performed by a local dealer which, of course, is more expensive than doing it yourself. Items in this expense include 10 sets of breaker points (5 sets of plugs), a new distributor, 4 voltage regulators, a new battery, new master cylinder, brake reline, 4 wheel alignments, repainting, tune-ups, and miscellaneous small items.

As to general remarks on the car, the engine with stock 6.8 compression is much smoother and quieter than earlier V-8s. Milling the heads resulted in restoring the older model type of roughness, a phenomenom receiving much attention these days and one that Cadillac engineers state was a considerable factor in their decision to change from side valve to OHV. Aluminum alloy heads would reduce the present necessity for a steady diet of "premium" motor fuel even

Many readers have inquired about the "shaving" of Technical Editor Bond's car. The hood ornament and Ford name above grille were removed as were the license plate holder and trunk latch on the rear deck. This common California modification aroused considerable interest in the East.

—PHOTO BY JACK CAMPBELL

on a slightly retarded spark, tho I doubt if the roughness would be reduced appreciably.

The car is fairly comfortable on long trips. On five different occasions, 1200 miles were covered in 24 hours with 2 drivers, alternating at the wheel. Handling qualities, however, are not good. On smooth straight roads, the heavy front end and low rate front suspension shows up well—on rough or winding roads it is a different story. The front end seems to pitch up and down, and at the same time to "corkscrew" in a manner that can only be compared to a small boat in a "quartering" sea. On turns, the roll is appreciable, tho not particularly detrimental to cornering power if you get accustomed to it. Caster, or return action, is much too powerful and very tiring. The steering is not definite—normally there is a bare trace of understeer but turns taken really hard show evidence of oversteer up to the point where the rear end begins to slide—which then produces drastic oversteer. The above conditions are not by helped by a steering ratio of just over 23 to 1 requiring $4\frac{1}{2}$ turns of the wheel, but then what American car of equal or larger size is any better?

Incidentally, lowering blocks were fitted and gave a definite improvement in handling qualities and are very fine, provided that the car is not over-loaded.

Engine cooling can only be described as passable in comparison to other American makes, nearly all of which will boil under summer driving conditions readily found in California.

The Bendix duo-servo brakes give a very light pedal pressure and are satisfactory for average American road conditions, tho lining life is very short (30,000 miles) and some brake fade can be induced.

The E.L.P. (extra low pressure) tires which I was forced to take in order to get delivery are generally unsatisfactory. Ford is to be commended for continuing 6.00-16 tires as standard equipment. Tire squeal can be reduced somewhat by carrying higher

pressures which also improves the tire mileage by a very considerable amount. At 48,000 miles my car still has the original 5 tires, albeit with no tread pattern left. I recently tried 6.50-15 tires and it was almost impossible to get squeal and the car handled much better.

The Ford transmission has always had a good reputation and the '49 is virtually unchanged, except in minor detail. The gear ratio in 1st (2.82) is much lower than necessary with a such a "tail-light" car and the blocker-type syncro-mesh falls short of the standard of fool-proofness of the cam type syncro-mesh. Fast shifts are hindered by the flexible remote control system, which is very lightly constructed but has given no trouble even tho bent nearly double trying to "stay" with competitive minded Olds 88s. The clutch remains the Long semi-centrifugal type—one of the best, and action is still smoother by virtue of the more flexible Hotchkiss drive now used.

The 1949 Ford with its completely new (to Ford) design of chassis and body is not without faults. On the other hand, many of the minor irritations have been corrected on the 1950 and 1951 models. These include door rattles, fan belt squeal, and cold piston slap. I do not hesitate to recommend the Ford—the chassis design is sound, the powerplant time proven, and the body design functional. I particularly like the reversion to 56-inch tread, low frontal area, simple lines, box section frame, low weight, large displacement engine, ideal 3.73 axle ratio, servo brakes, Hotchkiss drive, hypoid axle gears, and much improved ease of servicing. As to the earlier rather critical comments, these are faults found on virtually any American stock car—remedied, perhaps, on the sports car mentioned in the first paragraph which should be completed by Spring. With wheelbase reduced by 10 inches to 104, engine aft by 18 engines, and a light 2-seater body, it should prove an ideal all-around car for my purposes.

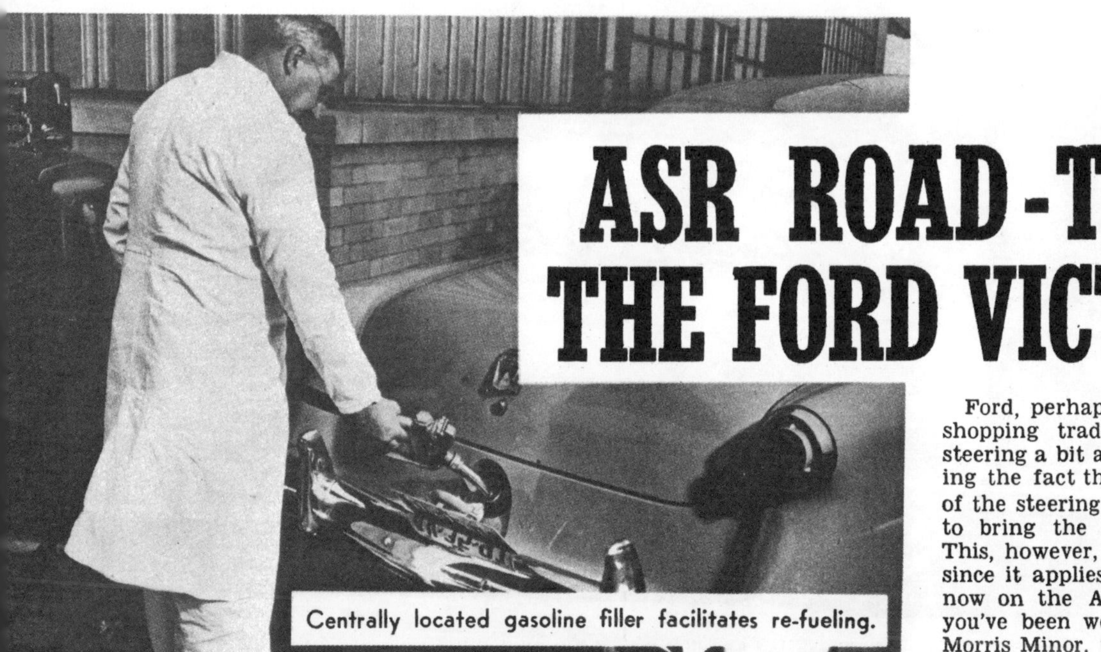

ASR ROAD-TESTS THE FORD VICTORIA

Centrally located gasoline filler facilitates re-fueling.

By

MORGAN MORRIS

THE 1952 Ford has received so much praise lately by various testers that AUTO SPORT REVIEW decided to run a road test and see for itself.

Right off the bat it could be seen that the '52 Ford is a "fat cat." It's plush, it's beautiful—in fact old Henry probably would not recognize it.

Despite the full styling treatment, the current Ford remains a Ford fan's Ford. It still has the personality and character that have made it the basic hot rod and custom job from coast to coast.

The car tested was a V-8 Victoria with Fordomatic transmission. If it seems to be heresy to use an automatic transmission car for test, it should be pointed out that automatics are here to stay. Whether we like it or not, in a few years shifting gears will be as obsolete as cranking the telephone before making a call.

Granted that there is some power loss and that the price is higher, the fact remains that Americans just don't want to develop their wrists by out-guessing road load torque requirements. In any case, the Ford-o-matic is just about the finest automatic transmission on the market.

The car was provided by Palmer Motors, Staten Island, New York. This outfit was sure enough of the product to pick a car off the floor and send it out with no holds barred. There were only about 800 miles on the speedometer, so it wasn't pushed too hard.

Ford, perhaps in response to the shopping trade, has softened the steering a bit and there is no denying the fact that quite a few turns of the steering wheel are necessary to bring the car around a bend. This, however, is a minor criticism since it applies to almost every car now on the American market. If you've been weaned on an MG or Morris Minor, the Ford makes you feel as though you are wading through the turn, but the steering could be a lot worse and there is good solid feel to the car while cornering.

Acceleration, despite the automatic transmission, is good. Zero to fifty is under 12 seconds, although no very close check was made, considering the car's low mileage. It should be remembered, too, that this is done with an engine relatively unchanged since 1932. The new overhead V-8, which will be out soon, should set a new standard for performance, judging by what the old V-8 can do.

STATEN ISLAND (New York) is an ideal test ground. It has high crowned macadem, six-lane concrete, dirt lanes and what the British like to call pave (paving blocks to you). Road surfaces range from excellent to impassable. The Ford took them all in stride. The

Ford Victoria holds road; has good cornering qualities.

Spare tire is easy to remove from trunk compartment.

Extended headlights and jutting tail lights give Ford Victoria sleek look.

steering wheel was far from "dead" but it showed no tendency to bounce, no matter how hard pot holes and ruts were hit. A strong side wind failed to deflect the car from its course, even at 90 M.P.H.

The speedometer, oddly enough, was a bit low, a nice change from the optimistic instruments commonly installed. Considering that this was a dealer's car right off the floor, it seems likely that the Ford Company doesn't belong to that group of car makers who believe that they are making for safer and saner driving by kidding the driver about how fast he is going.

There is one thing which can do with a little improvement and that is weight distribution. The tail end is light and a rough surface on a steep grade is best taken carefully. Wet paving blocks stopped this

CONTINUED ON PAGE 39

Controls are conveniently grouped to the left of steering wheel.

Uphill acceleration from a standing start is good.

Eight-cylinder Ford negotiates rough terrain easily.

The Golden Anniversary Ford, with its distinctive grille, has been chosen as the pace car at the 1953 Indianapolis race.

'03-FORD-'53

Fifty years ago the "Boss of the Road" was the Fordmobile. The Golden Anniversary model also qualifies for that title in the ride department.

Speed Age Staff Research Report
Photos by DON O'REILLY

FIFTY years ago a company—with $28,000 in cash and the plans of a man who at 40 was twice a failure—sallied forth in Detroit to engage the already well established automobile industry.

The man behind that venture, the designer whose faith in his own horseless carriage couldn't be shaken by adversity, was Henry Ford.

History has long since credited Ford as the man most responsible for the evolution of mass transportation and its accompanying social and industrial benefits.

That first production model in 1903 was the Fordmobile, the "Boss of the Road." By the time models N, K and S had given way to the now famous T, the slogan "Watch the Fords Go By" was a household by-word. Then came the Model A and B and, finally the V8.

For more than 20 of the Ford Motor Company's 50 years, the V8 has been one of the most popular powerplants in the low price field. Introduced in 1932, this engine has retained its position as one of the production leaders of the world without undergoing any radical design changes.

Its straightforwardness, economy of replacement parts, sturdiness and potential has made it one of the most popular blocks for the hot rod, sports car and even racing car builders. That it has stood up, and in many cases produced more than twice its original rated horsepower, is a tribute to the genius who designed it.

The Ford for 1953 continues this basic V8 which was stepped up to 110 HP last year. A conventional L-head, this engine

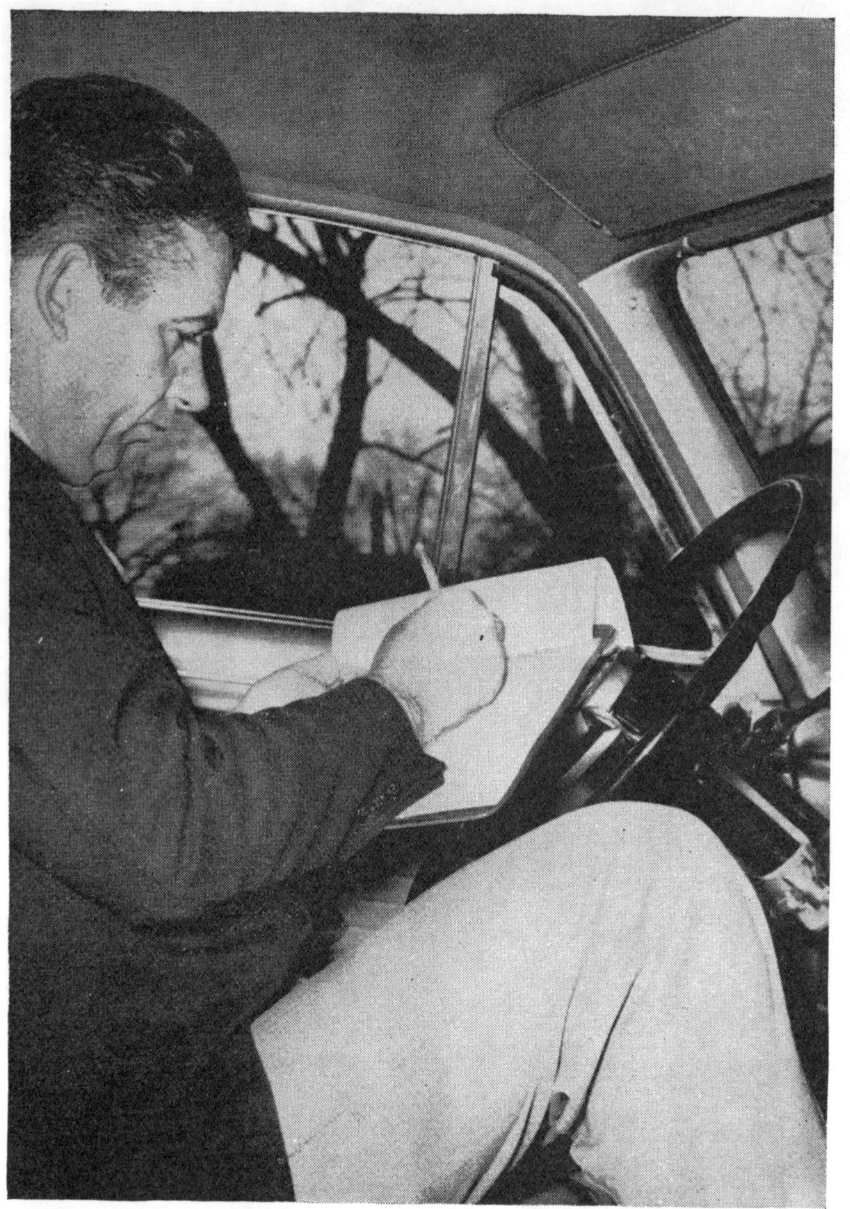

Vince McDonald, a member of the research team, makes notations of the Ford's performance after trial run using a PerfOMeter, mounted on steering column.

$1,991.42—plus taxes—Customline standard equipment includes two sun visors, half-circle horn ring with special button at center, metal exterior molding at windshield and rear window, two interior lights operated by automatic door switches in addition to manual control, metal molding on side panels, front and rear arm rests, one ash tray in rear compartment of Fordor and two in others, Customline nameplate and bright metal molding on instrument panel, cigarette lighter, pebble-grain rubber mat in rear compartment harmonizing with interior trim, bright metal cap moldings on side embossments, illuminated clock and wheel rings.

In city traffic where most of the testing was done, the ease of handling and its snap up to 35 MPH is equal to any. Beyond this point, however, the automatic transmission won't satisfy the nervous individual who must 'beat the pack'. A torque converter coupled with a gear box, the transmission shifts without hesitation and so smoothly it can hardly be felt. This results in a snappier pickup than the ordinary fluid or torque converter coupling, but is not as positive as the automatic mechanical gears. Using the kickdown switch for passing or hill-climbing results in an immediate revving of the motor, but no great transfer of engine speed to the rear wheels as could be expected.

Although this year's Ford is a long way from the top in the horsepower race, the car's ease in handling leaves you with a light airy feeling and is somewhat that has been attained heretofore only with power steering. Much of the new ease built into the '53 Ford can be traced directly to a stronger frame and redesigned front and rear suspension systems.

One of the motoring public's major gripes about low-priced cars has been the handling and steering qualities of these automobiles.

Ford has attacked the problem—in its Mainline and Customline sedan and coupes—by using a K-bar frame. This is essentially a box frame with five cross members, if those closing the box are

runs a 7.2 to 1 compression ratio. Also available is the Mileage Maker Six, the overhead valve, 101 HP engine introduced last year. Both powerplants operate on standard fuel. Since most manufacturers are swinging to the V8 engine, the Six can very well become the economist in the Ford line. Both engines are offered with a choice of three transmissions, conventional, overdrive and Fordomatic.

But Ford's emphasis this year is on riding and handling qualities and the Customline Fordor sedan, equipped with Fordomatic, tested by the SPEED AGE staff, held some pleasant surprises.

This car was picked up at the Chester. Pa., assembly plant, the largest of 15 such plants where 4,000 parts are put together to make an automobile. Since there are 12,000 pieces involved in the manufacture of a Ford, it is obvious much subassembly has been done before individual operations begin at these branch plants.

Delivered in Washington, D. C. for

The car was put through rigorous braking tests. A Speed Age driver is beginning to apply the brakes at 50 MPH in a panic stop. Brake fade was negligible.

As brake pressure is applied the Ford's rear end lifts sharply from the road.

counted. The 'K' effect is achieved by extending a strut from each front corner of the box diagonally to the next cross member. This additional stiffness results in a flatter ride, softer steering and helps prevent body rattles.

In conjunction with the chassis changes, Ford doubled the up and down distance the front wheels can travel before the compression bumpers 'bottom' against the frame. These bumpers are small, cone-shaped rubber pucks located between each

With full brake power on, the rear of the car starts to come around.

front wheel control arm and the chassis. The shock absorbers also have been re-valved, probably with smaller holes in the pistons to slow down the flow of fluid and more quickly snub wheel movement. The semi-elliptic rear springs are softer, and mounting the new shock absorbers diagonally helps take the tilt out of turns. Altogether, the ride is very much like that of a heavier car.

These changes have done wonders for cornering ability. Body pitch is reduced considerably, thereby keeping weight distributed more evenly over all wheeels. After diving into a few turns at speeds that normally would be considered unsafe, and coming out with the feeling there was something to spare, one develops a healthy respect for a frame and

All instruments are plainly marked for easier operation. Glare is kept to a mini-minimum by sparing use of chrome. Unlighted quadrant was major objection.

suspension that makes this a safer car for John Q. Public.

Although the sloppiness and bad road behavior of the '52 Ford has been eliminated, steering is still slow—five turns from lock to lock. A longer, stiffer linkage with its added leverage gives a much easier and more positive control.

Ford brakes are excellent with no tendency to fade, even under severe punishment; however, without the weight of passengers in the rear seat, extreme caution must be exercised in emergency stops. The back end has a tendency to lift and swing, so that all too quickly the car is sideways on the road. For the unwary or a person with slow reflexes, this could be disaster.

The hand brake, once referred to as an emergency brake, can again come under this heading; when set, it locks both rear wheels.

At top speed, there is no feeling of discomfort, the car flattens out and control is as positive as when in normal driving.

Gas mileage with the Fordomatic is not as good as that with the manual transmission and certainly not as good as the overdrive. Heavy city traffic recorded 14 to 15 miles per gallon, but at 35 MPH on the open road the mileage jumps to 19 MPG. At 50 it drops off to a little better than 17 MPG and at 60 MPH goes to 16 MPG. In overdrive one could expect a substantial gain in mileage and top speed.

Seating room at shoulder height is less than in many standard size automobiles and riding for any distance with three people on one seat is decidedly uncomfortable. However, leg room, especially in the rear seat, is much better than average, even with the front seat pushed full back. Front seats have automatic posture control and a mechanism for fore-and-aft adjustment of four inches. During this adjustment the seat cushion rises a half inch while the back tilts forward 1.8 inches.

Instrumentation is well designed and convenient to the operator—with one exception. The Fordomatic indicator quadrant is not lighted and, when driving at night, the operator must grope or guess to find the right position whenever the automatic selector is moved.

The glove compartment, is just that. Out of reach for the driver and entirely too small to be of any use. Free of excess chrome, the instrument panel's flat finish is eye resting and without dangerous reflections. Controls are of the push-pull type and so located that they do not represent a hazard in event of a collision.

The steering wheel, with a 50th anniversary medallion in the center, has a single crossmember and the horn ring only on the lower half. This is a commendable safety feature. The gauges are grouped around the speedometer, so that a glance is all that is needed to read one, or all, without interference and a full circle, one-piece windshield, low hood lines and wrap-around rear window provide excellent driving visibility.

There is very little road noise or shock transmitted to the body, and engine noise is effectively muffled by a glass fiber padding under the hood. This adds greatly to the comfort of the passengers and normal conversation can be carried on with ease. This is an improvement on the Fords of a few years ago.

Nature cooperated during the SPEED AGE test, providing a week of steady downpour. In addition to this, a high pressure hose test failed to reveal any body leakage. This year's body appears to live up to the company's claim that it is dust and draft free.

Body lines have not been changed appreciably from the previous year's model although the grille has been redesigned

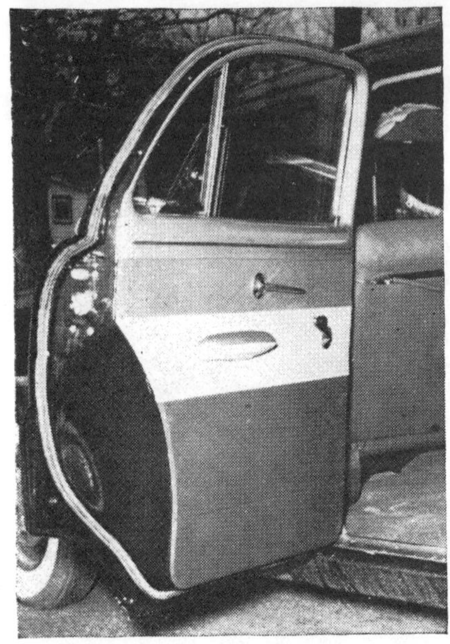

Rear doors open in the same way as the front ones, allowing easy entrance.

with a single chrome center spinner. A chrome molding also runs through the center of the rear fenderline and the tail light lenses have been altered to be more easily seen from the side and rear.

Continued is the centerfill gas cap styling and the mounting of brake, and clutch pedal on those cars so equipped, by suspending them from the rear of the dashboard.

Equipping the doors with 2-stage door checks is a big help to the shopper who, previously, after swinging open the door to place an armload of parcels inside, was in turn helped inside when the door swung shut.

Door handles are on the push button type and the doors themselves are large enough to permit easy entrance and exit. Those in the rear, in the 4-door sedan, follow modern styling in that they serve as a side to the seat.

Both the trunk and hood lids are counterbalanced and swing upward easily. The hood however, is unlatched from

The Ford features doors that will open to half or full-open positions, a convenient device for laden shoppers. The car also has the suspended pedal setup.

The door at the full-open position, below, allows more than ample room for entering or leaving the car. The body gave no indication of drafts or rattles.

ROAD TEST REPORT STATISTICAL DATA

Engine Specifications

ENGINE:
Number of cylinders. 8
Arrangement ....90 degree V
Valve arrangement ....L-Head
Bore ....3.19 inches
Stroke ....3.75 inches
Displacement ....239.4 cubic inches
Taxable horsepower 32.5
Brake horsepower ....110 @ 3800 RPM
Maximum Torque 196 foot pounds @ 19-2100 RPM
Compression ratio ....7.2 to 1
Numbering system
  (front to rear)—Left bank 5-6-7-8
            Right bank 1-2-3-4
Firing order 1-5-4-8-6-3-7-2

PISTONS:
Material ....Aluminum alloy
Description.....Autothermic, solid skirt cam-
  ground, spherical head, tin-plated
Weight ....13.05-13.19 ounces
Compression rings 2
Oil rings 2

PISTON PINS:
Material ....Alloy steel, heat treated
Type ....Full floating

CONNECTING RODS:
Material ....Forged steel
Length, C to C ....6.998-7.002 inches
Weight ....18.66-19.01 ounces

CRANKSHAFT:
Material ....Precision-molded alloy iron
Weight ....62 pounds
Number of main bearings 3
Connecting rod journal diameter.2.1385 inches

VALVES:
Material ....#1 Silchrome
Diameter of head ....1.505-1.515 inches
Angle of seat ....Not listed
Intake valve opens ....5 degrees BTC
Intake valve closes ....41 degrees ABC
Exhaust valve opens ....48 degrees BBC
Exhaust valve closes ....3 degrees ATC

MISCELLANEOUS:
Oil Capacity ....4 quarts
Fuel capacity ....17 gallons
Water capacity ....23 quarts
Battery ....15 plate, 90 ampere

TRANSMISSION:
Automatic:
Number of forward speeds 2
Gear ratio, power range
  2.44—1 Plus Torque Converter
Gear ratio, drive 1.48
  1 Plus Torque Converter
Gear ratio, reverse
  2.00—1 Plus Torque Converter
Downshift possible up to 62 MPH

Interior Specifications

Width of front seat
  (shoulder height) 55.2 inches
Width of back seat
  (shoulder height) 54.7 inches
Depth of front seat cushion..........18.2 inches
Depth of rear seat cushion..........19.0 inches
Total adjustment of front seat at floor.4.1 inches
Vertical distance, wheel to seat.......5.9 inches
Head room, front seat ....35.4 inches
Head room, rear seat ....34.2 inches
Leg room, front seat ....42.8 inches
Leg room, rear seat ....41.5 inches

Chassis

FRAME:
Type......Ladder with box section side rails,
  five cross-members and 'K' bracing.
Wheelbase ....115.0 inches
Tread:
  Front ....58 inches
  Rear ....56 inches
Weight:
  Shipping ....Not available
Overall length ....197.8 inches
Overall width ....74.3 inches
Overall height ....62.3 inches

REAR AXLE:
Type ....Semi-floating
Gearing ....Hypoid
Ratio..(Automatic) ....3.31 to 1

FOOT BRAKES:
Drum diameter ....10 inches
Material.Pressed steel disc and cast iron drum
Effective area ....173.52 square inches
Type.....Hydraulic, internal expanding, Duo-
  Servo, single anchor
Linings ....Molded asbestos

Ford V8 Customline

STEERING:
Type.......Ford, worm and triple tooth roller
Turns, lock to lock 5
Ratio ....26.3 to 1
Turning radius ....Not available

ROAD CLEARANCE:
Minimum ....7.1 inches

SUSPENSION:
Front....Independent-coil spring incorporating
  two unequal length transverse control
  arms
Rear ....Longitudinal leaf
Shock absorbers....Monroe, Gabriel or Houde

TIRES:
Size ....6.70 x 15
Pressure: front ....26 pounds
        rear ....23 pounds

Performance Data

	INDICATED	ACTUAL
East-west run ...	94 MPH	88 MPH
Opposite direction ...	92 MPH	86 MPH
Average ...		87 MPH

Rate of Acceleration

0-20 MPH ....3.3 seconds
0-30 MPH ....6 seconds
0-50 MPH ....14 seconds
0-60 MPH ....19 seconds

Brakes

Efficiency 78%

Prices, delivered at Washington, D. C.

	SIX	V8
MAINLINE		
Business coupe	$1,655.70	$1,731.90
Tudor	1,759.96	1,835.57
Fordor	1,808.84	1,884.46
Ranch Wagon	2,140.77	2,216.94
CUSTOMLINE		
Tudor	$1,866.86	$1,942.52
Fordor	1,915.76	1,991.42
Club Coupe	1,876.36	1,952.57
Country Sedan	......	2,409.31
CRESTLINE		
Victoria	......	$2,259.55
Sunliner	......	2,369.24
Country Squire	......	2,548.56

Bumper Guard—Front $24.50
Bumper Guard—Rear 25.70
Cigarette Lighter—Mainline 3.90
Clock, Stem Wind—Mainline 11.60
Clock, Electric—Mainline 19.00
Coronado Deck 45.90
Directional Signals 15.26
Fordomatic Transmission 184.00
Heater—Magic Air 71.43
Heater—Recirculating 43.89
Hood Ornament 6.50
Horn Ring—Deluxe 5.10
Leather Type Trim 30.53
Light, Back-up (pair) 12.05
Light, Glove Compartment 3.15
Light, Luggage Compartment 1.80
Light, Under Hood 2.15
Overdrive 109.70
Paint, 2-tone 19.35
Radio—6-tube 87.50
Radio—8-tube 99.50
Radio—Rear Seat Speaker 11.50
Seat Covers—*(Tudors-Fordors-Coupes)*
Check Weave Fibre 31.40
Parade Plastic 40.60
Premier Nylon 54.15
(Victoria)
Fiesta Fibre 36.60
Candy Stripe Plastic 46.60
Premier Nylon 54.15
Signal—Hand Brake 4.75
Spotlight with Mirror 23.80
Sun Visor—Outside, painted 25.00
Tinted Glass 23.13
Windshield Washer 9.59

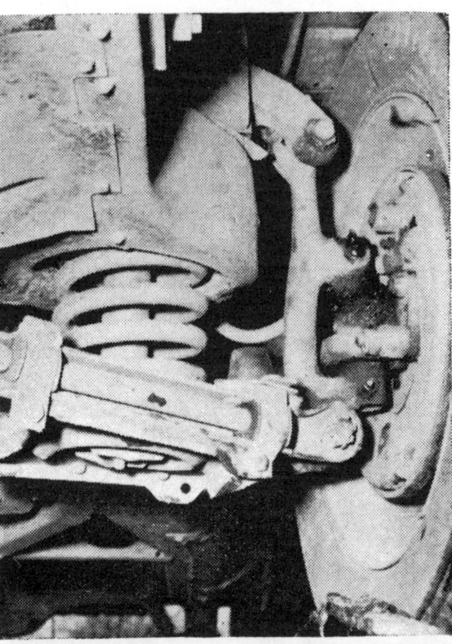

The independent coil spring suspension of the new Ford gives a smooth ride.

the outside, an obvious economy measure which also has drawbacks. The inside release is a great deterrent to under-the-hood burglars.

This Ford, unlike some of its bigger brothers, also will be a mechanic and serviceman's delight since there is hardly any unit which cannot be reached readily for repair or replacement.

Safetywise, the Ford rates high. Interior protrusions are very few and the car's steadiness on any type of roadbed puts it in a class by itself, safety-wise.

A few years ago Ford led the field in total sales. It still ranks high in volume—second only to Chevrolet—and this model may make Ford's Golden Anniversary year the company's best. ☆ ☆

Shocks are mounted at an angle on the improved, sturdier rear suspension.

In profile, the new Ford could easily be mistaken for last year's model. This is the Crestline Sunliner, which is available in 12 colors with blending two-tone leather and vinyl upholstery.

testing the

1953 FORD

by george greer

There are few external changes, but Ford has made some major refinements since 1952

THE 1953 Ford hit the market with very few changes except for a new grille, new tail lights, new chrome strips on the rear fenders, and some chrome strips on the dashboard which further improve the appearance somewhat. There are some mechanical changes involving the riding quality. When the 1952 Ford was introduced last year its enthusiastic acceptance and resultant demand worried a number of prominent gentlemen in the low-priced car sales department. That their worries were legitimate has been borne out by the sales record of the 1952 model, which at the moment is knocking on the door of the sales leader of past years.

It's no surprise, then, that the 1953 Ford retains the same body shell. The dimensions are the same inside and it could be mistaken for a 1952 Ford at first glance.

But don't let this fool you. The 1953 Ford is a much better automobile than its older brother. One may say that the 1953 Ford is a thoroughly refined version of the earlier model.

On the day the new Fords were shown in New York City, a new eight-cylinder Customline four-door sedan was made available for AUTO AGE to test. A thorough road test was made of this car, extending over a period of two weeks and covering a total of over 1,000 miles. Ironically, the car was used for an emergency call at night between 2:30 and 6:30 a.m. the first day of the test. The usual break-in routine had to be dispensed with, and the car was pushed through gears (it was a standard shift model, not

Greatest difference is found in the grille, which still features the familiar central spinner but is considerably cleaner and handsomer than before.

TESTING THE 1953 FORD

equipped with overdrive) at RPM's which would have made Henry Ford Jr.'s hair turn gray, considering that the odometer showed all of 5/10ths of a mile when the test started. Neither the engine nor the rest of the running gear seemed to object to this treatment, and during the remainder of the test nothing showed up which would indicate that it had been too rough for the car.

The doors now have a two-position door check which will keep them open in either the half-way position or all the way. This comes in very handy in close spaces, such as you encounter in parking lots or public garages. It also helps in dense traffic, where it is usually dangerous to open the door all the way when getting in or out of the car.

With the exception of the above-mentioned changes, the general interior appointments are the same as in the 1952 Ford, quiet and conservative. The only objection I could find was the loudspeaker grille in the dashboard which looks cheap and has a tendency to rattle. The radio speaker, when turned on at over one-quarter volume, has a lot of distortion, and I believe this is due to the poorly constructed grille.

The front seat is of good height and gives you adequate support where it is needed. The seat adjustment, though, should be easier to operate than it was on the model tested. The rear seat also is very comfortable and there is plenty of leg and headroom for most people. It is not an obstacle course getting in and out of the car as it is with some. Doors open and close easily. Windows, including vent windows, are easily operated.

The trunk lid is countersprung, so that it opens practically by itself as soon as the key is turned in the lock. There is certainly enough usable trunk space to house the baggage of an average family of four. And while we are on the subject it should be mentioned that the trunk deck emblem has also been changed this year.

SITTING in the driver's seat, one has plenty of vision both forward and to the rear. A one-piece windshield is used as well as a large one-piece wrap-around rear window. Believe it or not, you can actually see the right front fender from the driver's seat. The ignition key also operates the starter (this is now becoming standard procedure on a lot of new models). Both brake and clutch pedals are suspended from underneath

the dashboard instead of projecting from the floorboards; this also makes it possible for the master cylinder to be mounted on the firewall at about the same height as the engine intake manifold. This is obviously a better place than the old position and makes it easy to service the unit. In fact the whole engine compartment is clean and uncluttered, and evidently an effort was made to allow easier servicing of the main engine components.

During the first few hours of the test run it became quite obvious that this car handles very easily in traffic, with a very smooth clutch and smooth powerful brakes that do not require very much foot pressure to stop the car. The car steers very easily; in fact, it is geared so that the steering wheel can be turned without any great effort while the car is standing still. This makes it easy to park the car in the closest spaces, and women will love it. But—and this is a big but—in order to accomplish this feat a steering ratio had to be used which means nearly five turns from lock to lock. And brother, that doesn't mean quick steering. It means mushy long-winded steering every time you turn a street corner, and what happens if you want to steer out of real trouble quickly at high speed is something that the writer did not even try. This super-easy clock-wind steering is about the worst fault of the automobile. Up to about 70 mph the car maintains a nice level ride but above that speed a definite steering wander is noticed which requires continuous correction. In my opinion this is definitely a dangerous factor!

The suspension is good both front and rear. The car will hold to the inside of a highway bend where more expensive makes will not—but here again the steering ratio louses up a really good spring set-up. There is very little sideway of the body and practically no up-and-down motion even on a rough and rutted road. Very little road shock is transferred through the steering wheel, but one is continually steering the car to keep it going straight. This annoyed the writer as well as two other people who drove the car, and none of us can understand why this was not corrected on the 1953 models, since the 1952's had the same steering ratio. It is recommended that anyone who intends to use a Ford for high-speed work consider altering the steering by lengthening the pitman arm or adopting the Ford truck F1 steering gear set-up.

This would give an overall ratio of about 18:1 or about 3¾ turns from lock to lock.

The brakes acted very well over the entire test route. They are powerful, with brake fade only becoming evident after four emergency stops in succession were made from 75 mph to zero. Even then they recovered their full strength within a few minutes. Under other conditions they will not fade. They are also watertight as far as could be determined.

The clutch is still of the centrifugal type and the amount of abuse it got on the test proves once again that it is one of the toughest on the market. No chatter, either! We purposely shifted the car from 3rd gear to 2nd at 69-73 mph, letting the clutch out rather fast, with no bad results to either clutch, universals or transmission. This was done repeatedly with no ill effects. Under extreme acceleration from a standing start there is a small amount of rear spring "wind up" which produces some wheel spin, but even this is very negligible. Suspension-wise this car leaves very little to be desired, and that only in the steering department.

AS far as the eight-cylinder, 110-hp engine is concerned, the least that can be said is, "Give it all you can and it will ask for more." This only proves that Ford really knows how to make V-8's. This engine performs at its best at over 30 mph in high gear or above 1,200 rpm. Below this speed it is somewhat sluggish, especially if the gas pedal is suddenly floorboarded all the way. However, this engine will pick up from eight or even six mph in high gear smoothly if the throttle is opened gently.

During our test run we hit all kinds of weather—sun, snow, ice and plenty of rain. This gave us a chance to observe the car under all conditions, and among other things we noticed that the body is absolutely watertight. The general behavior on ice and snow is fair. There is a lack of rear-wheel traction because of the somewhat unequal weight distribution. This, however, is true of most late-model passenger cars.

In the writer's opinion, this car would be a much better buy if it were equipped with overdrive at no extra cost. In the first place there would be less engine noise at high speeds, and better gas consumption figures would be realized. Our test car was not equipped with overdrive and carried a rear axle ratio of

CONTINUED ON PAGE 39

FORD FOR '54

Introduction of the 1954 Ford with its all-new overhead valve V-8 engine and many other features is a highly significant development on the motoring scene. Impressed with the importance of this in advance, MOTOR LIFE sent Correspondent George Johnson to Detroit. His assignment: Put the new car through its paces, bring back a first-hand report. To round out the coverage, MOTOR LIFE had Engine Expert Barney Navarro prepare an analysis of the modification possibilities of the new overhead valve V-8 engine, which will be found on page 18. But, first of all, Johnson's story.—Ed.

BY GEORGE JOHNSON

WHAT KIND of a car does Ford have for '54? It was a hot, sunny day in early fall when I arrived in Detroit to get the answer to that important question. For nearly a week I drove the cars, studied them and weighed the results. Let's have a look, on paper, at the facts and figures.

Ford's big proving ground is the ideal course for testing a car. Rugged is too mild a word to describe the man-made conditions. Roads full of chuck holes, bumpy track crossings, steep grades, frame-wrenching twists in pavement—plus a banked track for long, easy speed runs. And we went over all of them!

The testing and detailed examinations covered a variety of cars. A few were 1953 Fords equipped with the new '54 ohv V-8, put together primarily for engine checks. The rest were complete '54 models, prototypes set up for shakedown runs

of all the features. In fairness to Ford, I should say that not all of the cars were in top condition, some having been through very rough treatment before my arrival.

Since the '54 models mark the first major engine change by Ford in more than 20 years, performance was the first item I had in mind. To point up the improvement, tests were made with stock two-door sedans using standard transmission. Here are comparison figures, listing the new engine's acceleration alongside that clocked by one of the old faithful flathead V-8s:

	'54 OHV V-8	'53 FLATHEAD
0-30 mph, seconds	5.4	6.1
0-45 mph, seconds	12.1	13.1
0-60 mph, seconds	16.2	20.1
Standing Quarter-Mile, seconds	18.7	21.5
Top Speed, mph	93.9	87

Acceleration, of course, was not the only yardstick we used to measure the new engine's performance. Its efficiency is also indicated by miles per gallon. So under a similar setup, we made another comparison:

	'54 OHV V-8	'53 FLATHEAD
Steady 30 mph	22.4	21
Steady 45 mph	20.3	19.2
Steady 60 mph	17.7	16.0

The figures speak for themselves and any comment on them would be superfluous. However, they do not demonstrate the smoothness of the new engine. The familiar old

Trailing a fifth wheel, a Ford convertible samples the pulling power of the new ohv V-8 on the 17 per cent grade of an artificial hill at company's proving ground track

Switch in engines has had good and bad points from accessibility angle. However, the change in the suspension and frame clears oil pan area, permitting much easier removal

Test driver has a look at the new plexiglass top which is tinted to eliminate most of heat rays from the sun. Overall view of the model showing styling is at top of opposite page

Ford made a major dash change. Most notable is unique mounting of speedometer made of transparent plastic. Instrument panel and knobs are recessed for increased safety

Rough treatment received by cars at Ford's track is illustrated as a '53 model powered by new ohv V-8 takes railroad crossing setup with a high bounce. Tests like this also gave new front end suspension system a severe beating and demonstrated the easier handling characteristics as well as simpler repair operation

The ball joint front end on Ford for '54 is compared with arrangement used on 1953 and earlier models. Originally introduced on the '52 Lincoln, the suspension system has longer arms which reduce road shock. The kingpin is eliminated and lubrication points have been trimmed from 16 to four. Principle used is similar to the human arm; it can move up and down and at the same time rotate for steering movement

throb of power strokes has been softened, I found. In fact, they've been virtually silenced and, at any speed, the operation is scarcely audible. The only apparent sound of movement while at speed comes from the windstream flowing over the body and the steady hum of the tires on the pavement.

More comment on the engine is due. But at this point it's appropriate, when speaking of over-the-road travel, to touch upon another important item in the '54—the front suspension system.

Engine improvement has received much attention in the postwar years. Far too little notice has been given to the handling qualities of the American automobile. Ford now steps smartly into the spotlight with its ball-joint suspension system which was first introduced on the '52 Lincoln. The system has now been extended to the complete Ford line of cars.

In the ball-joint suspension system, the front wheels are connected to the spring-supported arms coming out on each side of the frame by two simple ball-and-socket joints on each front wheel—one connecting to the top supporting arm and the other to the bottom supporting arm. This allows a four-way movement with a dual purpose: up and down for the road shocks; back and forth for the turning movements.

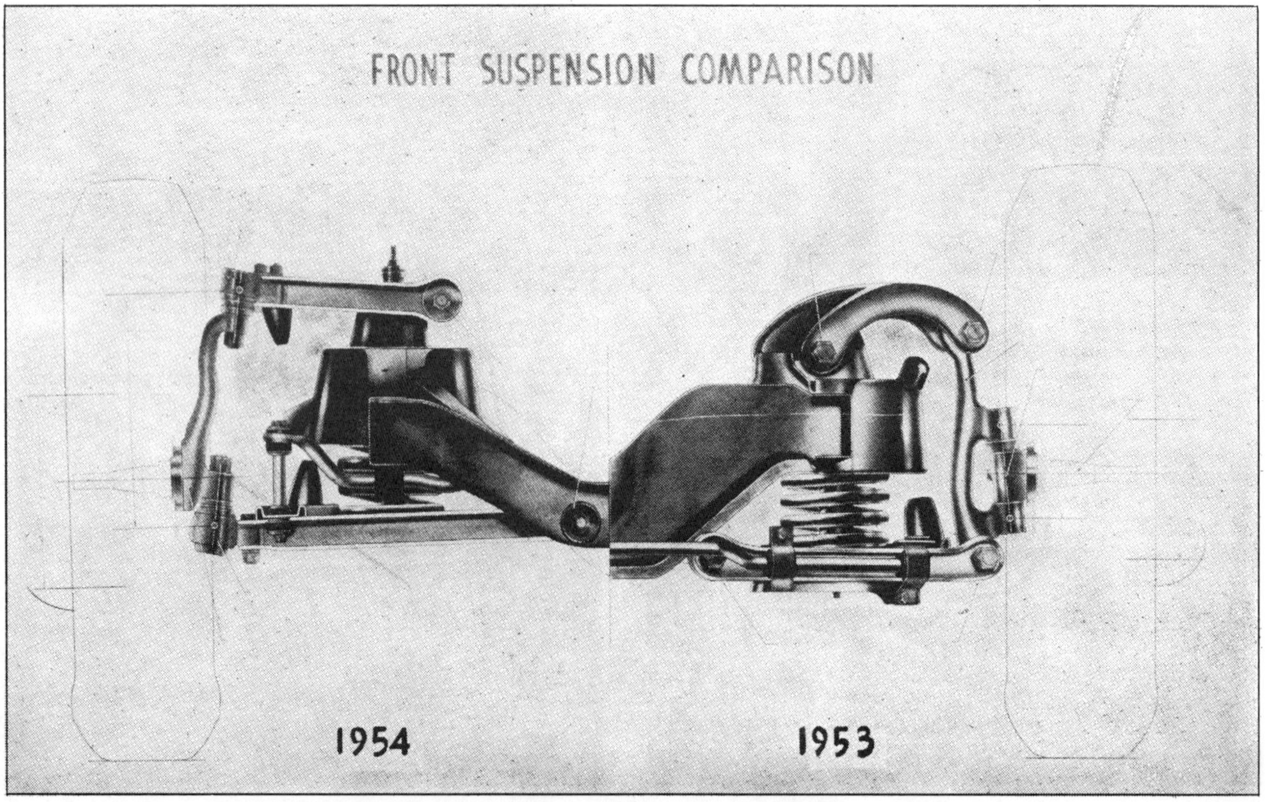

The benefits of this arrangement are twofold. First, servicing and repair work are simplified. The servicing is easier since lubrication points in the front end are reduced from 16 to four. Repair work is facilitated because the units can be removed and replaced in half the former time, while wheel alignment is no longer a major operation.

Secondly, a valuable improvement in handling is achieved. Steering is much lighter and requires less effort on the part of the driver. At moderately high speeds, the '54 Ford was swung into a tight circle with only a slight body roll. Furthermore, the tiresome vibration and road shock transmitted through the steering column was markedly reduced.

NOW LET'S get back to the engine. I found that the power plant under the hood was the product of some five years of research by Ford engineers who worked their way through more than 600 variations in design. The one finally decided upon contains a displacement of 239 cubic inches with a bore and stroke of 3.50 x 3.10. Using a compression ratio of 7.2-to-1, it produces a maximum output of 130 hp at 4,200 rpm with torque (lb-ft) rated at 214 from 1,800 to 2,200 rpm. It is important to note that the power increase over the former 115-hp flathead V-8 has been achieved without boosting the displacement.

The greater efficiency comes, naturally, from the combination of new features. In addition, the design promises greater reliability through its rigid construction. To cite all of the improvements that have been incorporated would be impracticable in this report. But a number of them should be noted.

One item pointed to with pride by Ford engineers was the cast, rather than forged, crankshaft which now has five main bearings, as against three in the flathead. The number of counterweights has been brought up to a total of eight, a factor which will assure smoother operation and greater resistance to vibration.

The ohv arrangement has reduced the surface area in the combustion chambers which means less heat loss through the cooling jacket. Valve size has been increased with improved timing. Better breathing of the engine, an essential item for increased power and efficiency, has been accomplished with redesigned porting and manifolding for both intake and exhaust systems.

A sidelight on the engine is the fact that the new frame and suspension setup permits lower seating and easier accessibility to the oil pan area from below.

IN STYLING, the '54 Ford incorporates a few major and many minor changes. Greatest single innovation is the appearance in the Ford lineup of the plastic-topped model. My first reaction, aside from personally approving the attractiveness of the model, was what will it be like on a scorching summer day?

Since the weather already was hot, I had an ideal opportunity to check this car for comfort. After switching between it and a normal steel-roofed sedan, I could detect no noticeable difference. The en-

CONTINUED ON PAGE 69

Overall view of '54 Crestline convertible shows that Ford has retained the basic styling lines that proved so popular in 1953. The long, clean look is unchanged and minor refinements made in grille and trim are designed to give the car a lower and wider look. Note the new transparent plastic speedometer in front of the steering wheel

Chassis arrangement for the 1954 Ford models shows the revisions made in frame, suspension system and engine seating. Area below engine has been cleared for servicing through relocation of tubular cross-member, while lower positioning will permit reduction in hood height. Frame side members are of full box section and now surround the coil spring pockets for increased strength and rugged durability

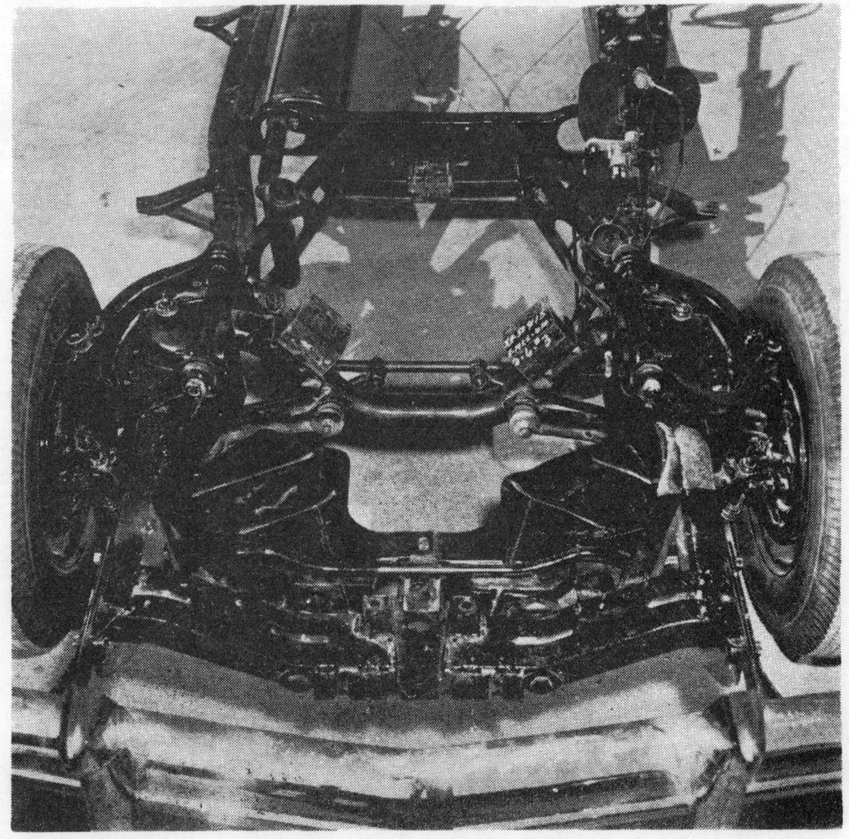

Skyliner goes through paces in wet sand to prove stability.

Testing FORD'S OVERHEAD VALVE V-8

IF **YOU** happen to be one of the many Ford devotees of long standing, this is your year to howl. Because the new overhead valve V-8 engine, the ball-joint front suspension and some other points of good design combine to make the 1954 V-8 as satisfactory a car as Ford has yet produced.

That ball-joint suspension system, by the way, is just about as good as Ford claims. The car corners like a mechanical rabbit chased by a greyhound, settling into the curves easily and confidently and hanging on all the way around with no strain. In our lateral sway test, the Ford took a 285-ft.-radius circle at 40 *mph* with a side-tilt of only 4°—the best performance of any car tested this year. Road shock is reduced considerably—thanks, also, to power steering—and the bumps aren't nearly so evident as they were in last year's Ford.

The model tested for us by Professional Engineering Consultants was the Skyliner V-8 with Fordomatic transmission, power brakes, power steering and an eavesdropping roof. Now about that famous plastic roof insert: Since it already has given rise to several thousand transparent observations of one kind or another, let's just stick to the facts. The transparent molded plastic insert covers an area of 11.2 sq. ft. over the front compartment. It is supposed to have five times the impact resistance of laminated plate glass and should not be subjected to temperatures over 180°. Ford claims that the blue-green tinted plastic eliminates 60% of the sun's heat rays and 72% of the sky glare; but with the sun entering about two inches back of the leading roof edge the glare was noticeably irritating. However, if you object to this you can get a curtain,

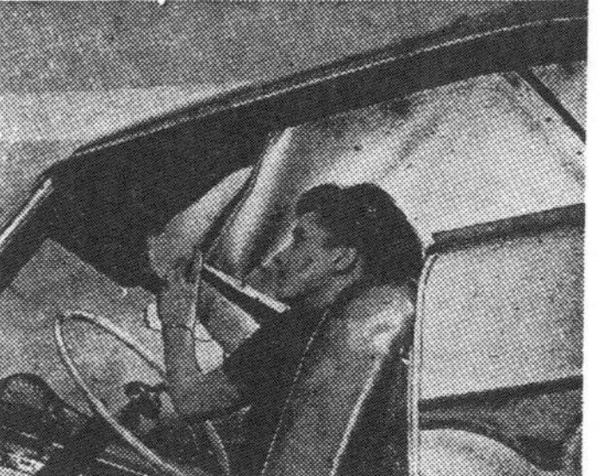
With transparent roof insert passengers can view tops of flagpoles, pesky pigeons and registration numbers on low-flying planes. Note distortion of lower part of pole.

If you don't like overhead eavesdroppers while you're driving the Skyliner you can get a special curtain to snap on the inside to cover the transparent section.

Ford instrument panel is excellently designed, with all gages apparent to driver at a quick glance. Rear of speedometer dome (A) is transparent plastic to give daylight illumination of speedometer. Note location of directional signals (B) and high beam indicator (C).

Fig. 1—Brake fade test. Pedal pressures for Ford V-8 to decelerate from 60 to 30 *mph* at rate of 7 ft. per sec./per sec. Cycle repeated 11 times.

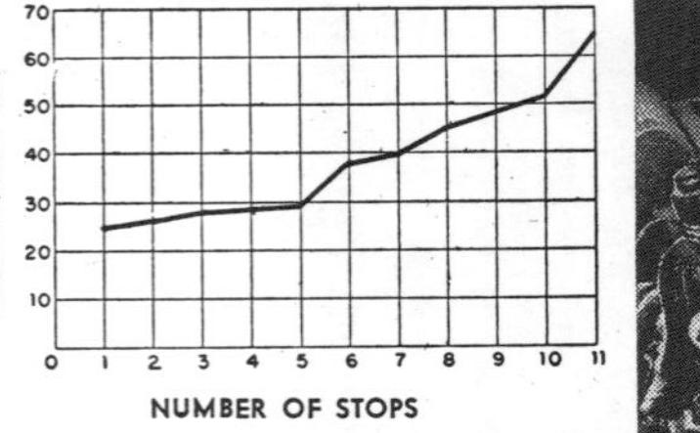
Close-up (left) shows structure of independent ball-joint front suspension. Two ball-and-socket joints (A) and upper and lower control arms (B) are principal components. Design is simpler than hinge joint and kingpin front suspension previously used in Fords (right).

matching the headlining, to snap on (shades of the old roadster side curtains!) over the inside of the transparent section. The rubber seal around the insert looked rough, but the roof on our test car didn't leak a drop, even in the hardest kind of rain, nor during our water penetration tests.

The new 130-*hp* V-8 engine runs quietly and is under no strain in normal operation; apparently it has been built for long and efficient life rather than hot rod performance. Nevertheless, there was a definite performance gain over the 110-*hp* V-8 we tested last year.

Although the Ford is still no demon on acceleration, it went from 0 to 60 in a true 18.5 seconds—about 2 seconds better than the time turned in by last year's test car which had a standard transmission. Up through 30 *mph* the 1953 car was able to reach its speed about 1 second sooner than this year's Fordomatic-equipped model. Our tests showed that the least possible time in which this Ford can accelerate from 0 to 60—with no wind, best spark-setting and driver alone—is 17.5 seconds.

The top speed test with the Ford turned up some unique results. On the first trial, a top of only 93 *mph* on the speedometer was attained (and this baby was supposed to have a potential of 105 *mph*). Following the advice of a helpful Ford field service representative, the push rods, which had been set at 0.015 in. hot, were loosened to 0.018 in. and the tests were re-run. Again, the car "hung" at 93 *mph* for half a mile. But at that point the Ford descended a slight grade and hit 101 (90.6 *mph* true speed), then leveled off and held at 98—a true 88 *mph*.

So you can have your choice as to top speed,

Drivers' Observations

ROADABILITY: Big improvement over previous Fords in road-holding, curve-hugging abilities. Settles into the corners well, with relatively little overthrow. Power steering, which helps in cornering (best in Fords to date), lets you keep most of the feel of the road; there's no sensation of being out of touch with the front wheels. Rough road ride not especially "soft," but front suspension handles hard bumps easily without transmitting shock through steering wheel. Still somewhat susceptible to wind wander, as was last year's Ford, but tracking ability has improved. Wind noise only moderate at 60 *mph* with vents open. Rear-end howl at that speed definitely noticeable.

RIDING COMFORT: If you're sensitive about your bald spot you may not like the Skyliner's transparent roof panel, which also admits quite a bit of sky glare into the driver's compartment during the day. Shiny top of dash glares considerably, too. Seats firm but comfortable. Front seat wide enough to accommodate three good-sized adults, although rear seat might cramp them a bit. Leg room in rear quite limited when front seat pushed back all the way. Arm rests well located for comfort. Dash board ash tray angles upward rather sharply when pulled out, making it awkward to stub out cigarettes and flick ashes. Engine noise and vibrations seem minimum—certainly are not annoying. Head room seems less than last year. A six-footer, a hat and this Ford just

INSTRUMENTS AND CONTROLS: Instrument grouping extremely well-planned for swift, easy reading by driver. Half-circle horn ring an asset here. Red bulls-eye lights indicate when oil pressure is low and generator not charging. Directional signal arrows (clearly audible click) neatly spotted on each side of speedometer. Flat glass on speedometer dial picks up perfect reflection of steering wheel hub at all times. Lower dials angled for easy reading, show up well against spot-finished aluminum with which dash instrument recess is lined. Rheostat-controlled dash lighting is comfortable on eyes, provides good readability. Gear shift positions are (left to right) Park, Reverse, Neutral, Drive, Lo. Starter will work only when gear selector is in Neutral. And they still haven't lighted that gear quadrant. Adjustable speed wipers function well but leave usual corner blind spots. Heater threw out plenty of warmth for comfort in 20° weather. With car sitting on clean, dry surface, it took 4 ft lbs to turn steering wheel with power on, 17 ft lbs to turn it with the power off.

don't fit together very well, especially in the back seat. Map light under dash—operated either by a manual switch or by opening of doors—offers good readability. Two dome lights illuminate rear seat. Average-size glove compartment unlighted.

SPECIAL COMMENTS: Accessibility of service points generally satisfactory—generator (lower left front of engine) fair; master cylinder (left side on cowl) good; transmission dip stick (right rear of engine) good; distributor (right rear of engine) fair; fuel pump (left front of engine) not too handy; adjustment of valves (overhead) good; spark plugs not very accessible. Plastic bag (instead of glass jar) for windshield washer water is mighty good idea. Doors have two hold-open positions, leave plenty of entry room when opened wide. Spring-loaded trunk lid opens easily when key is turned in lock; however, it takes a sturdy push to get it closed again. Interior door locks are push buttons which still allow inside handles to be turned. Easily operated bumper jack is well constructed, showed no tendency to slip. Double action ratchet lifts lip a notch on both up and down strokes of handle. Rear-view mirror large enough to give good vision through wrap-around rear window. This car had an exterior driver's door mirror on it, and why don't they make this key driving safety aid standard on all cars? They're a positive boon in the heavy traffic driving we have to contend with these days. Doors can be closed when front seat backs are folded forward. Rain-storm water test showed slight to moderate leakage into trunk, more severe penetration at both vents, front and rear windows and around doors. Engine did not miss at all when water sprayed downward through grille and at all probable angles from beneath car.

which isn't vitally important to the average good driver anyway; but the point is that the results of these tests bring out some interesting facts. One is the claim of the Ford engine experts that the new engine is sensitive to push rod adjustment. On the other hand, it's possible that the relatively new engine in our test car required an extra long time at high speeds to loosen up and achieve the equilibrium of its parts necessary before it could reach its maximum speed.

Curiously, the chassis dynamometer test we ran on this Ford followed a pattern similar to that of the speed runs. At first the maximum power output at the rear wheels was 72 *hp*, which held constant for several minutes. However, when the engine was allowed to overspeed and then braked, the power increased to 78 *hp* and held at that point. But after a shutdown, a new test was run which again turned up the 72 *hp* value.

Nevertheless, despite the certain sluggishness of our test car, the engine—sturdy and built for punishment—is an excellent job for normal driving. And with 10,000 miles under its fan belt and, perhaps, a larger carburetor it probably will be a good deal more lively.

What kind of gasoline mileage does this 8-cylinder, 130 *hp* plant get? According to our tests, it is better at all speeds than its V-8 predecessor of 1953. At the constant true speeds of 30, 40, 50 and 60 *mph*, this year's car showed a miles-per-gallon advantage of from 1.75 to 3.5—a gain in economy worth considering. The best observed constant speed mileage figure for the '54 Ford was 21.2 *mpg* (true) at 28 *mph*. In our economy fuel consumption test, a combination of traffic and open-road driving, the car showed that it would go 85.1 miles on five gallons of gas for a true *mpg* average of 17.02.

Regular fuel is specified for use in the Ford V-8; however, during the course of our tests a light, rhythmic knock—decreasing with speed and not audible above 40 *mph*—was noted with regular gas in the tank. This was with the specified spark setting of 6° before top center. Using premium fuel there was no knock at any speed. Our engineers thought that the spark timing might have to be retarded to 0° or 3° *btc* for hot weather driving with regular gasoline.

In our braking tests—both panic stops and fade—Ford's power brakes showed excellent stopping characteristics, although serious slewing developed in panic stops from 50 *mph*. Nevertheless, stopping distances from those speeds attempted all were within the National Safety Council's standards for good brakes.

Our fade test—revised this year—works like this: The service brake is applied at 60 *mph* to decelerate the car to 30 *mph* at an even rate of 7 ft. per sec./per sec. The car is immediately brought up to speed (60 *mph*) again, and the procedure repeated. On the Ford, the pedal effort required for the first deceleration was 25 lbs., and it took a total of 10 such consecutive decelerations to double that initial pedal effort (Fig. 1). The number of rapid-fire decelerations needed to produce serious fade was set at "something over 10." This is a rugged test, and its results indicate that for all normal driving purposes the Ford power brakes won't fade enough for you to worry about.

Ford's power brakes, as a matter of fact, are very well designed. The power booster has been added to the conventional braking system to achieve a set-up that is not overly delicate to the touch and allows a comfortable safety margin because the pedal height (5 in. above floor) is sufficient to provide good mechanical leverage in case the power should fail. The reverse side of the coin, however, is the fact that the brake pedal is 2½ in. higher than the accelerator pedal (normal in most cars), which means slower reaction time than if the two were on the same level.

But what about the slewing that showed up in the panic stops? It was not actually a fault of the brakes but rather of weight distribution. Ford's proportion of curb weight on the front wheels (2,150 lbs. or 60%) and rear wheels (1,465 lbs. or 40%) makes it more front heavy than other cars tested this year. With only the driver in the car making a panic stop, the car has a tendency to "nose over" when the front wheels lock. This loosens the grip of the rear tires on the road, and the rear wheels are inclined to whip around. With two or three passengers in the rear seat, no slewing occurred, which means that more weight is needed in the back to stabilize the braking.

You can buy this Skyliner V-8 for $2,240.50, the factory-suggested retail price, which includes federal taxes and delivery and handling charges but does not include transportation costs, state and local taxes or optional equipment. Fordomatic is optional at $184 extra. Power steering costs $134 and power brakes $41.

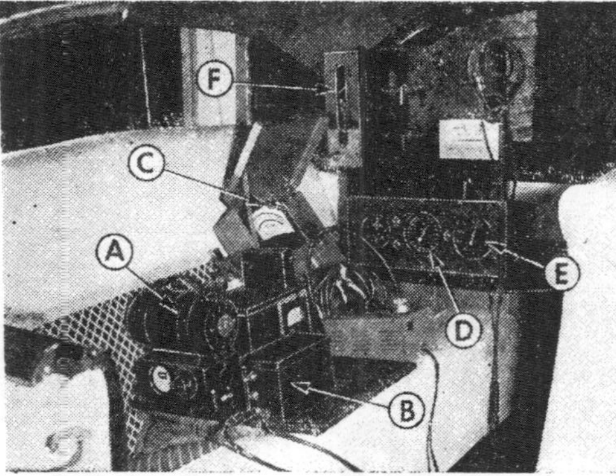
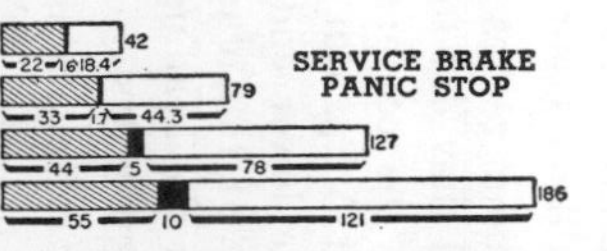

Instruments used in testing the Ford: (A) motor-generator to convert 12-volt *dc* current to 110-volt *ac*, (B) amplifier to detect engine knock, (C) tachometer to record *rpm*, (D) electric counter, (E) electric timer, (F) fuel burette to measure gasoline consumption.

MAKE OF CAR: Ford V-8 Skyliner

START OF TESTS: February 1, 1954

GENERAL ROAD CONDITIONS (for gas mileage and acceleration tests): Portland concrete, dry, smooth and level

MILEAGE AT START OF TESTS: 1790 **MILES COVERED IN TESTS:** 895

GAS USED: Regular **OIL USED:** 20W

CURB WEIGHT: 3615 lbs. 60% on front wheels; 40% on rear wheels

TIRE PRESSURES: 26 lbs. front; 23 lbs. rear for all tests. **SPARK SETTING:** 6° BTC

TEST DATA

GASOLINE MILEAGE (checked with fuel volume flow meter and 5th wheel. Temperature 42° F. Relative humidity 80%. Barometer 29.2 in. Hg. Carried weight 595 lbs. Two runs made in opposite directions on same road):

True Speed (5th Wheel)	True Miles per Gallon	Odometer Miles per Gallon	Ton Miles per Gallon (true)
20	20.5	21.3	43.2
30	21.1	21.9	44.4
40	20.1	20.8	42.3
50	18.3	18.8	38.6
60	17.2	17.6	36.2
70	13.1	13.3	27.6

TRAFFIC FUEL CONSUMPTION (simulated traffic pattern of city driving—stops, acceleration, braking. Carried weight 485 lbs.): True mpg 12.8. Odometer mpg 13.2. True ton mpg 26.2. Maximum claim that can reasonably be made for the car—slow acceleration and coasting): Odometer mpg 29.0.

ACCELERATION (timed with 5th wheel. Carried weight 441 lbs. Temperature 42° F. Relative humidity 80%. Barometer 29.0 in. Hg. Spark 6° BTC. Figures are average of two runs in opposite directions):

True MPH	Gear Range	Average True Time (sec.)	True MPH	Gear Range	Average True Time (sec.)
0-20	Lo	4.02	0-70	Lo, Inter & Hi Shift at 38 & 57	28.2
0-30	Lo	6.24	0-80	Lo, Inter & Hi Shift at 38 & 57	47.5
0-40	Lo	9.0	20-40	Hi	7.5
0-50	Lo & Inter. Shift at 38	12.8	20-60	Hi	16.6
			20-70	Hi	25.7
0-60	Lo, Inter & Hi Shift at 38 & 57	18.5	20-80	Hi	44.5

Minimum time for 0-60 mph (true) over level road with no wind, best spark setting, premium fuel and driver alone: 17.5 seconds.

ACCELERATION FACTORS (Temperature 42° F. Relative humidity 80%. Barometer 29.0 in. Hg. Carried weight 441 lbs. Spark 6° BTC. Figures are calculated from average of two runs in opposite directions):

True Speed	Gear	MPH per Sec.	Ft. per Sec.
10	Lo	5.0	7.3
20	Lo	4.5	6.6
30	Lo	3.9	5.7
40	Inter.	3.1	4.6
50	Inter.	2.3	3.4
60	Hi	1.5	2.2
70	Hi	0.75	1.1
80	Hi	0.50	0.7

HILL CLIMBING (calculated from accelerometer readings with allowances made for rotational inertia. Data same as preceding test):

Approx. MPH	Gear	Grade in %	Pull in lbs.
15	Lo	31	1230
40	Hi	10	406

TOP SPEED AND SPEEDOMETER-ODOMETER CORRECTION: Odometer distance 10 miles; true distance 9.666 miles; odometer error at 35 mph 0.334 (plus):

MPH Speedometer	True Speed	% Error Speedometer	Engine RPM	MPH Speedometer	True Speed	% Error Speedometer	Engine RPM
Top Speed 98	88.0	10	3810	50	45.5	9	2030
90	81.0	10	3500	40	36.7	8	1650
80	72.0	10	3100	30	28.0	7	1310
70	63.3	10	2710	20	18.5	7	1000
60	54.4	10	2310				

STOPPING ABILITY (Surface, Portland concrete, smooth and dry. Grade level. Surface temperature 42° F. Tires 7.10-15, 4-ply. Drag factor of road [average coefficient of friction between tires and road] 0.68. Pedal pressure 100 lbs. on all stops):

SERVICE BRAKE PANIC STOP

Actual Speed	Segment distances	Total stopping distance (ft.)
20	22, 16, 18.4	42
30	33, 17, 44.3	79
40	44, 5, 78	127
50	55, 10, 121	186

Distance traveled during average driver's reaction time (¾ sec.)

Brake lag: Distance covered between time brake pedal is depressed and wheels grip pavement and lock.

Braking distance: Distance covered between time wheels grip pavement until car comes to stop. Figure at ends of bars indicate total stopping distances in ft. (sum of reaction, brake lag and braking distances).

PARKING BRAKE TEST: Brake applied hard and suddenly from 20 mph actual speed

Breaking Distance 49 ft.

Did Rear Wheels Lock? Right Yes Left Yes

HORSEPOWER AT REAR AXLE (values calculated from accelerometer readings with allowances made for efficiencies and rotational inertia):

MPH True	RPM Engine	Equiv. Engine Torque (lb. ft.)	Axle Horsepower
90	3900	119	88
70	3000	137	78
37	2000	142	54

Per cent of advertised engine horsepower supplied to rear wheels: 68

CHASSIS DYNAMOMETER CHECK (Tests supervised by Glen Kunz, regional representative, Clayton Dynamometer Co. Temperature 65°. Relative humidity 50%. Barometer 29.1 in. Hg):

Speedometer	Engine RPM	Horsepower
26	1730	46
54	2380	63
79	3100	76 (max.)

PERFORMANCE FACTORS (Calculated)

MPH (true) at maximum advertised horsepower 97 and torque 27. Engine rpm at 60 mph (also revolutions per mile) 2560 rpm. Average piston speed at 60 mph (also, ft./mile) 1320 ft./min. Cu. ft. per minute of mixture at 60 mph (also, cu. ft/mile) 177. Maximum engine horsepower (adv.) per ton of car (curb weight) 72. Reciprocating load factor (piston weight, bore, stroke, connecting rod) 15.9. Reciprocating load factor at 60 mph 1040. Maximum engine horsepower (adv.) per cubic inch displacement 0.545.

SPECIFICATIONS

ENGINE: 90° V-8; bore 3.50; stroke 3.10; advertised maximum brake horsepower rated 130 at 4200 rpm; advertised maximum torque 214 ft. lbs. at 1800-2200 rpm, corrected to 60° F. and 29.92 in. Hg.; compression ratio 7.2 to 1; piston displacement 239 cu. in.; fuel specified regular.

TRANSMISSION: Fordomatic, torque converter; rear axle ratio 3.31.

STEERING: Turning circle 41.2 ft., curb to curb. No. wheel turns, lock to lock 4.5.

EXTERIOR: Wheelbase 115.5 in.; overall length 198.3 in.; overall width 74.2 in.; overall height 64.1 in.; curb weight 3615 lbs. (10 gal. fuel, oil and water); minimum road clearance 8 in. at rear shock absorber.

INTERIOR: Headroom, front seat 37 in., rear seat 34.2 in.; legroom, front seat 41 in., rear seat 25.5 in.; hiproom, front seat 58.9 in., rear seat 48.6 in.; total front seat adjustment at floor 4.1 in.

VISIBILITY: Windshield area 940 sq. in.; rear window area 1270 sq. in.; driver's eye to road over left front fender 48 ft., over hood center 40 ft., over right front fender 40 ft.

EQUIPMENT: Battery 6 volt, 17 plate, 90 amp. hours, located right front under hood; tires 7.10-15, 4-ply; recommended pressure 26 lbs. front, 23 lbs. rear, cold; spring, front coil, rear semi-elliptic leaf.

CAPACITIES: Fuel tank 17 gals.; crankcase 5 qts.; cooling system 21 qts. with heater; differential 3.5 pts.; transmission 9.75 qts.; luggage 27 cu. ft. usable (approx.).

CERTIFICATION

I certify that the test results in this report are the true and accurate findings in tests conducted on the automobile named under the conditions specified.

Edw. F. Obert

Edward F. Obert, Member SAE
Chicago Section Chairman, ASME
Director, Automotive Research Laboratories
Professional Engineering Consultants
1204 Noyes Street, Evanston, Illinois

FORD 6 ... *IT GOES, TOO!*

By DON WERNER

AMONG all of the automobiles of the world, Ford has the unique distinction of being the only make that offers a genuine choice between two modern overhead valve engines, either inline or V-type, in all its cars, ranging from the bottom to the top of the line.

This option, which can be exercised at the modest cost of less than $100 in any area of the United States, often may be the source of some indecision on the part of a car buyer. The situation further is aggravated by the fact that both of the engines are honestly new. The ohv V-8 (MOTOR LIFE road test, February 1954) made its initial appearance this year. The ohv 6 is in its third year as a production model.

Engines, in some respects, are like people. Soon after they are born, certain behavior characteristics quickly generate a reputation. This often is misleading and tends to obscure other important factors. The case of the Ford 6 proves the point and an extensive road test by MOTOR LIFE was revealing.

The Ford 6 selected for study was a four-door Customline sedan equipped with almost every available accessory, including Fordomatic, power steering and power brakes. Testing was conducted in congested city traffic, through the spacious desert and on up into the high mountains where altitude, ice and snow provided punishing conditions. Now let's evaluate the data accumulated in nearly 2,000 miles:

MILEAGE

In the economy department, of course, the Ford 6 really shines. This is the reputation it already has, as we mentioned a moment ago. The luster which it acquired shortly after its introduction in 1952 found fresh radiance with the 27-mpg sweepstakes victory scored by Driver Les Viland in the 1953 Mobilgas Economy Run, where conditions favor a heavier car with an efficient engine.

Using the same brand of gasoline, in the regular grade, the test car registered a maximum of 25.1 mpg, according to the exceptionally accurate McCullough fuel meter. And this reading was obtained at an altitude of 3,000 feet, where the hp loss at the flywheel is roughly 16—five hp drop for each 1,000 feet. In addition, the torque converter in the power train was a further limiting factor in obtaining peak results.

As a sidelight, we might mention that another Ford 6, with overdrive, was used to make a fast 300-mile trip that included considerable city driving in two metropolitan areas. The overall average: 23.5 mpg for the entire distance.

SPEED

Here's where most of the surprises were met. The car makes no pretense at being a fireball. And it isn't. But its big name as an outstanding economy vehicle has created some misconceptions. In its class, it's lively and responsive. One driver, in fact, had to get out and look under the hood to make sure the engine compartment wasn't occupied by a V-8. Top speed and acceleration in the lower ranges compare favorably, and in some instances even surpass, rival makes. Generally speaking, it's time the car's performance, within the limits of its cubic inches, is recognized for its true worth. The punch it packs is no knockout, but it lets you know it's in there swinging.

ENGINE

Let's look at the power plant whence all these goodies come. Don't make the glance too casual or you'll miss something.

First off, skip the idea that this '54 version represents only a slight change from '53. Granted that all they did to hitch another 14 horses to the team was boost the compression and increase the bore to bring the total to 115 hp. But some real engineering improvements went into the lower end for more strength, while the dip stick and some of the other fixtures swapped positions. All this comes under the heading of working the bugs out of the system after a few years.

For the devotee who likes to tinker but is something less than another Clay Smith, the Ford 6 is made to order. It's about as simple as a modern design can be, with parts easily available and at low cost. There is another item, in this connection, that makes the package a joy. The engine is small and the compartment is big, so you can crawl all over it and whistle while you work. The same factor also figures in repair bills and makes the mechanics good-natured when you want a professional to do the job for you.

Before dropping the engine subject, we might include a word here for those who yearn to modify. You can't make it into a bomb for Bonneville, but respectable increases are possible with some reworking. However, keep in mind that this is an overhead and don't start thinking of a special high compression head. It'll cost you a small fortune.

HANDLING

So far we've had nothing but good to say about the Ford 6. Some of the bad features will crop up in a moment, although not until we get beyond the handling department.

Kicking out the kingpin and bringing in Lincoln's famed ball-joint suspension is a milestone for the low-priced field. Ford always did steer easily, but now it leaves you searching for adjectives. Some body sway is there; yet it isn't noticed because of the positive line the car follows through a turn. In fact, control is so good that the addition of power steering is merely a refinement rather than a major improvement. The number of turns from lock-to-lock could be trimmed and, somehow, the wheel itself seems to be abnormally large and cuts into forward vision for drivers who are built low to the ground.

Simplicity of the new suspension system will help out your pocketbook. Repairs cost less, as do replacement parts, while alignment and lubrication are vastly easier.

TRANSMISSION

Nothing new here to discuss, except to mention, for those who have been out of touch, that the torque converter Fordomatic works right along with the best, is trouble-free and has the handy selector arrangement of reverse and drive positions that permits rocking in snow or sand. Operation is smooth and noiseless, and not too hard on mileage.

RIDING QUALITIES

Here, too, there's been no important change except for that contributed by the ball-joint suspension. It, naturally, brings substantial improvement, not so much in providing a billowy effect as it does in really leveling out the bumps. Too, there is the feeling of security with less roll and pitching.

INTERIOR

Chief new touches inside are on the dash. This is a fresh treatment for 1954 with the novel and very steady speedometer, and red warning lights being substituted for oil and amperage needles. The latter are nice, but maybe the indicator needles could have been retained along with them.

Rest of the dash and instrument panel represents a step forward, but not far enough. Some controls have been recessed (good), although safety features still are insufficiently stressed (bad). Windows need too many turns of the crank to raise and lower. The balance of the interior is colorful, has quality workmanship and is highly satisfactory. The heater ventilators let in a little too much engine noise.

EXTERIOR

Despite the mechanical advances, styling is the thing that makes Ford the big seller. Basic lines of 1953 have been retained with the normal grille and trim alterations. Looks are a matter of taste but few disagree with the conclusion that Ford rates right at the top in clean appearance and fine lines without trying to incorporate the Italian influence. General finish is good, both on paint and chrome trim.

(Continued on page 69)

PERFORMANCE

TOP SPEED:
Average of two-way runs: 95.95 mph
Fastest one-way run: 100.3 mph

ACCELERATION:
0-30 mph: 5.7 secs.
0-45 mph: 10.1 secs.
0-60 mph: 18.5 secs.
Standing Quarter Mile: 21 secs.

EMERGENCY BRAKING DISTANCES:
From 30 mph: 46 ft.
From 45 mph: 101 ft.
From 60 mph: 182 ft.

FUEL CONSUMPTION:
At constant 30 mph: 25.1 mpg
At constant 45 mph: 21.7 mpg
At constant 60 mph: 19 mpg

SPEEDOMETER CORRECTION (Above readings all taken at corrected speeds):
Indicated 30 mph: 27.60 mph actual
Indicated 45 mph: 41.66 mph actual
Indicated 60 mph: 53.70 mph actual

Ford 6 tops a steep mountain roadway upon which it displayed remarkable agility for a car of its power and size

Here's the brightest spot in the whole car. Relocated dip stick indicates basic engineering changes made for '54

Most overlooked in the Ford 6 is its speed performance which, for an economy vehicle, rates extremely high in field

Ford
THUNDERBIRD

Luxury cockpit of Ford's new "personal" car.

Underhood space with a V-8 is at a premium.

THE FIRST truly American "personal" car is the way the Ford Motor Company describes their new 2/3 seater, high-performance, Thunderbird model scheduled for its first public showing late in October.

To the purist the Thunderbird has far too much luxury to qualify as a sports car, but even *that* group will find much of interest in the specifications of this car. The design concept alone proves that, for included in the list of desiderata were such items as high performance, good handling, quick steering, firm suspension and good brakes.

How the above sports car features have been combined with passenger car comfort, safety and convenience is our story. The Thunderbird has a wheelbase of 102 inches, weighs 3147 lbs. at the curb. The V-8 engine is 15% larger than the current Mercury, and while no horsepower figures have been re-leased, something like 190 bhp can be expected. The resultant ratio of 16.6 lbs/bhp insures high performance, even by competition sports car standards.

Good handling qualities may come by accident, by long evolution, or by good design and thorough testing. The Thunderbird falls into the latter category and its design features include a weight distribution of 52/48, ball joint front suspension, a 3-piece ride stabilizer, and rubber bumpers to reduce rear spring "wind-up" during fast acceleration. The steering gear ratio is given as 20 to 1, (equivalent to about 3.7 turns lock to lock). As is well known, good handling with independent front suspension requires an extremely rigid frame and the Thunderbird's frame has box section side rails, four cross members and an I-beam type X-member.

The Ford Thunderbird undergoing rough treatment on a special staggered-bump test road.

No data is available on the suspension characteristics other than the statement that the car has passenger car comfort with "firm springs for stability and security".

The brakes are Bendix duo-servo types with 11-inch drums. Front linings are 2 inches wide, rear linings are 1.75 inches. A vacuum booster is optional at extra cost. Wheels and tires are specially designed to withstand continuous high-speed driving and the Thunderbird becomes the first American car to use tubeless tires as standard equipment.

Reverting back to the powerplant, the new 292 cu in. Y-block V-8 has .125 inch more bore, .200 more stroke than the 1954 Mercury. The carburetor has 4 barrels supplied with cool air through a hood bulge that is not a dummy. Exhaust system is dual with reverse-flow mufflers. The clutch is 11 inches in diameter and of the conventional sdp (single dry plate) type.

There are 3 transmission options: conventional 3 speed, conventional with overdrive, or Fordomatic. For the Zephyr-gear enthusiast, 1st speed has the same ratio as the 06H model L-Z (2.33:1), 2nd speed is nearly the same as the 26H Lincoln Zephyr (1.48:1). Control of all transmissions is by a very neat floor-mounted lever.

The rear axle housing is similar to the Spicer-type, with hypoid gears. Axle ratios are 3.73 with 3-speeds, 3.92 with overdrive and 3.31 with Fordomatic.

Body construction is all-steel with convertible-type windows and wrap-around windshield. The single seat provides hip room of 60.2 inches, but is designed for two people. A middle passenger can be carried, but cushion depth over the propeller-shaft tunnel is restricted. The top is black rayon cloth and folds to a protected position behind the seat. An optional hard-top, weighing only 65 lbs. is available, made of fiberglass. It is insulated against sound and heat and retained by 4 toggle-action clamps at the rear, 2 similar clamps on the windshield header. The fiberglass top is finished in the same color as the car.

Instruments consist of a large speedometer flanked by a 5000 rpm tachometer on the left and an electric clock on the right. The clock has a sweep-second hand and matches the tach. Fuel and temperature gauges complete the instrumentation, with warning lights for no-charge and low oil pressure.

Upholstery is all-vinyl in white with trim to match the body color. Color choice will be black, torch red or turquoise. No price has been announced, but it is expected to be under $4000. ●

SPECIFICATIONS

Wheelbase, in.	102
Tread, front	56
rear	56
Tire size	6.70-15
Curb weight, lbs.	3147
distribution	52/48
Engine	ohv V-8
Bore and stroke	3.75 x 3.30
Displacement, cu in.	292
	(4787 cc)
Bhp	not available
Gear ratios (oa. - std. trans.)	
high	3.73
2nd	5.52
1st	8.69

CONTINUED FROM PAGE 22

Ford cold as far as a fast start was concerned. This is usually overcome by adding weight to the trunk but it seems a shame to hobble an otherwise outstanding car in this way. The reason seems to be the far forward position of the engine. Let's hope that the next Ford series will be a little closer to the 50-50 weight distribution which makes for better handling.

THE paint job is excellent. The interior is in better taste than the living rooms of most of the owners. The dashboard is easy to see and does not reflect light into the driver's eyes. The seats hold you up to the work in a safe, sensible position. Visibility is excellent and there is an air of roominess about the car which is surprising in view of the relatively short (115 in.) wheelbase. The trunk is big and the spare tire is sensibly positioned vertically to one side, where you can pull it out without unloading everything in the trunk.

In the actual test, this Ford was put through some pretty rough handling. It made a hill climb which would be a credit to any club meet, a tortuous dirt and rock 40 per cent grade, practically impassable for an ordinary car. The light tail caused some swinging from side to side as the hill was climbed, but car and crew arrived at the top in good order, leaving a trail of flying dirt and stones over half the country side.

We have come a long way from the Model T. This Ford is a luxury car. It's got looks and guts and it ought to run, as a family sedan, approximately forever. After that it can be rebuilt as a roadster, lakester or what have you. It's still a Ford.

THE END

CONTINUED FROM PAGE 29

3.90 to 1, whereas the same car with overdrive would come equipped with a 4.10 to 1 rear axle which with the overdrive in operation would give a total ratio of 2.87 to 1. Obviously this is a much better combination, which will give better acceleration and top speed.

WE made some acceleration and speed runs; however, in all fairness to the automobile it should be stated that the engine was not broken in at the time and better figures would have been obtained had the car travelled over 3,000 miles before the test. When we made the speed runs the odometer showed only 876 miles. The car was *not* specially tuned for the test.

During night driving the instrument panel reflects in the left front vent window. Headlights are good for road speeds up to 55 mph. Overall gas consumption for 1,000 miles, of which 40% was city driving, was 14 miles per gallon. On the highway, strong cross winds affect the car's stability so that it becomes necessary to reduce speed at times. All the accessories work very well, especially the heater and defroster which are tops in all kinds of weather. The windshield wipers are quiet and efficient. The speedometer is about 7% fast at 80 mph and about 3% fast at 50. The engine consumed 2½ quarts of number 10W oil during the first 1,000 miles. The rear main bearing seal was improperly installed at the factory which caused the oil to leak out completely at one time, and we found ourselves with *no* oil pressure at 60 mph. We don't know for how long this condition existed before we noticed it—but there was no harm done to the engine.

All in all the 1953 Ford is a good buy if equipped with overdrive—unless it is to be used in the city exclusively. It is a car which has everything a family man would want—room, speed, comfort and low upkeep cost—with a good trade-in value even after two or three years.

1953 Ford Specifications

Engine: V-8 L-head, 90 degree V. Piston displacement 239.4 cu. in. Bore 3.19". Stroke 3.75". Brake hp 110 at 3800 rpm. Compression ratio 7.2 to 1. Oil capacity 5 quarts with filter. Gas tank capacity 17 gallons.

Wheelbase: 115". Length overall: 197'8". Width overall: 73'9". Height overall: 62.3". Ground clearance: 8" at lowest point. Front tread: 58". Rear tread: 56". Tire size: 6.70 x 15 on 5" rims.

Transmission: 3-speed synchromesh (on car tested), overdrive or Fordomatic optional at extra cost.

Steering: Overall ratio 26.3 to 1. Turning diameter 40 feet (approximate).

Performance: Acceleration 0 to 30 in 5.4 seconds. Acceleration 0 to 50 in 13.00 seconds. Top speed average of 4 separate runs 91.5 mph.

Note: These figures are not indicative of best performance as the car was not broken in—nor was the engine specially tuned for these tests.

Driving around with Walt Woron

Heel-over gives evidence of good ride, ability to stick in turns without drifting over line. Speed here was 55 mph

THE ACCUSATION that American car manufacturers couldn't build a sports car—even if they tried—is no longer valid. The first indication was the Chevrolet Corvette. And although the Ford Motor Co. is the first one to deny it, they have a *sports car* in the Thunderbird, and it's a good one.

Ford prefers to call it a "personal car." The thinking behind this, as brought out in a discussion with W. R. Burnett, Chief Passenger Car Engineer for Ford, is that "although the Thunderbird has the performance and attributes of most sports cars, management also felt that it should have a few more comforts to make it more appealing to a wider segment of the public." Besides having the power-operated four-way seat (which is actually for making the car usable for more people of varying builds and heights, rather than just comfort), the Thunderbird has power steering (optional) for more ease in city driving, power brakes, and complete weather protection in the form of a standard Fiberglas hardtop (that can be placed over the optional soft top when it's folded up behind the seat), and roll-up windows (power optional). This follows our thinking about the new type of sports car. You'll recall that we pointed out at the time of Thunderbird introduction (June MT), "The pattern [of sports car acceptance in this country] became evident. America was definitely interested in a *personal* car that was *fun to drive* and *feasible to own.*"

Enough for that. The car's been kicking around long enough for almost everyone to know most of the stories about it (except some of the finer points we're going to bring out here). So let's get on to the hottest news about the car. Wot'll she do? To find out, Don MacDonald and I visited the Ford Proving Ground (Dearborn, Mich.) on one spottily sunny day in between two rainy ones. Having the car for the better part of the afternoon enabled us to become familiar with it quickly.

Vision over the low hood is good, although there is a slight amount of distortion in the corners of the wrap-around windshield. With top up you feel pretty closed in, mostly because it's not like most of the new car "glass bowls."

All instruments (including a tach) are well-positioned and easy to read. Of interest to rally drivers is the sweep-second clock. The emergency brake is up under the dash, like passenger cars, instead of being "fly-off" *à la* sports cars. The foot pedals are far enough apart so that you don't get your feet tangled. You don't even have to reach across the wide bench-type seat to raise or lower the passenger's window, if you pay the extra loot for power-operation of it.

After getting it out on the grounds and getting acclimated to the car (with a Ford engineer beside me), I began to put it through its paces. The more I drove it, the more I liked it. The happiest thing to me was not that it could burn rubber from a standstill (which it will), nor that it can burn rubber when changing gears (even with a Fordomatic), nor that it feels so solid to driver and passenger alike, but—that it handles so superbly.

There's definite oversteer built into the car (which means that it will break loose in a turn before it drifts, unlike the true competition sports car). It hangs so well in the corners that you can take any given curve at 10-15 mph more than the '55 Ford (an improved version of the top handling car of '54). Most important is the feeling of security you get from the car. Ater pushing it around the handling course (asphalt, varying-radii turns) a few times I soon got confident enough to begin taking them at 55-65 mph. With more practice behind the wheel I felt sure that I could up the speed—that's how the car impresses you.

With all of these good handling characteristics, the Thunderbird is also easy to drive, having an exceptionally short turning radius, a steering ratio of 20 to 1 (3.5 turns lock to lock, both with and without power steering). You can adjust the wheel to your own liking merely by loosening the adjustment on the column and pushing in or pulling out the wheel (three inches of movement).

The ride is unlike that which the diehard sports car addict has come to expect from a sports car. It's firm enough to prevent too much bobbing coming out of a dip or flying over a bump, yet it's soft enough to be kind to a weak sacroiliac. There's a certain initial lean going through a corner, but it doesn't increase appreciably during severe cornering.

The standard power brakes make the Thunderbird squat down right now. Last year Ford brakes were among the best in their class, while the combination of larger brakes (11-inch drums instead of 10-inch) and the lighter weight make the Thunderbird brakes well above average.

Drag? Why not? The Thunderbird will go with the best of them, even with Fordomatic. Normally, a fast speed-shifter could outdrag an automatic car, but here's one case where they're even. After driving the Fordomatic job I had a chance to drive a couple with stick shifts. From first to second the gate wasn't exceptionally smooth, and though you can keep your foot down on the throttle all the way, it's asking a lot of the clutch, day-in and day-out. In shifting from second to third, you can keep your foot down and just "pop" the clutch. Going through this procedure, you'll wind up just about even with a Fordomatic 'Bird. Why? With Fordomatic, a hotter engine, rated at 198 horsepower, is used. The stick-shift engine has 190 hp.

FORD THUNDERBIRD

No car has caused so much conjecture as Ford's new Thunderbird. We looked for a lot, and when we drove it, we found it.

The Thunderbird's looks change considerably with its fender skirts removed

A time of 11 seconds is what we got for 0 to 60 mph, putting it into sports car company. The needle of the electric speedometer hit 80 mph just 19.4 seconds after the standing start. Axle "wind-up" is kept to a minimum by the use of rubber bumpers on the frame which the semi-elliptic rear springs contact on sudden take-offs before the springs distort too far.

Fordomatic for '55 now uses the low-gear starting feature (available on all '55 Ford products), which permits you to start in low gear instead of second by pushing the throttle all the way to the floor. It will then shift to second at about 30 mph, and to third gear around 60 mph. This is all accomplished while the selector is in DRIVE; it isn't necessary to use LOW, then to manually shift to DRIVE.

MT's Editor removes 'Bird's chrome air cleaner, exposing four-barrel carburetor; valve covers bear special insignia

Downshifts can be made to LOW at any speed. This puts you manually into second gear, then an automatic downshift to LOW comes at around 20 mph. Downshifts are considerably smoother.

The Fordomatic transmission lever, located above the driveshaft tunnel, is short and stubby (like that of most sports cars), giving you the feel of a conventional transmission. An interesting safety feature incorporated in the lever knob is a pushbutton lock on top of it to prevent inadvertent shifts from DRIVE to REVERSE or vice versa. You can go from LOW to DRIVE, but not through NEUTRAL into REVERSE unless you push the button.

Acceleration at passing speeds is impressive. We averaged times of 4.2 seconds to get from 30 to 50 mph, and 11 seconds from 50 to 80 mph. That's enough to indicate that the 'Bird meets its advertising claims of "sports car . . . performance."

Despite claims to the contrary, no-one outside of Ford personnel had tested the car for top-speed at presstime—and Ford people aren't talking. My guess, though (and I have reason to believe it's fairly accurate) is that it will fly along in the range of 120-mph-plus (if overdrive-equipped). That's as fast as most popular sports cars, or faster.

As I see it, the Ford Thunderbird has three basic points in its favor: a rakish, ground-hugging style; performance to match good sports cars; and a design that has built-in comfort for driver and passenger, with no penalty whatsoever to pay for their fun. It certainly seems like the right combination to make the car appealing to a fairly broad cross-section of the motoring public.

It takes two to do a quick, neat job of folding the Thunderbird's top down behind seat. Fiberglas hardtop is standard

Scanning Thunderbird's instrument layout, driver finds neat, legible setup with tach and clock straddling speedometer

The 1955 Ford

The Fairlane Crown Victoria has a chrome strip running across the top of the car. The model is also available with a transparent roof over the driver's compartment.

FORD introduced an entirely new line—the high-styled Fairlane series —as the leader of its four lines of passenger cars for 1955.

Included in the new Fairlane series, named after the home of the late Henry Ford, is a completely new styling idea— the Crown Victoria. The first Ford sedan under five feet in overall height, the Crown Victoria has an arch of chrome over the top like a tiara. It is also available with a transparent plastic roof over the driver's compartment.

The line also includes the Sunliner convertible, the Victoria, the four-door Town sedan and the two-door Club sedan.

Ford, which produces 47 per cent of all station wagons sold, has expanded the series to five models with all-steel bodies—one more than in 1954. They are the eight-passenger Country Squire, with side moldings of wood-grained glass fibre; an eight-passenger Country sedan; a six-passenger Country sedan; a Custom Ranch Wagon, and a Ranch Wagon.

The Customline series offers the Fordor and Tudor sedans with chrome molding along the sides to provide clean, classic lines and to serve as a 'bumper' to protect the finish when a car door opens in the next parking space.

The lowest priced series include three models—the new Tudor Business sedan, the Tudor sedan and the Fordor sedan.

The Thunderbird, Ford's 'personal car,' gave an advance hint of the company's styling trend when it was unveiled earlier. Measuring just 4 feet, 4.2 inches high in the hardtop model, the Thunderbird will accommodate three people, with rear compartment space for their luggage. It was designed for a combination of high performance with the comfort, convenience and safety of a conventional car. The adjustable steering wheel slides in or out three inches and can be locked in the position the driver prefers. A power seat is standard equipment.

Ford, which offered the first V-8 engine in the low-price field in 1932, has now introduced three new engines: a high compression Y-block V-8 engine of 272 cubic inch displacement and a 8.5 to 1 compression ratio; a powerful Y-block V-engine of 272 cubic inch displacement and a 7.6 to 1 compression ratio, and an improved six-cylinder I-block engine of 223 cubic inch displacement and a 7.5 to 1 compression ratio.

Dual exhausts, which provide extra power, are standard on all Fairlane V-8 and station wagon models.

The longer, lower bodies of the new Fords, with the wraparound windshield, is shown here in the Fairlane four-door sedan. Both the Y-block V-8 and the I-block Six cylinder engines are offered by the company.

A new, lower silhouette with modern styling inspired by the 'Thunderbird' distinguishes the four lines of passenger cars this year

Ford's new 'personal' car is the all-steel Thunderbird with a telescopic steering column. A semi-sports car, it is available either as a hardtop or a convertible.

How to Figure Your Repair Costs on the FORD

Job Description	1947	1948	1949	1950	1951	1952	1953	1954	Remarks
Adjust brakes	$4.00				$8.50			$9.25	Includes removing drums, inspecting and adjusting anchors
Reline brakes	$16.50			$16.00			$14.00		Parts will be extra
Adjust clutch pedal	$2.00				$.75				
							$.80		Manual control linkage Fordomatic
Replace clutch	$18.50			$11.25		$8.00		$7.50	V-8
	$18.50								Six
				$12.75		$10.50		$9.25	Overdrive
Overhaul transmission (synchromesh)	$24.50				$18.75			$15.25	Synchromesh
				$24.50			$23.00		With overdrive Parts will be extra
Overhaul transmission (Fordomatic)							$42.75		Parts will be extra
Replace generator	$28.50				$30.50				V-8
	$28.50							$30.00	Six
Overhaul generator					$7.80				Parts will be extra
Clean and adjust regulator					$1.25				
Replace regulator	$9.75			$10.25			$9.75		
Replace coil					$8.25				
Replace light switch	$1.50				$1.25			$1.75	Parts will be extra
Replace stoplight switch	$1.25			$1.75			$1.00		Parts will be extra
Replace starter motor	$26.75			$27.75		$28.00		$27.50	V-8
Overhaul starter motor	$6.75				$8.00			$7.75	V-8 Parts extra
Replace ignition switch			$3.00				$4.10		
Replace distributor	$19.60				$15.50			$18.00	V-8
	$18.50	$16.50		$15.75			$17.75		Six
Replace points	$7.00				$4.00			$3.25	V-8
	$4.90				$4.00			$3.25	Six
Clean and adjust breaker points and set timing	$5.60				$3.50			$2.80	V-8
	$4.50				$3.60			$2.80	Six
Adjust steering gear and linkage	$4.80			$5.00			$4.50		
Water hose	$3.20				$2.50			$4.00	V-8
				$2.50			$2.00	$2.75	Six
Water hose and reverse flush, removal and replacement of thermostat	$6.00					$7.20			V-8 Parts extra
	$5.75			$5.50			$5.25		Six Parts extra
Replace water pump	$23.25		$35.25			$37.75		$37.25	V-8 Both banks
	$18.25			$18.75			$17.25	$15.25	Six
Overhaul water pump using standard repair kit	$12.25		$20.00			$22.25		$22.75	V8 Both units
	$11.00			$11.25			$9.30	$9.75	Six
Replace fan hub	$4.00					$2.50			V-8 Parts extra
						$3.25			Six Parts extra
Replace fan blades	$3.25					$2.00			V-8 Parts extra
	$1.75			$4.00			$2.50		Six Parts extra
Replace fan belt				$1.75				$.75	V-8 Parts extra
					$1.20				Six Parts extra

Job Description	1947	1948	1949	1950	1951	1952	1953	1954	Remarks
Replace fuel pump	$5.55				$7.95				$7.50	V-8
			$7.35				$7.50		Six
Overhaul fuel pump	$2.00				$4.00				$3.25	V-8 Parts extra
			$3.75				$3.25		Six Parts extra
Replace cylinder head				$43.75					$126.50	V-8 Both banks
			$34.00				$64.00		Six
Replace cylinder head gasket	$13.25				$13.50				$30.50	V-8 Both banks
			$9.00				$18.00		Six
Tighten cylinder head bolts and adjust overhead valves				$2.00					$5.40	V-8
			$1.20				$4.30		Six
Valve grinding	$32.75			$46.75		$44.25			$41.50	V-8
	$25.00			$39.00		$33.75			$24.75	Six
Valve adjustment									$4.75	V-8
				$7.75			$2.70		Six
Replace rings	$43.50			$49.00		$62.00			$69.75	V-8
	$40.50	$43.75		$57.25		$50.00			$52.00	Six
Replace rings and grinding valves	$66.00			$76.50		$84.00			$83.00	V-8
	$57.75			$85.25		$60.00			$61.75	Six
Replace pistons, rings, pins and rod bearings (includes honing all cylinders)	$128.00			$134.25		$147.00			$154.00	V-8
	$106.50			$123.25		$116.00			$116.50	Six
Replace pistons, rings, pins, rod bearings, hone cylinders and grind valves	$150.50			$161.00		$169.50			$167.00	V-8
	$125.00			$151.25		$126.00			$126.50	Six
Engine, remove and replace complete with transmission	$15.60			$20.00		$18.75			$18.00	V-8
								$19.25	V-8 with Fordomatic
	$15.20			$18.50		$17.90			$17.75	Six
								$18.75	Six with Fordomatic
Overhaul engine in car, including honing cylinders, replacing rod bearings, piston rings, pins and grinding valves	$84.00			$98.00		$106.00			$104.00	V-8 Parts extra
	$77.00			$98.50		$78.00			$77.00	Six Parts extra
Rebuild engine	$145.00				$140.00					V-8 Parts extra
	$120.00			$128.00		$124.00			$122.00	Six Parts extra
Tune up: points, plugs, timing				$4.80					$5.25	V-8
					$4.50				Six
Tune up as above, including valve adjustment (overhead)									$10.75	V-8
				$10.00					$6.50	Six
Tune up as above, but including adjusting and/or cleaning spark timing, carburetor, fuel pump bowl, battery terminals, fuel lines; check coil, condenser, voltage control, compression and vacuum; tighten hose connection, manifold and cylinder head				$11.00					$15.25	V-8 Parts extra
			$12.00				$14.00		Six Parts extra
Compression test					$2.50					V-8
					$2.00				Six
Adjust headlights					$1.25					
Check and adjust toe-in				$2.00					$1.25	

'55 Ford V8

Roadability, handling, general responsiveness—all are top Ford points

Introduced into low-price class by the '54 Ford, ball-joint suspension allows confident, controlled hard cornering

Eye-level view of right rear fender shows how high fender line aids close-quarters maneuvering. All-around vision is good

Trunk's capacity is hampered by high sill (result of gas cap placed behind license plate) which complicates loading

By Don MacDonald

WE'VE JUST FINISHED 14 days and 1400 miles behind the wheel of a new Ford Customline V8 and enjoyed most every minute of it. Why the exceptionally long time and high mileage? The answer is simply that it's winter in the Midwest, and rain, sleet, and snow pour down on you by the bucketful. Although this delayed acceleration runs and other checks that require dry pavement, it gave us a good idea of what the Ford will do under conditions not normally encountered in MT Research road tests.

If you're thinking of a new Ford—perhaps a Fairlane, or a Mainline Six—you'll get the essential data from this test. Later in the model year we'll give you driving impressions on the Six, now a livelier car than before (with 120 horsepower) and of course a better economy potential than the V8. If high performance isn't your dish of tea, but good handling and balance are, you may like it even better than its big brother. At the other end of the price scale is the brightly glamorous Fairlane, and it of course has even more soup than the car tested here, having 182 hp, dual exhausts, a four-barrel carburetor and a taste for nothing but premium fuel. **Driver's Seat:** When you first climb into your new Ford, you face what is in our opinion the top instrument panel in the "popular" price field. We say this not from esthetic appreciation alone, but due to its exceptional readability, *night and day*. The eerie bits of ectoplasm that floated across the '54 windshield have now been laid to rest by lowering and flattening the speedometer's bubble top. Even secondary controls, such as heater and lighter, are identified by illuminated markings similar to those Ford pioneered four years ago. Directions on the more-than-adequate heater are admittedly confusing the first day or so, but you soon check out on the control. A feature well worth mentioning (after over 1000 miles of bad weather driving) is the handy cowl-suspended pedal for the optional windshield washers. The washers themselves are so placed on the hood that they accurately squirt the windshield at any speed.

Not so good are Ford's windshield wipers, which cover so little area that any advantage from the new wrap-around is less than useless on a wet and dirty day. The worst blind spot is in the center, as shown by photo on page 34. Another presumably unforeseen problem which we have noted in all cars that have the wrap-around windshield and resulting squarish "ventipanes" in the front door is excessive leakage

REAR WHEEL HORSEPOWER
(Determined on Clayton chassis dynamometer. All tests are made under full load, which is similar to climbing a hill at full throttle. Observe hp figures not corrected to standard atmospheric conditions.)

51 road hp @ 1800 rpm and 30 mph
57 road hp @ 2000 rpm and 38 mph
68 road hp @ 2500 rpm and 52 mph
Max. 75 road hp @ 2900 rpm and 61 mph

TOP SPEED
(In miles per hour over surveyed ¼-mile.)

Fastest one-way run 95.9
Slowest one-way run 94.8
Average of four runs 95.2

ACCELERATION
(In seconds, checked with fifth wheel and electric speedometer.)

Standing start ¼-mile (74 mph) 19.4
0-30 mph 4.5
0-60 mph 14.5
10-30 mph 3.3
30-50 mph 5.7
50-80 mph 19.8

SPEEDOMETER ERROR
(Checked with fifth wheel and electric speedometer.)

Car speedometer read 33 @ true 30 mph
50 @ true 45 mph
66 @ true 60 mph
81 @ true 75 mph
102 @ top speed

FUEL CONSUMPTION
(In miles per gallon; checked with fuel flowmeter, fifth wheel, and electric speedometer. Mobilgas Special used.)

Steady 30 mph 18.5
Steady 45 mph 17.4
Steady 60 mph 14.0
Steady 75 mph 10.9
Stop-and-go driving over measured course 11.9
Tank average for 1386.1 miles 13.4

STOPPING DISTANCE
(To the nearest foot; checked with electrically actuated detonator.)

30 mph 33
45 mph 82
60 mph 178

Nose-down during a panic stop is about average; even after repeated stops like this one, brakes would not fade out

when the pane is cracked open for ventilation and dehumidifying. As far as we know, Rolls-Royce is the only manufacturer to tackle this problem, and they solved it with an accessory that could cost no more than 10 cents in mass production. All it amounts to is a triangular piece of clear glass (or Plexiglas) pasted high-side-forward onto the outside bottom of the ventipane. It works effectively, and we suggest it to all in the hope that arrangements can be made to allow more people than just R-R owners to benefit.

This ventipane leakage, on U.S. cars if not Rollses, results from the fact that rain water wraps just as eagerly around a deep curve as does the scenery. An even more astonishing by-product is the lapful of water you may receive on opening your door on a wet day.

Steering: Our test car had standard steering; this year it's definitely on the stiff side for city driving and parking, but a delight on the open road. You feel what is going on between the wheels and the highway. The car tends to counteract any tendency of the driver to overcontrol going into a corner. A non-engineering explanation for this might be that the car always wants to straighten itself out. While not recommended practice, you can even whip the wheel of the Ford at 60 mph, let go, and it will straighten itself out with no protest.

Handling: Although the '55 Ford has an entirely new chassis and suspension, it has lost none of the qualities which made last year's model our top-handling road-test car. We are not sure that Ford will once again rate best this year (because some other cars have made dramatic improvement in this category); nevertheless, we don't know of a curve in this country that would cause the driver discomfort if taken at *posted*, repeat *posted*, speeds in this car. Passengers will be comfortable after a short orientation course puts them at their ease. Chassis changes show up best during severe cornering, as the rear end does not seem as light as in the '54 model. The new one provides a definite compromise between the extremes of oversteer and understeer, as Walt Woron pointed out in "Driving Around" two months ago. Also worth complimenting is Ford's stability at high speeds. It felt very good during our timed top speed runs (averaging actual 95, speedometer 102 mph), a quality you may never need but which you can be sure translates itself down through the speed range. Wind wander has been abolished for good, a fairly diffi-

cult trick in a car of this light weight. **Ride:** Ford's new ride is more on the firm side than ever. In town at traffic speeds, it feels stiff enough to remind one of a conventional car with "export" springing, but it is by no means uncomfortable. At highway speeds, the suspension neatly smooths out all but major irregularities, as any little Lincoln should. Although you will feel road shocks, insulation from any sound due to them is excellent. In the other car tested in this issue, you definitely heard every tar strip in a cement highway, but you didn't feel it—what's your choice in the matter?

Acceleration: In this department, Ford's family V8 (162 horsepower) with Fordomatic seems to be third in its field, but feels better than that. Still, the difference is so slight (from 0-60 mph, Chevy takes 12.5 seconds, Plymouth 13.5, and Ford 14.5—all with equivalent transmissions and engines) that certainly part of it could be attributed to the normal difference between equivalent production cars of the same make. Our average figure (culled from 10 "fifth-wheel" runs, half east, half west) jibes closely with the 14.1 seconds we got in an impression test of an overdrive-equipped '55 Ford (MT, Dec. '54). One would expect a stick-shift job

Advantages of 1955 Ford's new wrap-around windshield are soon forgotten in bad weather, when ineffective wipers leave blind spots at center and at sides

Wide-opening Ford doors ease sometimes-awkward problem of entry and exit. Driver clears windshield cut-back easily

Little Judy Unwin isn't looking out for traffic, but the Ford's driver can see her through wide-angled glass area at sides

After soaking up the cold from standing out all night, our Fordomatic shifted sluggishly and noisily for a few miles until it warmed up. When warm, shifts were very smooth both up and down.

Economy: The increase in horsepower, as might be expected, has had an adverse effect on gasoline economy. However, the bonus in performance will cost you not much more than the price of a few cartons of cigarettes for 10,000 miles that you drive each year. At a steady 45 mph, this year's Ford gets one less mile per gallon than last year's counterpart. At 30 mph, our figure of 18.5 mpg is well over three less than last year's car.

Despite the new 18 mm "Turbocharge" sparkplugs and a factory okay on regular gasoline for cars equipped with the standard (7.6 to 1) heads, we found it advisable to use Mobilgas Special throughout the test to avoid occasional mild pinging. Presumably, ideal spark timing gives you "trace" knock under full power, but we can't feel *sure* of full power unless there is *no* knock under any condition at factory-specified settings. The stopwatch seems to validate this argument.

Brakes: We had no trouble whatever with the brakes during the test, and they showed no sign of fade during our very severe checks on the slow-downability of the new Ford. These involve three "panic" stops each from 60, 45, and 30 mph, and the routine often necessitates that we sit by the side of the road between runs while things cool off a bit, but not so with the Ford. Actual stopping distances were not too much improved over last year's Ford, but if you will remember, those were well above average.

Details: You may have gathered that we like the new Ford in motion; we also like it standing still. Young Henry may not appreciate this (he'd rather sell Fairlanes), but we feel that the interior trim of the second-string Customline matches the varsity so far fielded by competition. The vinyl and nylon fabric combinations have a richness not usually associated with a workaday car. (*Continued on page* **69**)

to be faster than an automatic box, providing engines are equal. In any event, Ford's "Trigger Torque" power will more than cover up an occasional error in passing judgment—vital acceleration in the passing range (50-80 mph) is a good 30 per cent better than last year's car, and it was no slouch in its class.

Revamped Fordomatic: This automatic is easy to control with the new illuminated quadrant mounted on the instrument panel. Full throttle will automatically start you out in LOW range and will let you drop back to LOW at speeds up to 18 mph, making it unnecessary to move the selector lever except when needed for mountain driving and deceleration. We could find no material difference in our acceleration figures, using both methods. Our one complaint is a minor one and may be due to the viscosity characteristics of the transmission fluid used in the test car.

With air cleaner removed, Ford's ohv V8 bares most of its components for servicing

Overhead view of engine shows neat layout. Looking down on engine compartment: exhaust manifold, crossover are hard to avoid

FORD'S
Ranch Wagon

*One of the "surprise" cars of the
year in speed and economy—and can't be beat in
giving you the most for your money*

CAR TESTED:	FORD V-8
	RANCH WAGON

TEST CONDITIONS

Altitude	550	feet
Temperature	88	degrees
Wind	8	mph
Gasoline	STANDARD PREMIUM	

ACCELERATION AND TOP SPEED

MPH	0-30	0-45	0-60	30-50	40-60
Seconds	5	8.5	14.4	5-6	7.8

Standing ¼ mile	19.5	seconds
Fastest one-way run	108	mph
Top speed avg. 4 runs	104	mph

SPEEDOMETER CORRECTIONS

Car Speedometer	Actual Speeds
20	18
30	27
40	37
50	46
60	55
70	65
80	74
90	84
100	93

BRAKING DISTANCE

MPH	Stopping Distance	
30	50	feet
45	98	feet
60	176	feet

FUEL CONSUMPTION

MPH	Average	
30	26	mpg
45	21	mpg
60	18	mpg

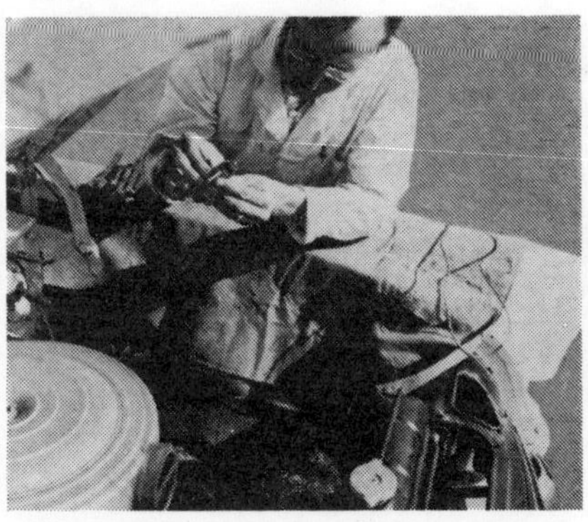

HANDLING, ride and braking qualities of the Custom Ranch Wagon are as good as the strictly passenger-bodied Fords. And, for 1955, that means they are hard to beat. The ball-joint front suspension has been refined each year and shows up to best advantage on wide, sweeping curves. Benefits of the power steering setup are appreciated most in city traffic and during parking maneuvers. Some tire rub was noticed when wheels were cramped sharply.

Riding comfort of station wagons has been questioned at times. While there are no standard items of test equipment to make a precision check on this feature, the personal reaction after many hundreds of miles behind the wheel is that such criticism is without foundation. The only exception to this may be found in the third or rear seat in the eight-passenger wagons (not a subject of this test report). Ford takes credit for introducing the four-way power seat into the low-priced field and it's an item that should be a must on anyone's list.

ENGINE of the Ranch Wagon was the ohv V-8, now in its second year. And it received more than ordinary attention during this road test. The reason was the remarkable top speed and economy figures which were obtained. In fact, following these runs, one of the crew (above photo) made a special check of plugs, compression and other factors to establish the fact that the engine was strictly stock. It was.

Much of the credit apparently belongs to the "power package," which is available (for $35) as a factory-installed extra on Ford station wagons and Fairlane models. While the engine seemed a little flat at low rpm and stalled occasionally, it obviously is a bargain in horsepower. The extras include a bigger air cleaner, four-barrel carburetor, cylinder heads with .9 higher compression ratio, special spark and intake manifold. It increases the rating from the standard 162 to 182 hp at 4600 rpm, boosts torque by about four per cent. Improvement is greatest at high rpm. Dual exhausts are stock.

INTERIOR finish in the Ranch Wagon is illustrated by the door opened for inspection in the accompanying photo. It should be seen in color to be appreciated. Plastic and basket-weave vinyls are bright, but easy to clean with ordinary solvents. Floor of the load space is covered in special linoleum so that it can be swept and hosed when necessary. Quality control in the cars seems to be higher than it has been for years and the only imperfection noted during a careful inspection of the test car was a slightly wider-than-it-should-be gap at the leading edge of the right-hand door. It, however, admitted no drafts or water to the passenger compartment.

Ford, like practically all manufacturers, is deeply conscious of the feminine influence in car buying. For this reason, it obviously has been paying especial attention to the design and finish of interiors. As a result, the Ranch Wagon (which lists at a surprisingly low price) has a luxury touch that is difficult to surpass for any kind of money.

PERFORMANCE of the Ranch Wagon, quite literally, takes the car right out of its class, particularly in top speed and in fuel economy. As the road testers aimed the car at a seven-mile straightaway, someone said, "I'll bet it won't break a hundred." It did—and more.

With an electric fifth wheel measuring the road, the needle on the Weston speedometer edged up to 100 mph . . . then 103 . . . 105 . . . 107 . . . and, finally, 108 as a curve came rushing up.

Equally sensational was the 26 mpg at a steady 30 mph. Other mileage figures up to 60 mph were exceptional.

Some of the factors that contribute to the impressive showing appear in connection with the engine report on the opposite page. The results, however, indicate that driving a station wagon means no important sacrifice in performance in any department, although the acceleration figures are not quite as spectacular as top end and economy. Yet they compare quite favorably with those obtained by the better vehicles in the big-car classes. It's obvious that in 1955 performance knows no price barriers.

UTILITY is what people look for in a station wagon. How many actually take advantage of what they buy is an open question. But there's no question that Ford engineers have been ingenious in creating a new kind of popular "convertible" for those who want a passenger-type vehicle with the carrying capacity of a light truck.

As a passenger car, the Ranch Wagon has two bench seats, with the front seat having a divided back like any conventional two-door sedan. Entrance and exit, however, is not too good and compares, in this respect, with a two-door hardtop. (This is eliminated, of course, in the four-door Country Sedans and Country Squire.) With both seats up, the arrangement is highly satisfactory for carrying six passengers comfortably. Only other important difference—common in the two-doors—is the rear side windows which slide open, rather than crank down.

When converting to cargo space, the bottom of the rear seat tilts forward and rests in a vertical position next to the back of the front seat. The rear seat back is then folded downward and becomes part of the floor. Thus, there are no seats to remove and carry outside the car or leave behind, as in the case of some other types of wagons. The spare tire and jack are located beneath a hinged lid in a recessed compartment next to the rear gate. With the rear counterbalanced, lift door up and the tail gate down, bulky objects up to eight feet long can be carried without extending beyond the car. If even this much load space is inadequate, a luggage rack is available as an accessory for mounting on the roof of the Ranch Wagon. It can be used to handle any gear that doesn't need protection from the weather.

STYLING may seem to be a secondary point with a utility vehicle, but nothing could be further from the truth when it comes to station wagons. As a matter of fact, the "ranchy" trend in living may have as much to do with the Ranch Wagon's present popularity as its all-purpose qualities. Furthermore, the car probably is the only one of purely American origin now in mass production. And its beginnings, as the estate car of wealthy families on Long Island, have enhanced its prestige.

However, it was Ford which first succeeded in wedding the station wagon layout to passenger car styling with results that were esthetically appealing. Functionalism is something often applied to sports car design, but it may have reached a more practical development in the Ranch Wagon than in any of the more exotic machinery found on either side of the Atlantic. It is safe to say that this is the "dream car" of Americans—and they are putting their money on the line to prove it.

FIVE CHOICES in Ford's 1955 Station Wagon Line

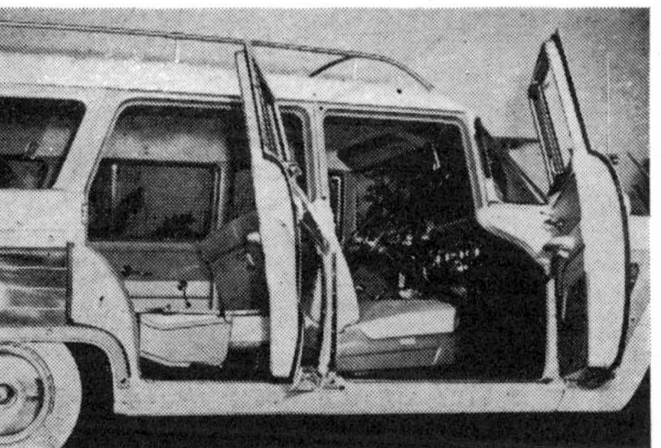

Four doors are feature of both eight-passenger station wagons, but simulated wood is only on the Country Squire.

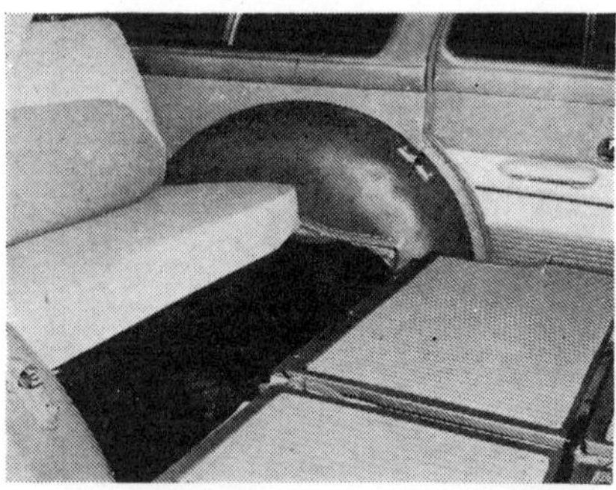

Converting interior of Country Squire and Country Sedan has many variations. Here middle seat folds down for cargo.

View from rear of Squire shows third seat removed. Note that only part of second seat can be folded down if so desired.

THE EIGHT-PASSENGER is one of two basic types of station wagons that Ford makes available. (The second type is the six-passenger unit described below.) All other important differences involve the number of doors or degree of custom trim—and the various arrangements add up to five choices in wagons. In the eight-passenger type, there are the Country Squire and the Country Sedan. The Squire costs approximately $100 more (base price) than the Sedan and for this the buyer gets the simulated wood finish on the side body panels of mahogany-grain type, along with wood-grain glass fibre moldings. Interior arrangement of the Squire and Sedan are identical and some idea can be obtained from the three drawings that appear below, although they do not tell the whole story. The eight-passenger capacity, of course, is obtained by using the three bench-type seats. Advantages over the six-passenger wagons are many. Not only may two more persons be carried comfortably, but when converted to carrying cargo, the load space is about one foot longer (because the second seat folds flush to the floor, while in the Ranch Wagons, bottom of the second seat only tilts to an upright position against the back of the front seat). However, the third seat in the eight-passenger models does not fold into the floor, but must be removed from the car or carried along with the cargo. An even greater advantage over the Ranch Wagons are the two extra doors, which contribute immensely to accessibility when carrying a cargo and during loading. In use, the variations are many. Space occupied by either or both the second and third seats may be converted to cargo space. And the second seat is divided off center so that either or both sections can be folded into the floor.

THE SIX-PASSENGER comes as three different models: Ranch Wagon, Custom Ranch Wagon, or six-passenger Country Sedan. The two Ranch Wagons are alike, except for trim. The Country Sedan has an exterior and four doors, like the eight-passenger Country Sedan described above, but carries an interior arrangement similar to the Ranch Wagons. In the two Ranch Wagons, both front and back seats are of the bench type, with the front divided at the center like any conventional two-door sedan so that the backs tilt forward to permit entry to the rear seat or, if the cargo space is being used, to allow access to the load area. The six-passenger Country Sedan, on the other hand, has the two extra doors to make entry, exit and loading easier. (Base price of the six-passenger Country Sedan is approximately $50 more than the Custom Ranch Wagon and $100 more than the Ranch Wagon.) From this it can be seen that buyers of a station wagon in the Ford line not only have to decide between six- and eight-passenger types, but also between two and four doors, in the various combinations. (The V-8 or six-cylinder overhead-valve engines are optional, also.) It's worth noting, too, that in the two-door models, the side windows in the rear compartment are opened and closed horizontally by sliding, a system not as satisfactory as in the four-door types where conventional cranks raise and lower the windows. The two Ranch Wagons offer maximum utility at a remarkably low price. But when considering the much greater versatility of the eight-passenger types, the rather modest extra cost (especially of the three-seat Country Sedan) seems to make it a better buy.

SPECIFICATIONS AND PRICES

ENGINES—V-8 ohv, bore 3.62, stroke 3.30, displacement 272 cubic inches, horsepower 162 @ 4400 rpm, compression ratio 7.6-to-1. Six-cylinder ohv, bore 3.62, stroke 3.60, displacement 224 cubic inches, horsepower 120 @ 4000 rpm, compression ratio 7.5-to-1. (Power package optional on V-8 includes special heads with 8.5-to-1 compression ratio, four-barrel carburetor, large air cleaner, special intake manifold and spark advance to increase horsepower to 182.) Standard carburetor on V-8 is dual downdraft, on six is single downdraft. Electrical system, six volts. **DIMENSIONS** — Wheelbase 115 inches, tread 58 front and 56 rear, overall length 197, width 75, height 62. **TRANSMISSIONS** — (rear gear ratios indicated) Conventional 4.09 or 4.27 optional, Overdrive 4.27, Fordomatic 3.54. (Note: suspension same as standard Fords, except for rear springs which have two extra leaves.)

(Factory-suggested retail prices include federal taxes and suggested handling and delivery charges, but not transportation costs, state and local taxes, nor optional equipment.) Ranch Wagon, $2043, Custom Ranch Wagon $2108, six-passenger Country Sedan $2156, eight-passenger Country Sedan $2287, Country Squire $2391, Fordomatic $178, Overdrive $109, radio $87, heater $71, power steering $91, power brakes $33, V-8 engine $100 extra, power package $35. •

Ford Customline

Four-Door Sedan

THE CUSTOMLINE four-door sedan is an above-average safe automobile. The V-8 engine of the car we investigated is of the usual Ford reliability and high performance. Although the suspension tends to be soft, the effect on roadability is not too pronounced. Steering is reasonable in comparison to the other cars we reviewed. The transmission system on all Fords has a reasonable safety factor when related to the power units employed and the rear axle assembly.

Road Test- 1956 FORD Fairlane

Photos by Joe Farkas

FORD'S production and sales volume has been growing significantly the past few years, so the company elected to stand pretty much pat with a proven winner for 1956—in most respects. While a number of styling changes were made, they aren't the type that are readily noticeable. A new grille was added, the roofline was lowered and exterior trim changed.

In its Fairlane models, however, the company joined the Cubic Inches Club by offering the engine used in 1955 T-Birds and Mercurys. This has been looked on in many quarters as an attempt to recapture the rating of top performer in the low-priced field from Chevrolet. Fords with this 292-cubic-inch engine have already proved successful in several stock car races.

The Fairlane also represents a relatively new philosophy in the auto industry. This line, Ford hopes, will permit the company to lure away some of the buyers who have habitually bought medium-priced cars in the past. Ford claims that it can give a buyer anything he can get in a higher-priced car in a Ford.

That the company has a point is obvious when you look at the situation closely. In a Ford you can get all accessories, from air conditioning to power seats and windows, that are available in any other make. Performance and handling are at least on a par with many of the cars in the price bracket Ford hopes to crack.

Fuel economy checks resulted in 21.4 mpg at 30, 20.2 at 45 and 16.7 at 60 mph. In 150 miles of driving, the tank mileage was 19 mpg.

Since addition of the bigger engine makes the Fairlane by far the most interesting of the new Fords, this was the model picked for MOTOR *Life's* road test. The car used had Fordomatic transmission, the 202-hp engine, manual steering and brackes. A four-door sedan was picked because this is still the most popular body style.

ACCELERATION is something Ford has long been noted for and the 1956 Fairlane is certainly the hottest performer the company has ever built. Detroit Editor Ken Fermoyle reported in MOTOR *Life's* first story on the 1956 Ford (November, 1955) that a pre-production Fairlane tuned by Ford engineers turned 0 to 60 mph in less than 10 seconds, so we knew what the car could do. The test car was purposely picked at random, had been given no special tuning because we wanted to find out what an *average* Fairlane such as a customer might buy off a showroom floor would do. Average 0 to 60 time was 11.6 seconds. From 0 to 30 averaged 4 seconds flat and 0 to 45 took 7.2 seconds. The 50 to 80 average was 13.8 seconds and the Fairlane turned the standing quarter-mile in 17.5 seconds. (Actual speed at the end of the quarter was just over 75 mph.) This shows that this car is fast even in average condition and the earlier tests demonstrate that it is capable of really startling performance with judicious tuning. The test crew felt that the transmission in the road test car was a bit slow in shifting and minor adjustments here would have improved performance noticeably.

Top speed of the new Ford Fairlane is one of its outstanding features. True speed on the fastest one-way run was 108.3! Average of several runs in opposite directions was just over 105 mph, which puts this model in the big class.

SPEEDOMETER ERROR on the 1956 Ford runs a nearly constant five per cent fast throughout the entire speed range. This is not only less than normal, but is unusual in that the percentage of error was so consistent. Most cars show relatively accurate readings at low speeds, tend to become progressively more optimistic as speed goes up. As the picture shows, however, the Weston electric speedometer registers 95 mph with the standard Ford unit reading 100 mph. At 30 mph, true speed is 29; at 40, 38; at 50, 48.5; at 60, 57; and at 80, 76.

GOOD HANDLING and excellent all-round roadability have been a Ford strong point for years—especially since the now-famed ball joint front end was introduced. The 1956 is no exception. The ease with which it can be whipped around tight turns and excellent acceleration out of corners furnished by the good low-end punch of the 292-cubic-inch Fairlane engine make this car fun to drive. Body roll is present only to a slight degree except during extreme cornering; even then you don't get a feeling of instability. Down-shifting for corners can be accomplished easily with the Fordomatic transmission and this gives a driver an extra margin of control; you can really barrel out of a turn in low range too! Ford traditionally has had a firmer ride than many other American cars and this is still the case. This is one reason why it handles so well. Despite this extra degree of firmness, ride is comfortable enough for all but the most critical drivers. Bad bumps are noticed perhaps more than in cars with softer springing, but under normal conditions ride is good.

RIDING QUALITIES of Fairlane were given extensive workout over graveled back roads, blacktop, rough paved stretches and smooth highways. Ride is firmer than most competitive makes—which helps account for excellent handling. However, don't think that comfort has been sacrificed noticeably. You might feel bumps a shade more than in some other makes when those bumps are really severe, but only the most critical will detect much difference between Ford ride and that of other cars under most conditions.

What FORD Makes for 1956

FORD has 18 body styles in four series —Fairlane, Customline, Mainline and Station Wagon and the six-cylinder engine is optional in all at about $100 less than the V-8 prices quoted below. Among the styles omitted here are Fairlane Crown Victoria Skyliner (which differs only because of a transparent roof insert), and the Custom Ranch Wagon and the six-passenger Country Sedan which are essentially the same as the Ranch Wagon and the eight-passenger Country Sedan, respectively. Prices shown include federal taxes and delivery charges.

Accessory Prices

Fordomatic $178; Overdrive $109; De Luxe Heater $71; Directional Signals $15; De Luxe Radio $106; De Luxe Air-Conditioning $435; Power Brakes $35; Power Steering $53; Four-way Power Seat $64; Four Power Window Lifts $102.

MAINLINE SERIES

• Four-door sedan—$1958

• Two-door sedan—$1913

• Business coupe—$1811

CUSTOMLINE SERIES

• Four-door sedan—$2050

• Two-door sedan—$2005

FAIRLANE SERIES

• Four-door sedan—$2143

• Two-door sedan—$2098

• Two-door hardtop—$2243

• Four-door hardtop—$2315

• Crown Victoria—$2387

• Convertible—$2409

STATION WAGONS

• Ranch Wagon—$2234

• Parklane—$2478

• Thunderbird—$3217

• Country Squire—$2582

• Country Sedan—$2478

CUSTOM RANCH WAGON

COUNTRY SQUIRE 8-PASSENGER

FORD'S LINE of station wagons is hard to beat. They have more plus factors in their design and operation than most of the wagons on the market. Though none of the car's features are outstanding in themselves, when they are all wrapped up in one solid package, they add up to an outstanding wagon "buy."

The engine choice of six or "Thunderbird" V8 offer either adequate performance with definite economy potential or just plain hot performance in all speed ranges. Several optional rear axle ratios permit the buyer to "gear" his Ford wagon to either heavy loads and hilly going or high speed cruising on super highways. (Overdrive is also available.) Fordomatic provides the most flexible of the automatic transmissions available in a low-priced wagon, with its combination of torque converter and three—instead of two—automatic speed changes.

Ford's chassis with ball-joint front suspension and good balance provides a stable underpinning for high speed traveling over rough roads. Brakes are smooth and easy to operate without power assistance.

Combined load and passenger space compares favorably with all the other low or even medium-priced wagons, yet the Ford has the shortest overall length of any full-sized nine-passenger wagon. The load space is as long as Chevrolet's and 4 inches wider than Plymouth's. The tailgate opening is average. Thus the overall load potential of Ford wagons is above average.

Although the ride is firmer than most straight passenger cars, especially when there is no load in back of the front seat, the combination of comfortable upholstery and tight control of pitching, bouncing or swaying makes for an overall degree of comfort seldom experienced in a wagon.

The solidity of construction is worth mentioning because the Ford wagons are almost completely free of "shake, rattle and roll" characteristics.

Summing up: Ford wagons are extremely well-built, rugged, roadable and practical vehicles with exceptional controllability and performance, a fairly comfortable ride and an overall aspect of good design and thorough construction. Ford wagons deserve their excellent public acceptance. ●

COUNTRY SEDAN 6-PASSENGER

COUNTRY SEDAN 8-PASSENGER

PARKLANE

<table>
<tr><td>

ford

</td><td>

☑ ☑ ☑ ☑ ☑
MEANS TOP RATING

</td></tr>
<tr><td>

Ford wagons have option of the well-designed and capable overhead valve six or the 202 bhp "Thunderbird" V8. With the V8, Ford wagons are the "hottest" in the low-priced field.

</td><td>

PERFORMANCE
☑ ☑ ☑ ☑ ☑

</td></tr>
<tr><td>

Generally pleasing and well integrated, from the smooth chrome-free two-door Ranch Wagon to the simulated wood paneling (painted metal and fibreglass trim) of the Country Squire.

</td><td>

STYLING
☑ ☑ ☑ ☑ ☐

</td></tr>
<tr><td>

Ford wagons ride firmly over rough surfaces but provide better than average comfort for all passengers, as the ride is well-controlled and free from pitch or sway.

</td><td>

RIDING COMFORT
☑ ☑ ☑ ☑ ☐

</td></tr>
<tr><td>

Excellent overall layout. Back seat of six-passenger models is comfortable with adequate room. Rear quarter window on four-door model slides open for extra ventilation of rear seat passengers.

</td><td>

INTERIOR DESIGN
☑ ☑ ☑ ☑ ☑

</td></tr>
<tr><td>

Ford's chassis design really comes into its own on the wagons, all of which have a firm, stable, over-the-road feel and precise control at high speeds and in sharp curves.

</td><td>

ROADABILITY
☑ ☑ ☑ ☑ ☑

</td></tr>
<tr><td>

Power steering is helpful here, although not an absolute necessity. Power brakes are not needed. Fordomatic gives superior control of acceleration and deceleration at all speeds.

</td><td>

EASE OF CONTROL
☑ ☑ ☑ ☑ ☐

</td></tr>
<tr><td>

Better than average with the capable 6-cylinder power plant. Conservative driving is needed to get average gasoline mileage with powerful V8s.

</td><td>

ECONOMY
☑ ☑ ☑ ☑ ☐

</td></tr>
<tr><td>

Very good on the Sixes, where engine components are readily accessible. Chassis is very simple and well designed. Some components on the V8 engine are tough to reach.

</td><td>

SERVICEABILITY
☑ ☑ ☑ ☑ ☐

</td></tr>
<tr><td>

Well above average. Exterior finish and trim are excellent, upholstery and interior paneling very good. Movable seat components and tailgate are neatly fitted.

</td><td>

WORKMANSHIP
☑ ☑ ☑ ☑ ☑

</td></tr>
<tr><td>

Excellent. Ford has a rugged chassis, and the wagon bodies are sturdily built and unusually free from squeaks and rattles.

</td><td>

DURABILITY
☑ ☑ ☑ ☑ ☐

</td></tr>
<tr><td>

Seats convert easily and tailgate, transom and latch operate smoothly.

</td><td>

OPERATION OF DETAILS
☑ ☑ ☑ ☑ ☐

</td></tr>
<tr><td>

Equal to or better than any low-priced wagon. Ford wagons have high resale potential, are all-around good buy.

</td><td>

VALUE PER DOLLAR
☑ ☑ ☑ ☑ ☑

</td></tr>
</table>

1956 FORD

RANCH WAGON

Flight Testing Ford's Bird

photography: Poole

R OAD & TRACK's original slogan was (from 1947 to 1954) "The Motor Enthusiast's Magazine" and this statement is still true today, despite its awkwardness. In accordance with our general policy of dealing primarily with interesting automobiles (which does not necessarily imply that uninteresting cars are impractical) we have allotted considerable space to American cars of the more or less special-interest type.

The mere fact that several special-interest types of cars are even offered by our volume-minded manufacturers is a modern phenomenon, but one which we are happy to find. The Ford Motor Company's Thunderbird is such a car; certainly not in the least bit dull, and appropriately cataloged as a "personal car."

Personal car is the right terminology, for the T-Bird has flown in sports car competition as if its wings were clipped—this is no sports car by any stretch of the imagination, and Ford never claimed otherwise. Furthermore it is now apparent that the Thunderbird's moderate price more than offsets its limited seating capacity, in comparing its sales figures to the luxurious Continental Mark II. While there have been rumors of a T-Bird competition version, the present policy of loading the cars with every conceivable option shows that the motoring enthusiast can go hang, and last year's sales of over 16,000 units proves that Ford found a new market of unsuspected strength.

Evaluating this car in its proper perspective, as a truly luxurious 2-seater convertible, the only conclusion that can be reached is that it succeeds admirably. At the same time our sports car outlook forces us to complain bitterly. It is so similar to a sports car that it seems a shame that it could not at least have been endowed with better steering and handling qualities, both of which are fair to good in comparison to domestic sedans, but abominable for a 2-seater machine.

If performance, without regard to engine displacement, were the only criterion, the Thunderbird would get very high praise. Last year's test (March, 1955) showed very good performance, and the 1956 model, with larger 312 cu. in. engine does even better. Yet it is true that a well known imported sports car with 100 less cu. in. will readily out-perform the best that Dearborn engineers can produce. In this respect our test car had, as last year, the automatic transmission. Despite all our efforts, we were unable to find a stick-shift Thunderbird within a 500 mile radius of our test strip.

As last year, we employed our "forced-shift" technique and this cuts the 0-60 mph and standing ¼ mile times by about .5 second. Normally the Ford automatic upshifts at a mere 3600 rpm but all the data recorded was made using 4500 rpm as a limit in 1st and 2nd gears. This is accomplished by starting in "LO" range, shifting to "DRIVE" at an idicated 43 mph, back to LO at 50 mph, and finally to DRIVE again at 80 mph.

On starting from a standstill, there is a definite pause before the car moves off. This is caused by slippage in the torque convertor (and not by rear spring windup) and does not affect the times recorded as our procedure does not start the watches until the first foot of car movement. Trick starts, such as holding the brake on, or racing the engine in neutral before pulling the lever into LO, give spectacular wheel-spin but no time improvement. When the throttle is depressed the Thunderbird rear end drops and the car moves off like a hydroplane getting up on its step. An honest 60 mph required an indicated 68 and our data showed an average of 9.3 seconds required, from 0-68, with one trial at 9.0 seconds dead.

The highest speedometer reading seen was 120 mph, during the best one-way timed run of 113.9 actual mph. The tachometer read 4600 rpm at the time and would go no higher, even with 5 miles available for peaking-out. Obviously this car was well tuned (by Bill Stroppe, well known Ford specialist) and the odometer showed 2300 miles at the time of the test. At this speed, the car was easy to control and high speed stability is excellent.

The twisting road characteristics of the Thunderbird might be described as Allard or Dellow-like, but with a difference. At the curb, with full tank, there is 60 lbs more weight on the rear wheels than in front. Two adults put the rear end weight up to 52.5% of the total. Accordingly the tail tends to swing out on

The Thunderbird Y-8 is smooth, quiet, dependable, powerful and crowded with accessories.

The spare tire must be tilted back and the trunk lid opened, before fuel can be added.

corners and the combination of very slow (4.3 turns) steering with a power booster and much too soft rear springs makes safe control questionable. However there is ample warning of too vigorous cornering by virtue of the rear tires rubbing on something when the body begins to roll. The power-steering is unobtrusive in normal driving, but lacks feel when cornering. We also found that a tricky corner entered conservatively could produce exciting results when the throttle was depressed to accelerate out. There is tremendous power available and any such car must always be treated with respect, especially by the throttle foot. In this case the tendency of the transmission to downshift could easily produce a spinout and in general it appears to be wiser to confine cornering experiments to LO range (second gear, above 20 mph.)

The Thunderbird has 11" brake drums with 170 sq. in. of lining area, enough for any car driven in average fashion and weighing under 4000 lbs., loaded. However the combination of a vacuum booster, which makes for a deceptively light pedal pressure, and an over 100 mph performance is not too fortunate. One moderate stop from over 100 mph produced signs of fade and two such stops within 3 minutes gave genuine fade and pungent odors. At this point there were still brakes, but pedal pressure was perhaps doubled. Despite all this we feel that no one would be foolish enough to drive this car for long at 100 mph, if only because of its original equipment tires.

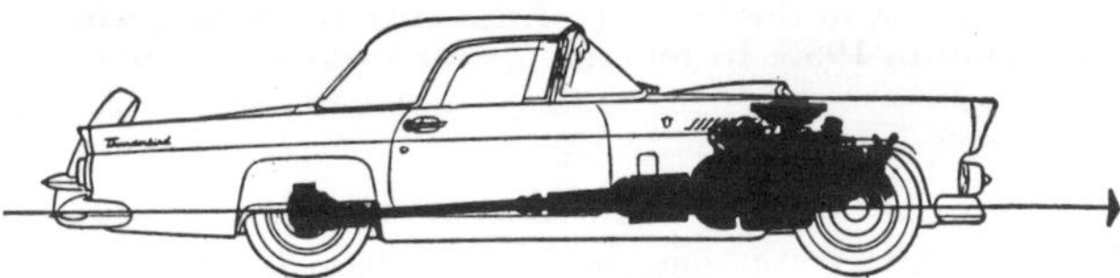

The Thunderbird engine is placed well behind the front wheels.

The bench type seat is wide enough for three adults except that the large transmission tunnel allows no room for the middle passenger's legs. Although the seats are very close to the floor, driving the car is comfortable due to the fact that either foot can be used for braking. The adjustable steering is a real boon but anyone over 5'-10" finds that the legs tend to hit the wheel when it is pushed well forward in Italian G.P. style.

As is usual with American cars, we quote the lowest basic list price. In this case the $3163.10 is for a bare car with stick-shift and hard top, although our test car had the following extras:

Fordomatic	$215.00
Soft top	290.30
Radio & heater	190.60
Power steering	64.00
Power seats	64.50

This adds up to $3987.50, to which freight and local taxes must be added.

The Thunderbird is a well-made, high performance automobile and fully justifies its title of "Personal Car." ●

The hard top is easily removed by two people and the new spare tire mounting gives a worthwhile increase in trunk volume.

R & T ROAD TEST NO. 109

FORD THUNDERBIRD

SPECIFICATIONS

List price (f.o.b.)	$3163
Wheelbase, in.	102
Tread, f/r.	56/56
Tire size	6.70-15
Curb weight, lbs.	3570
distribution, %	49/51
Test weight	3850
Engine	V-8, ohv
Bore & stroke	3.80 x 3.44
Displacement, cu in.	312
cu cm.	5115
Compression ratio	9.00
Horsepower	225
peaking speed	4600
equivalent mph	111
Torque, ft-lbs.	324
peaking speed	2600
equivalent mph	62.8
Gear ratios (overall)	
3rd	3.31
2nd	4.83
1st	8.94
1st + conv.	18.8

CALCULATED DATA

Lbs/hp (test wt.)	17.1
Engine revs/mile	2480
Cu. ft/ton mile	116.2
Piston travel, ft./mile	1420
Mph @ 2500 fpm	105.3

PERFORMANCE, Mph

Top speed (avg.)	112.2
best run	113.9
2nd (5000)	83
1st (5000)	45
see chart for shift points	
Mileage range	12/15 mpg

ACCELERATION, Secs.

0-30 mph	3.3
0-40 mph	5.0
0-50 mph	7.3
0-60 mph	9.3
0-70 mph	12.1
0-80 mph	15.8
0-90 mph	20.2
0-100 mph	26.6
standing start ¼ mile	17.0

TAPLEY DATA, Lbs/ton

3rd	360 @ 55 mph
2nd	450 @ 40 mph
1st	off-scale
Total drag at 60 mph, 183 lbs.	

SPEEDO ERROR

Indicated	Actual
30 mph	25.7
60 mph	52.3
90 mph	82.7
120 mph	113.9

Pair of 1957 Thunderbirds show off major changes from last year. Grille has been slightly enlarged, the bumpers are heavier, fins have been added and the rear deck stretched out.

The spare tire, carried on a continental mount for '56, has been returned to the interior of the enlarged trunk, where it started out in 1955. In general, the car looks better than ever.

THE 1957
THUNDERBIRD

STYLING—Moderate facelift, with revamped grille and bumpers, bigger trunk. The spare tire has gone back inside again.

PERFORMANCE—Not much improvement found in prototypes, but later production models should be up considerably.

ENGINEERING—Just a few changes in frame, brakes, springs. Overall length less. And 14-inch wheels and tires adopted.

BODY TYPES—Same as before, one body with choice of soft top or removable hardtop. Rumored four-seater some time away.

THE tremendous public acceptance of the Thunderbird was the big reason for Ford exploiting it via the "kissin' cousin" route to help sell standard Ford passenger cars. This automobile, universally and affectionately known as the "T-Bird," has achieved popularity that can't be measured by normal sales standards. Why? And will it continue to rate as highly in 1957? Let's see:

BY KEN FERMOYLE

LIKE NEARLY everyone else in the country I've been smitten by the Thunderbird since it first appeared. Earlier, really, since I was introduced to it before most people. It goes without saying then, that I was very anxious to see what had been done to it for 1957.

I was rather pleased after I first saw it early in the summer that it was still to be definitely a T-Bird—if you know what I mean. Frankly, however, I'm still partial to the original 1955 jobs. That's the trouble with success; it's *so* hard to top!

As far as styling changes for '57 are concerned, you'll have to judge for yourself whether the results are good or bad. There have been quite a few but they don't make a major difference in the total effect of the car. Most of them, naturally, have been aimed at keeping the T-Bird within kissin' kinship of the Ford passenger car line. (You might not agree with that, but it's important to Ford.)

The front bumper and grille have been revamped. Front wheel cutouts have been changed—and some bright-metal trim added to the formerly chrome-less side as a result. The body has been extended some 5 inches at the rear, but the spare tire has been moved back inside the trunk where it belongs! (In fact, the reason for the lengthened deck was to permit just that. Dearborn heard plenty about the continental mount!)

The contour of the deck lid has been reworked; it's higher now and has a reverse angle at the rear. Rear quarter panels have been restyled along '57 Ford passenger car lines. They feature the "canted blade" or fin effect along with the huge tail lights of the standard Fords.

There have been fewer changes in the chassis to which this sheet metal is bolted. Fewer, really, than in Ford passenger cars. The frame is unchanged except that number four cross member is now a box rather than channel section (because of the longer deck and extra weight).

Front suspension is virtually the same as in earlier models. Ball joints and coil springs are still used.

Semi-elliptic springs are retained at rear, but five leaves are now used. (There were four last year.) They are the same length (55 inches) and width (2 inches).

Effective brake lining area has been increased from a fraction under 170 inches to 176 inches, despite the switch to 14-inch tires and wheels. This was done by enlarging front brake area slightly, keeping rear brakes the same size as last year.

Wheelbase is the same—102 inches—and tread is still 56 inches front and rear. Overall length has gone from 185.12 inches to 182.01—but this is deceiving. As mentioned earlier

With the spare back in the trunk, the T-Bird still has more luggage space than in the past. This is possible because of increased length. The Bird now looks less like a sports car.

Engine modifications have been few, although output is now up to a top rating of 245 (which is optional with stick shifts). New four-barrel Carb here with air cleaner off is lower.

the body is some 5 inches longer; last year's overall figure included the tacked-on continental tire mounting. Overall height is down from 52.14 to 51.54 inches with the hardtop in place (from 52.50 to 51.90 with soft top), due principally to the smaller tires.

In engines, the 312-cubic-inch V-8, standard on Ford-O-Matic and overdrive models, is rated at 245 hp with 9.7-to-1 compression ratio. This engine is 265 hp when equipped with optional four-barrel carburetor. A 292-cubic-inch V-8 is standard on standard shift models, is rated at 212 hp with 8.6-to-1 compression. However, the bigger engine is optional on the manual shift T-Birds.

So much for the tangibles. What's more important to T-Bird admirers is how these changes have affected the car on the road. That's what I was anxious to find out when I slipped behind the wheel of an engineering prototype out at Ford's Dearborn proving grounds.

The job I drove was one used to check out the engineering changes for 1957. It was standard '57 all the way thru except for a few unimportant pieces of chrome. Unfortunately, it was a fully-equipped model—power seats, windows, brakes, steering, Ford-O-Matic; the works—and had covered a lot of long, hard miles. Perhaps that's why the performance wasn't up to my expectations.

But let's take handling first:

The T-Bird is no sports car and Ford has never made that claim. It has, however, been a car which put a lot of the fun back into driving. It still is.

If anything, the changes made for '57 have improved handling. Weight distribution is better due to the extra poundage added at the rear by the longer body. Engineer Jim Aldridge of the Thunderbird development group, who rode with me, said their tests indicated that rear end stability was improved as a result. I'm inclined to agree.

There seemed to be less rear end steering effect in hard cornering; the difference wasn't great, but it was there. Of course, a few short hours driving isn't conclusive proof but I can certainly say that the '57 T-Bird handles at least as well as its predecessors and be accurate.

My major handling complaint is—again—the very slow steering. It requires nearly 4½ turns of the wheel to go from lock to lock—even with power steering. It would seem that if they must use this power assist, they could at least lower the steering ratio in cars so equipped. As it is, you're kept pretty busy getting thru a tight radius turn.

In general, the Thunderbird still falls somewhere between a true sports car and a standard passenger car as far as overall handling and maneuverability are concerned.

The same is pretty much true about the ride. It certainly can't be called harsh or uncomfortable. Going from a normal sedan to a T-Bird, you might notice a little extra firmness and a shade more pitch due to the shorter wheelbase—not, however, if your sedan was more than four or five years old.

You get an extra measure of comfort in the new T-Birds as a result of a new seat design, by the way. It doesn't look much different than seats in earlier models, but the development engineers swear by it. They claim it is a big help in reducing fatigue on long trips in particular.

Now we get to performance; and, frankly, it was disappointing. The car tested just didn't deliver the acceleration you expect from a T-Bird. (Probably, however, the production models will be much better.) Top speed would almost certainly have been better; unfortunately there are no facilities for maximum speed runs at Ford's Dearborn test area.

Let me give you the figures I got first, then we'll look at some of the whys behind them. (Figures quoted were the result of stopwatch timing with the speedometer corrected for error. All runs were on a dead-level straight.)

Best I could do from 0 to 60 mph was 11.5 seconds. From 0 to 70 took 16 seconds. (This time was for a one-way run only; all others are two-way averages.) From 0 to 80 took 21.2 seconds and the 50 to 80 time was 15.1 seconds. Only low and intermediate were used from 0 to 60 and 70 mph but I had to shift into high range just over 70 which accounted for the long time it took to get up to the 80 mph notch. The 50 to 80 runs were made by running in drive range and just flooring the throttle to get into intermediate. Downshifting to low—and thus going into intermediate and being able to hold it there longer—might have cut the time but I wanted to simulate normal highway conditions.

One of the big reasons for the relatively lackluster low- and mid-range performance was the axle ratio. It has been lowered (a higher gear) from 3.31 in '56 to 3.10 with Ford-O-Matic. With three-speed manual transmission the change is from 3.73 to 3.56; with overdrive, from 3.92 to 3.70. And, as the specification table shows, there isn't a lot more horsepower than last year. (There is also some added weight.)

Top speed will undoubtedly be better especially compared to '56 models which had the added drag of the outside tire mounting. Economy will probably be slightly better too. •

FORD ROAD TEST

AN EARLY INTRODUCTION DATE, and a wise policy of stockpiling sufficient '57 models to flood the road immediately afterward, gave Ford a head start this year. What kind of Ford is this?

Basically, it has more of almost everything than its '56 counterpart. It's lower by four inches, longer, more powerful, still competent on the highway. There is no revolutionary change in the car's behavior.

Our test car was a Fairlane 500 four-door that looked like a true centerpost-less hardtop, but wasn't. The combination of narrow posts and chrome window trim would fool almost any bystander except when both side windows are down. The combination of looks and sturdiness is top-notch and should be copied, but probably won't, by other manufacturers.

The car had the 245-horsepower Thunderbird Special engine, Fordomatic, power steering, no power brakes. To compare it to Ford V8s with less power, dock our performance figures a little and increase our fuel mileage figures. Cars with stick shift should show no significant performance difference but will give better economy, especially if they have overdrive.

On the highway we liked the car better that in town. Once you give it its head, it responds like a high-spirited but essentially amiable steed, requiring no constant correction on straight roads. A crowned road does cause a sharp pull to the right, and recovery when the wheel is whipped from side to side—we do this to simulate an accidental tug—is not as good as it should be. Wind has less effect than on previous models, as it should considering the new weight of 3800 pounds. Steering wheel vibration is very slight. It's an unusually pleasant car for the drivers on a long trip—untiring mentally or physically.

Has Its Roadability Rating Changed?

To some extent, and not for the better. The new weight distribution, though far from ideal as on nearly every V8, is much improved over last year and should theoretically give better roadability. Last year it was 59.5 per cent at the front, and this year that proportion is down to 55.4; yet on sharp curves, or even normal ones taken too fast, the rear can break away with disconcerting suddenness.

For those madmen who yearn to "let 'er out," the Ford feels

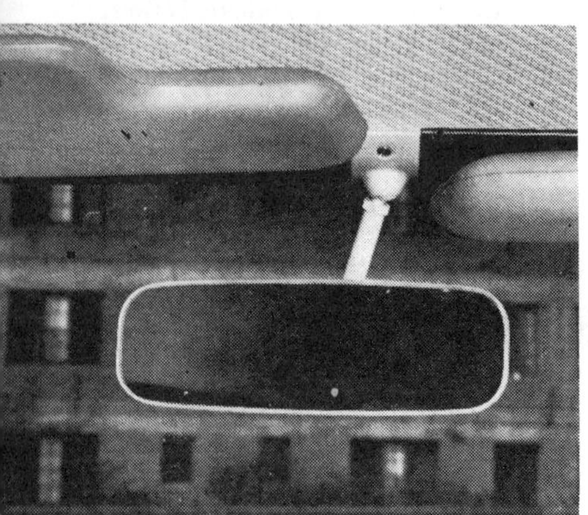

HIGH-MOUNTED MIRROR has universal joint that adapts it to all sizes of drivers or to clear obstructions at rear.

THIEVES will welcome this handy push-button, situated just inside the small vent. It's not so easy for driver.

LINCOLN INFLUENCE appears in slim pillars, lined with chrome for a hardtop look. Nothing lined up well on test car.

Is It Still Up Top in Handling?

It's not the stand-out car that it was by comparison with other makes when Ford was first with ball-joint front suspension. Broken-field running in traffic demands lots of winding from the power steering, which takes 4.75 turns from lock to lock just like its manual counterpart. Opinions on Ford's power steering are very different among various MT testers: "Best power steering I ever tried—gives you a real feel of the road"; "Feels like a fairly easy-steering older car without power"; "Gives no advantage to the driver except in parking." Take your pick!

An exceptionally broad, though not very high, windshield gives the driver a good vantage point. He sits rather close to the roof, particularly in Fairlane models, behind a massive cowl. This year's steering wheel is a half-inch smaller in diameter than the 56's (but seems enormous beside that in the Plymouth) yet the lower portion of its rim hung down too far for some drivers. Big rear fins and modern all-around vision make parking easy. The Fairlane's nine-inch length increase does not. Customs and Custom 300s, the sober buyer will note, can fit into slots half a foot shorter.

good right up to its top speed and excellent at the speed limit on any U.S. highway you can name.

There is a certain un-Ford-like wallowing when coming out of severe highway dips, the penalty of 57's new softer ride. If you leave the pavement there's no cause for panic, but take it easy on your braking or sudden turns on rough or washboard surfaces.

How Does It Go This Year?

Just a little better from a standing start than in '56 despite the big rated horsepower difference. Half a second separated the new quarter-mile and 0-60 times from those with last year's Fairlane. There's a European-style torque increase at higher rpms in this Thunderbird Special engine that reminded us of an entirely different kind of car, the Mercedes 190-SL. At 2000 to 2500 rpms, it's almost as though you had cut in a blower or shifted instantaneously to a slightly lower gear. And that's not just a seat-of-the-pants increase either: Ford's newly available power to pull out of tight spots is proved by the stopwatches. At both lower and higher speeds, passing times show about a second's improvement this year, and 45-60 is a hasty 4.3. (We have substituted this more realistic figure for our former 40-60 acceleration test, used up through last year.)

Has Economy Suffered?

Surprisingly, only at lower steady speeds. At a steady 75 this large engine can loaf along and deliver marginally better mileage than the 292-cubic-incher did last year, and our tank mileage went up two miles per gallon when we weren't doing actual fuel, braking or acceleration tests.

Are Ford Brakes Still Good?

They're a lot better. It's not a cinch to increase a car's weight by 100 pounds and bring it to a panic stop in 14 less feet from 60 mph, but that's what Ford has done. There is obvious fade but a minimum of dangerous darting from one side to the other, even when it smells as though the brakes were aflame. Pedal pressure on our non-power-equipped car seemed high to those used to a booster, but not to others.

Can You Reach Anything Under the Hood?

If you like to tinker with your own engine, you'll run into a little trouble. Plugs are concealed under the exhaust manifold, the oil filter is well hidden by power equipment. The battery, oil dipstick and filler are handy and the transmission dipstick is not too hard to reach.

Is the Ride Smoother?

Yes. Awareness of road surface is no longer disturbing, though it's there. As yet Ford shows no signs of abandoning its mechanical, keep-the-driver-in-touch feel which can be refreshing after the plush-swathed way that some cars drive. If you enjoy the act of driving, you'll like a Ford; your passengers might prefer to be better insulated, though they'll note an improvement over last year.

It's now easier to bottom a Ford when storm drains cross the road, and passengers won't stay so securely in their seats on highway dips. When rounding a curve the body leans somewhat, but your passengers will stay put easier than in many larger cars.

What's Different About a Ford?

Mostly you'll get some careful attention to small details. The Fordomatic transmission, a Class A box in every regard, continues basically unchanged and the buyer is not expected to pay an extra fee for it, as he is for Plymouth's and Chevy's new automatics. Upshifts are accomplished with little fuss, and creep is noticeably slight. It still offers something that may loom larger to us as test drivers than to you, and that is its quadrant. The shift pattern is toward you and down for LOW, as on other automatics, but toward you and up for REVERSE, as on a car with a stick shift. This is a safety feature, if you drive automatics and stick shifts interchangeably. It's truly valuable only in a tight spot, but we like it. Snowbound drivers will note a disadvantage to the Ford quadrant: you can't rock directly from LOW to REVERSE and back.

Ford's windows roll faster (2⅝ turns up or down) than they used to, and a fine British feature has at long last been adopted: the driver's window requires a whole turn less than the others for a total of 1⅝, a real safety device. Ford's tail lights, while they irritate some people, can certainly be seen better than almost any others you can name, and after all, that's what tail lights are for. Two-position door checks, a blessing in a tight spot, are still a Ford Motor Co. exclusive.

And now for a couple of '57 innovations that didn't come off so well. The odd flip-open ashtray is a menace: its door didn't fit on the test car, and stabbing at a dark hole seems an unnecessarily complex way to remove the ash from your cigarette. We

FORD ROAD TEST

nominate this feature for revision in '58, as we do the position of the front inside door locks. These are now pushbuttons, presumably to get on the bandwagon, but they interfere with the operation of the new narrow windwings. (These are hard enough to manage anyway.) When one realizes that the new buttons don't affect the interior door handles at all but only block the exterior opening mechanism, the mixup seems utterly pointless.

The new Thunderbird-type hood is something we could also do without. We cheer the return to the safer interior latch, and we'll go for the greater protection if the hood should blow open. Still, hoods have to be latched, and if you can handle this one with ease you're better than we are.

Will It Wear Well?

Ford's reputation for durability in rough service is an enviable one, and seems to bear little connection with the obviously hasty assembly of many Fords. The test car was startlingly bad in this respect. Nothing seemed to fit. Great gobs of lead were hanging on the rakish left rear fin. The driver's window tended to jam. Three fuses (high beam indicator, cigarette lighter, radio) blew during our test. The left rear door wouldn't shut unless the window was rolled down. The trunk, like the hood, was nearly impossible to latch.

We're deliberately making all these detrimental observations for a reason. They are points for the prospective buyer to watch out for, not in evaluating all Fords, but in microscopically examining the one Ford that is to be his. We've seen Fords badly assembled that seemed to wear forever, and other Fords put together beautifully. Naturally, if you buy a '57 car, you'll want it to be as perfect as possible, so take your time when you take delivery.

FORD ROAD TEST

VISIBILITY out the sides of new car is limited by low roof line. A tall person has only limited knee room.

WRAP-AROUND will block entrance for the less nimble. Dished wheel and padded visors, plus excellent safety belts, continue.

TRUNK LATCH hangs menacingly over tester's head as he checks extra-large trunk in Fairlane. Spare comes out with ease.

P E R F O R M A N C E

'57

(245-bhp engine)

ACCELERATION
From Standing Start
0-45 mph 6.9   0-60 mph 11.1
Quarter-mile 18.2 and 77 mph

Passing Speeds
30-50 mph 4.3   45-60 mph 4.3
50-80 mph 12.4

FUEL CONSUMPTION
Used Mobilgas Special
Steady Speeds
20.6 mpg @ 30   17.0 mpg @ 45
14.15 mpg @ 60   13.6 mpg @ 75

Stop-and-Go Highway Driving
15.6 mpg tank average for 569 miles

OIL CONSUMPTION
Two quarts added in 575 miles

STOPPING DISTANCE
160 feet from 60 mph

BRAKE FADE
(Series of slow-downs at rate of 15 feet per second per second from 60 mph, slowing to 20 mph, accelerating at full throttle back to 60, repeating 12 times) Burning odor began on third stop. Some fade on seventh stop. Pedal very hard on eighth stop. Deceleration rate 10 feet per second per second below 30 mph on 10th stop. Deceleration rate five feet per second per second below 30 mph on 12th stop. No swerving during test.

SPEEDOMETER ERROR
Read 32 at true 30, 49 at 45, 54 at 50, 65 at 60, 79 at 75, 85 at 80

'56

(202-bhp engine)

ACCELERATION
From Standing Start
0-30 mph 4.0   0-60 mph 11.6
Quarter-mile 18.6 and 75 mph

Passing Speeds
30-50 mph 5.3   50-80 mph 13.3

FUEL CONSUMPTION
Used Mobilgas Special
Steady Speeds
21.4 mpg @ 30   18.8 mpg @ 45
16.1 mpg @ 60   13.5 mpg @ 75

Stop-and-Go Driving
13.5 mpg tank average for 536 miles

STOPPING DISTANCE
174 feet from 60 mph

SPEEDOMETER ERROR
Read 32 at true 30, 50 at 45, 64 at 60, and 80 at 75

By DELL ROBERTS

GARAGEMEN and dealers have had ample time now, with the model year almost at an end, to find any "bugs" in the '57 Ford and learn how to deal with them.

It pays for the owner to know the trouble spots, however minor, in any car. No secret success formula, no special technical knowhow are needed to guarantee you a happy time with your 1957 Ford. It's just a matter of knowing:

(1) Exactly how your car differs from previous models;

(2) How to maintain it properly;

(3) Whether or not your repairman is giving you good service.

A thorough understanding of the car's special features can save you lots of money and trouble by enabling you to do your own repairs intelligently and to guide your garageman in the work he does for you. The following rundown on the anatomy of your '57 Ford will help you make the most of your car.

FUEL SYSTEM, RELATED EQUIPMENT

Carburetor — Your Ford may be equipped with a Holley, Ford or Carter carburetor, depending on the model. The Ford and Holley may appear on any engine in the line. The six-cylinder is now being equipped with the Holley only. The Carter—a four-barrel type—comes only on the eight.

The Holley single-barrel job has a manual choke; all others, an automatic choke. The Ford dual barrel has two main assemblies — air horn and main body. The Holley dual-barrel has four — main body, throttle body, fuel bowl assembly and metering body. The three four-barrel carburetors also differ. Check you car to see which kind you have.

Service procedures, which differ with each carburetor, are beyond the skill of the average car owner — especially in the case of dual- and four-barrel models. But make sure that your mechanic doesn't overlook all these differences.

Air cleaner — All engines are now equipped with a dry-type air cleaner, which has a replaceable cellulose-fiber filtering element. This element should be cleaned every 5000 miles, replaced every 20,000.

To clean the element, just tap it gently against a hard surface. Do not immerse the element in cleaning solvent, and do not blow it out with

compressed air. This will ruin the cellulose fiber.

Before you replace the filter element, clean the body and cover of the air cleaner. Here, cleaning solvent can be used.

Oil filter — This is a new item, a self-contained throwaway element that should be replaced every 4000 miles.

To service, the car must be put on a lift so that the filter may be removed. Place a drip pan under the filter. Unscrew it from the cylinder block. Check to see whether the filter adapter plate is properly positioned. (The word "top" should be opposite and parallel to the outer edge of the car.) Clean out the filter recess.

The gasket on the filter should be coated with oil. Then place the filter

SERVICING OUT THE "BUGS" IN YOUR '57 FORD	
TIP ON THE CARBURETOR	Servicemen find that the Carter four-barrel carburetor needs periodic adjustment, especially for owners who do a great deal of stop-and-start city driving and are interested in gasoline economy. This adjustment should never be made by a mechanic not well versed in the Carter carb.
TIP ON BRAKES	The parking brake sometimes works rather hard, occasionally sticking in top position. After dropping some penetrating oil at the juncture of the exterior brake housing, mechanic should brake and unbrake repeatedly.
TIP ON THE HEATER	Some owners have been annoyed by a whistling noise when the heater is on. Chances are, it's just dirt impeding the flow of air. Dirt should be blown out.
TIP ON SPARK PLUGS	Better gas mileage for around-the-town driving may be achieved, one serviceman tells us, with spark plugs colder than Ford specifications — that is, on V-8's equipped with the four-barrel carburetor. Car in question was equipped with a spark booster, too.
TIP ON OIL FILTER LEAD-IN PIPES	Does your Ford seem to be burning oil? Check the fittings on the pipes leading into and out of your oil filter for "bleeding." If the fitting is wet and sticky, it may have been loose. Retighten it, or replace the tubing if necessary. A too-tight gasket-to-adaptor plate may be the culprit.
TIP ON WHEEL NOISES	A few customers have been plagued by wheel noises. Servicemen recommend tire pressure checkup, then wheel balancing and a check under hubcaps for bits of dirt and tiny rocks. Next, check wheel alignment.
TIP ON INTERIOR NOISES	Rattles have been reported on custom front seats. Such noises can be easily corrected by tightening the retaining screws. . . . Also, the glove compartment seems to be so constructed that loose articles set up quite a racket when they roll around inside.
TIP ON THE EXTERIOR	Edging on the chrome came through rough on a few models. Servicemen can correct this easily. . . . Check rubber moldings around rear windows. If there is not a firm bond, correct promptly to avoid water leakage later on.

into position on the engine block. Tighten the new filter by hand until the gasket contacts the adapter face, then tighten it half a turn more. Don't tighten the filter too much.

Operate the engine at fast idle for a while and look for leaks. If there are leaks, check the whole unit and the pipes leading into it. Then test the oil level. Nine times out of ten, one of these areas is the source of the leak.

ELECTRICAL, IGNITION SYSTEMS

Distributor — There's a new distributor for eight-cylinder engines. On the six, the spark advance of the distributor is regulated entirely by vacuum differential at the carburetor, but the eight now has two interacting spark advance systems. A centrifugal advance mechanism is located beneath the movable breaker point, and a vacuum-operated spark control diaphragm is located on the side of the distributor base.

Idea of this setup is to get better performance at any given speed. This is what the vacuum provides for at low speed and part-throttle operation; at high speed and full-throttle operation, the centrifugal portion takes over.

The centrifugal weights make the distributor cam advance, opening and closing the breaker points earlier by means of a slotted plate which fits over pins in the weights. Rate of advance is controlled by calibrated springs; the slots determine maximum amount of advance.

Cleaning and adjusting the distributor is a job that requires real know-how, and it is better left to someone with the proper tools and test instruments.

There are several facts to remember about this distributor:

Breaker arm and bracket assembly should be replaced whenever the distributor is overhauled.

Engine oil should never be used in lubricating interior parts — especially the cam.

If the engine has been cranked while the distributor is out, the car must be completely retimed.

The distributor should always be installed so that the rotor points to the No. 1 spark plug wire terminal in the rotor cap.

Gauges—Fuel gauge and temperature-sending unit of the Ford have been furnished with a new rheostat, designed to eliminate wild fluctuations and to make readings much more accurate. The part of the gauge (remote register) you see on the dashboard operates in the usual way—gauge point controlled by bimetallic arm and heating coil.

Here's how the fuel gauge operates: When the tank is empty, the grounded sliding contact is at the high end of the resistance. Thus, very little current flows through the circuit.

As the tank is filled, the float—which is connected to the grounded sliding contact—rises, moving the contact up the wire and lessening the resistance. This allows more current to flow through the heating coil, forcing the bimetallic arm to deflect the pointer toward "full."

Temperature of the bimetallic arm changes slowly, thus minimizing effects of sudden changes in fuel level.

The temperature-sending gauge operates in the same way, except that it is mounted in the cylinder head and resistance is varied by engine temperature.

AXLES, WHEELS, SUSPENSION

Axles—The Ford rear axle is all new. It's constructed ruggedly, and it's easy to maintain. It can now be partially disassembled without removal of the entire unit.

Specifically, the new design is a "banjo-housing" hypoid — housing is shaped like a banjo—in which the drive pinion is mounted 2¼ in. (formerly 2½ in.) below the center line of the drive gear. The pinion shaft is straddle-mounted; that is, two opposed tapered roller bearings support the pinion shaft at the front of the pinion gear and a straight roller bearing supports it at the rear of the pinion gear. All this is assembled in a pinion retainer, bolted to the carrier housing.

Other characteristics to remember: Right and left axle shafts are not interchangeable. (Left is shorter.)

Two carrier and differential cases are used to accommodate the two bearing sizes.

Axle shafts and drive pinion seal can be replaced without removing the differential.

Before blaming the rear axle for noises, make sure they don't originate in areas where repairs are less expensive. What sounds like axle noise can often be traced to improperly inflated tires, or to the engine, the exhaust or the wheel bearings.

Check for tire noise by driving the car over various kinds of road surfaces. If you hear a hum over a blacktop surface, try switching the tires—after inflating them properly, of course. (Note: Ford recommends 24 psi in front and 21 psi in rear on all models, except Thunderbird and station wagons. T-bird tires should be 22, front and rear; station wagon tires, 24 front and 26 rear.)

Check for wheel bearing noise by jacking up each wheel and feeling for roughness as the wheel is rotated.

Sometimes, simply braking lightly while you are coasting the car slowly downhill can eliminate wheel bearing noise.

Still getting excessive noise in the vicinity of the rear axle? Well, before you start working on the axle itself there are additional possibilities to test — loose or broken fenders, body bolts, brackets, or undercoating on the driveshaft.

Suspension—Front suspension on the 1957 Ford has been beefed up considerably. Added strength has been gained by making the upper and lower control arms in one piece — on all models except the T-bird, which has an entirely different suspension arrangement.

The new front stabilizer bar is bolted to the lower control arm. Torsion-type rubber bushings at the inner ends of the suspension arms insulate the frame from road shock and vibration. There is now more rubber insulation between the frame and the coil springs; also, between the frame and the torsion-type stabilizer.

Better stability has been achieved for the front suspension by mounting front ends of springs outside the frame rail.

What appears to be front suspension trouble is often the result of incorrect tire pressure, so it's a good idea to check your tires frequently. Irregular tire wear, sag at one wheel, hard ride, wheel shimmy, side-to-side wander, body roll, pull to one side—all these can be caused by the tire pressure.

Before you check the suspension, also test for bad bearing adjustment, out-of-round wheel or brake drums, poor brake adjustment, lack of lubrication, misaligned frame or loose parts.

BRAKING SYSTEM

Ford brakes have been redesigned to provide extra strength. A fixed anchor pin that goes through the wheel spindle to the brake backing plate gives the front brake additional stiffness.

On the T-bird's front brake, the anchor pin fastens to the carrier plate.

On the rear brake assembly of all Ford models, the parking brake lever, link and spring are now attached to both primary and secondary brake shoes.

An adjusting screw compensates for brake wear. But if the linings are worn to within 1/32 in. of the rivets, it's time to reline or replace the brake shoes. When lining wear has reduced the brake pedal reserve to less than half the total travel to the floor, brakes should be adjusted.

If, when you apply the brake, you feel as though you were pushing down on a wet sponge, there's probably air in the brake lines. Have it bled out.

If the pedal retracts slowly after being pushed to the floor, chances are there's a leak in the hydraulic system.

What happens in the rare (fortunately!) emergency when you push the brake pedal down to the floor and the car doesn't stop? Well, if you—and the car—survive, you can be sure that you've either forgotten to fill the master cylinder reservoir or you've got a leak that has let all the fluid run out.

Disastrous locking like this can also be caused by dirty brake fluid, a clogged bypass port in the master cylinder, sticking brake cylinder pistons or swollen master cylinder cups.

Brakes can be released by bleeding off a few drops of brake fluid at a cylinder bleeder screw. But this will not attack the real cause of the trouble, which should be taken care of immediately.

Brake squeal, grabbing and pulling also indicate a trip to the serviceman. The trouble may simply be dirt in the rivet holes or drum — which can be scraped off and blown away. Oil or grease on the linings, or lining glaze, can usually be removed by sandpaper.

After any one of these operations, adjust the brakes.

HEATER SYSTEM

Ford's new fresh-air heater system finally switches to cowl intake for its air. (A recirculating-type heater is also available.)

On the fresh-air system, the blower connects to an outlet in the right side of the fresh-air intake chamber. Two types of temperature control units are used. Here's how they operate:

The tube control unit uses a capillary tube valve, which automatically regulates the flow of water through the heater. Action of the tube control is regulated by the temperature control lever (the top lever) in the heater.

Naturally, the temperature control lever also operates the bimetallic control unit. This, in turn, controls a bimetallic thermostat valve, which regulates a vacuum-operated water valve attached to the heater core.

These two valves automatically regulate the flow of water from the cylinder block to the heater. When no heat is needed, the temperature control level is simply pushed all the way to the left. This closes the valves and prevents water circulation in the heater core.

If you're not getting enough heat, check first for air leaks under the dashboard area. Then, let an expert have a crack at the problem.

It should be noted, in conclusion, that the durability of your 1957 Ford —like that of any other product—depends on how you maintain it. ●

FORD ROAD TEST

(*Continued from page* 37)

SPECIFICATIONS

POWER UNIT:
   Type: inline 6
   Maximum brake horsepower: 115 @ 3900 rpm
   Maximum torque: 193 lbs.-ft. @ 2200 rpm
   Piston displacement: 223 cu. ins.
   Bore and stroke: 3.62x3.60 ins.
   Compression ratio: 7.2 to one
   Valve arrangement: overhead
   Carburetion by: single Holley downdraft
   Oil Filter: full flow

DRIVE TRAIN:
   Automatic transmission: Fordomatic: torque converter
   Ratios: Drive: 1.48 & 1; Low: 2.44; Rev: 2.0

CHASSIS:
   Suspension, front: Coil spring independent
      rear: semi-elliptic leaf
   Shock absorbers: Monroe, 1.0-in. piston dia.
   Steering type: Master-Guide (Bendix) power
   Steering wheel turns: 4.5 from lock to lock
   Steering turning diameter: 41 ft.
   Brake type: Power hydraulic
   Brake drum diameter: 10 ins.
   Brake lining area: 173 sq. ins.
   Tires: 6.70x15
   Wheelbase: 115.5 ins.
   Tread: front 58 ins.; rear 56 ins.

GENERAL:
   Overall length: 198.3 ins.
   Overall width: 74.2 ins.
   Overall height: 62.3 ins.
   Weight: 3260 lbs.

RATING FACTORS

Bhp per cu. in.: .52
Pounds per bhp: 28
Pounds per sq. in. piston area: .87
Piston speed in ft. per min. @ max. bhp: 2373

MAINTENANCE DATA

ELECTRICAL:
   Ignition timing: 3° BTC
   Spark plug gap: .033-.037 in.
   Breaker point gap: .024-.026 in.
   Battery: Ford

VALVES:
   Timing—Intake opens: 13° BTC
      Intake closes: 68° ABC
      Exhaust opens: 55° BBC
      Exhaust closes: 22° ATC
   Operating clearances: Intake .015 in.,
      exhaust .019 in.

WHEELS:
   Tire pressures: front 26 psi, rear 23 psi

RADIATOR:
   Capacity—without heater: 15 qts.
      with heater: 16 qts.

FORD TEST

CONTINUED FROM PAGE 33

gineers later provided me with test data to substantiate my impression. Experiments with instruments have shown there is less than one degree rise of measured temperature in the plastic job. The quarter-inch thick transparent top is tinted to turn back the heat rays.

Another novel treatment appeared on the dash of the '54 Ford. The speedometer, mounted high and in direct line of driver vision, is also of transparent plastic. Rest of the instruments are recessed into a burnished metal panel and are easily accessible for anyone behind the wheel. I noted also that interior dimensions of the glove compartment have been nearly doubled, while the former amperage and oil needles have been replaced by red warning lights.

Exterior changes have been directed at giving the '54 Ford fresh styling and a wider look. Finish on the models I inspected was not important since they were not production units. However, the wide range of optional equipment listed as available for '54 did cause me to reach one conclusion.

Ford is going to make it very difficult for the normal big car buyer to convince himself that he cannot get most of what he wants in a Ford for '54.

'55 Ford V8 Road Test

(*Continued from page* 48) Yet, we know from experience that the residue from a two-year-old's muddy feet can be brushed off quite readily.

Mention of two-year-olds reminds us of the distaff side and their problems. During the course of the test, we lent the car to the gals for a shopping expedition and went along with a camera. Parking, for once, was not a problem, as you can see by our eye level picture from the driver's seat. The wrap-around windshield afford-ed us excellent forward visibility.

There are some small items which we could quibble about, such as the high trunk ledge (necessitated by the gasoline filler located therein) and the lethal-looking (to good leather luggage) hinges on the lid, but this wouldn't be fair, as all cars seem to have their fair share of design quirks. Overall, the Ford Customline sedan was designed and built to satisfy the day-to-day needs of your family, and we wouldn't be at all surprised if it turned out to be your choice with just that purpose in mind.   —*Don MacDonald*

ENGINE: OHV V8. Bore 3⅝ in. Stroke 3³/₁₀ in. Stroke/bore ratio 0.909:1. Compression ratio 7.6 to 1. Displacement 272 cu. in. Advertised bhp 162 @ 4400 rpm. Bhp per cu. in. 0.596. Piston travel @ max. bhp 2420 ft. per min. Max. bmep 143.0 psi. Max. torque 258 ft. lb. @ 2200 rpm.
DRIVE SYSTEM: STANDARD transmission is three-speed synchromesh using helical gears. RATIOS: 1st 2.57, 2nd 1.63, 3rd 1.00, reverse 3.13. AUTOMATIC transmission is Fordomatic, three-element torque converter with planetary gears. RATIOS: Drive, 1.47 x converter ratio and torque converter only (2.40, 1.47 and converter only, at full throttle through downshift detent); Low, 2.40 x converter ratio; Reverse, 2.00 x converter ratio. Maximum converter ratio at stall 2.1. OVERDRIVE transmission is standard shift with planetary gears. RATIO: 0.7.
REAR AXLE RATIOS: Standard 3.78, 3.89 optional; Fordomatic 3.31, 3.55 optional; Overdrive, 3.89, 3.55 optional.
DIMENSIONS: Wheelbase 115½ in. Tread 58 front, 56 rear. Wheelbase/tread ratio 2.03:1. Overall width 75⅞ in. Overall length 198½ in. Overall height (empty) 61 in. Turning diameter 41.1 ft. Turns lock to lock 4½. Test car weight 3525 lbs. Test car weight/bhp ratio 21.8:1. Weight distribution 57% front, 43% rear. Tire size 6.70 x 15, tubeless.
PRICES: (Including suggested retail price at main factory, federal tax, and delivery and handling charges, but not freight) MAINLINE, business sedan $1706, two-door sedan $1807, four-door sedan $1853. CUSTOMLINE, two-door sedan $1901, four-door sedan $1945. FAIRLANE, two-door sedan $2014, four-door sedan $2060, hardtops $2195, $2302, and $2372 (plastic top), convertible $2304. STATION WAGONS, $2143, $2209, $2256, $2387, $2492. (Six-cylinder models approximately $100 less; add $38 to above Fairlane and station wagon prices for 182-horsepower V8 engine.)
ACCESSORIES: Radio $99, heater $71, power brakes $32, power seat $64, power windows, $102, overdrive $110, Fordomatic $178, white sidewall tires (exchange) $27.
PARTS AND LABOR COSTS and **ESTIMATED COST PER MILE** for the '55 Ford will appear in an early issue.

Jimmy Reece TESTS the '57 FORD

No one knows as much about Detroit's production cars as the nation's top stock car race drivers. Day after day, on all kinds of road surfaces and under all conditions, these men put stock cars through grueling trials and tests in competition with one another.

In view of these facts, SPEED AGE has arranged for a series of tests of all Detroit cars by some of the nation's leading race drivers. We feel it will assure our readers of the inside story on performance and handling as interpreted by the men best qualified to judge.

This month Jimmy Reece brings you his EXPERT TEST of the 1957 Ford.

Next month Johnnie Tolan will report on his tests of the 1957 Chevrolet and the fuel-injection Corvette.

SPECIFICATIONS:
1957 FORD
CUSTOMLINE 300

ENGINE:

MODEL	T-BIRD SPECIAL
CYLINDERS	Y-8
VALVES	OHV
DISPLACEMENT	312 CU. IN.
BORE	3.8 IN.
STROKE	3.4 IN.
COMPRESSION RATIO	8.6:1
MAX. H.P.	245 @ 4600 RPM
MAX. TORQUE	332 @ 2600 RPM
CARBURETION	DUAL QUAD

DIMENSIONS:

WHEELBASE	116 INCHES
TREAD-FRONT	59 INCHES
REAR	56.4 INCHES
LENGTH (OVER-ALL)	201.7 INCIES
WIDTH (OVER-ALL)	77 INCHES

GEARING:

REAR AXLE	3.10:1
TRANSMISSION (FORDOMATIC)	2.40:1 LOW
	1.47:1 INTER.
	1.00:1 DRIVE
	2.00:1 REVERSE

PERFORMANCE:

TOP SPEED	115.85 TWO WAY AVERAGE
	116.75 BEST ONE WAY
STANDING QUARTER	17.9 SECONDS
0-30	3.9 SECONDS
0-40	5.1 SECONDS
0-60	9.4 SECONDS

By JIMMY REECE

FORD definitely has it for '57. And by it, I mean a new, low-slung bombshell that might well become the new leader in sales over all other 1957 cars. The new Ford is loaded for bear against all comers. All new from the ground up, it's one of the best looking cars for '57.

Recently, a '57 Ford broke all existing American stock car records for Class B closed cars at Bonneville, Utah, under sanction of the United States Auto Club and the FIA. In twenty days, the car traveled 50,000 miles at a hot average speed of 108.16 mph, including all pit stops. That's impressive! It points up the all-out efforts to make '57 the hottest year ever for Ford.

In a gruelling test for SPEED AGE, I put a 1957 Ford Customline 300 through more than 1,200 miles of brutal test driving that covered everything from harsh cornering and panic stops to rapid acceleration runs over a drag strip, and I was just as impressed with the results as the Ford factory must be with the Bonneville records.

Ford this year, has put together a car with many changes designed to improve handling, performance and comfort that will count with new car enthusiasts looking for these qualities. In addition, the '57 Ford has been designed for the kind of performance that counts in stock car racing which, of course, really interests me as a professional race driver.

Our Custom 300 test car was equipped with the 245 hp V-8 and Fordomatic,

Jimmy demonstrates the lowness
of the new 1957 Ford. It fits under
his arm and he's no giant.

and it proved to be a virtual bomb at any speed. Still stiff with newness when we picked it up at San Marino Motors in San Marino, Calif., we broke it in on a trip up the California coast from Los Angeles to Sacramento. To insure that the car was at its peak, we had it tuned by Les Richey, service man for San Marino Motors who tunes most of the Fords used in competition at drag strips in the Los Angeles area.

Before beginning our runs we had the speedometer calibrated by the Automobile Club of Southern California. It showed an error of 14 per cent at 60 mph. Later, in acceleration tests, our speeds were checked according to the auto club's calibration so that our findings were as accurate as possible.

On the trip to Sacramento, we made a constant check on economy, although the engine was still tight. On the open highway, at an average speed of 60 to 70 mph, we averaged 15 mpg, which wasn't bad at all for a brand new automobile. In city traffic, the mileage fell off to approximately 13 mpg.

We saved the acceleration runs until last, so that the engine would be fully broken in, and started up the Coast to make handling and riding tests. They told quite a story.

Getting away in traffic was a cinch. The speedometer really walked up the numbers and there didn't seem to be any end to the rapid acceleration. It had punch, and plenty of it, at all speeds. It was really surprising to stand on it at 75 or 80 mph, and still feel the mill pull like a demon. But more about this when we get to the acceleration runs.

As for handling, the car was definitely outstanding. I barrelled into corners at considerable speed and never heard a squeal from the tires. Only under really rugged cornering conditions was there any noticeable body lean. Most of the improved handling may be attributed to the new lower front suspension, contoured frame and outrigger springs.

The car itself rode like a much heavier machine. Improved shocks were responsible for that. In all of our severe cornering tests, we failed to experience any rock and roll movement, and the car never felt unstable at all. I'm all for heavier shocks, and have them on my own car, but for normal driving, I think Ford has shocked

Hood on the Ford hinges forward providing better access to engine. Jimmy had trouble with latch.

Comfortable seating and good visibility are one of the new Ford's best features.

Lock button on door has been moved forward out of the reach of children. No-draft has larger catch.

Trunk lock is neatly hidden behind Ford crest. Sliding arrangement covers lock when not in use.

Rear of the new Ford offers clean, attractive lines. Gas filler is concealed under license plate. Note very little squat under acceleration and practically no wheel spin.

their '57 models perfectly.

Another impressive feature was the quietness of the ride. After switching over to an entirely new car, one of the first from the assembly line, you would expect a few body rattles at least. But our test car had none. The ride was quiet and comfortable, even over rough roads and railroad crossings. There was, however, a slight shaking of the front fenders, but this was due to the action of the front shocks.

Steering was just right for highway driving. Not too fast or too slow, you could handle the corners without effort, and that wonderful location of the steering wheel keeps you in a natural driving position. The front end dipped slightly on panic stops, but I was able to bring the car to a controlled stop from 70 mph without a lot of skidding and sliding.

For acceleration, we took the car to the Lion's Club drag strip located at Long Beach, Calif. We took the machine through speed runs up to 60 mph, using the calibrated speeds on the speedometer, and we checked it through the measured quarter-mile course. The results were impressive.

Speedometer Error Calibration Curve

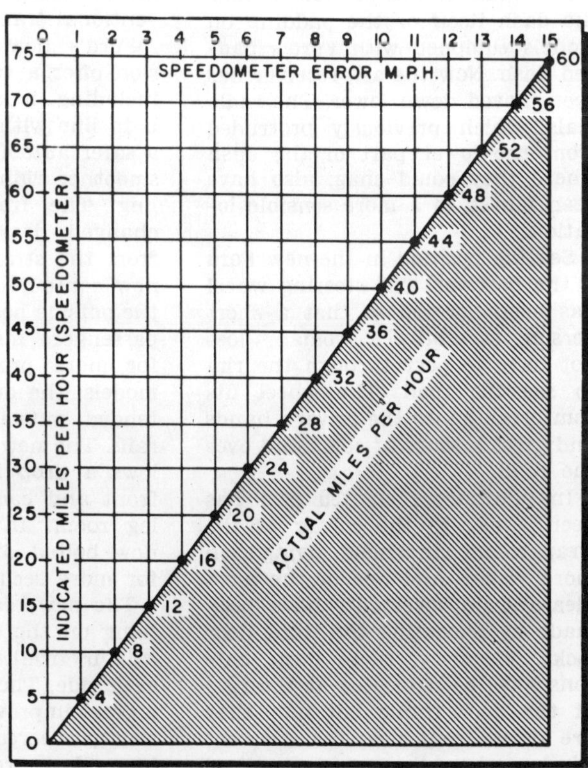

Discrepancies between actual speeds and those indicated on the speedometer are shown in this chart. Error increases as speeds get higher. Average was about 25 per cent.

Biggest trunk in Ford history permits Jimmy Reece (right) and friend plenty of squatting room.

Our Custom 300 ripped off the quarter-mile in a hot 17.9 seconds, using a start both from drive and from low range. It hit 0-30 in a rapid 3.9 seconds; 0-40 in 5.1 seconds; 0-50 in 7 seconds flat; and 0-60 in 9.4 seconds. In all cases, our take off was made without rear wheel slippage, made possible by the new off-set rear axle.

The '57 Ford's interior is good looking although a bit meager on seat padding which is very thin. A well grouped instrument panel shows careful planning, and the accessory switches, lights, vents, cigaret lighter and windshield wiper switch, are lighted at night which makes them easy to find.

Two faults, which we found in our test of the 1956 models have been eliminated this year, and they include relocation of the ash tray and radio dials. On the '56 Fords, the ash tray was located just under the lip of the dash board. Butting a burning cigaret was a problem because it was possible to mar the dash itself or the padding on models equipped with Ford's padded dash. Now the ash receiver has been moved down lower. The radio dials, which previously protruded from the lower part of the dash where they could snag, also have been moved to a more sensible location.

Seating position in the new Ford is the best yet. The steering wheel has been lowered so that a short person, especially a woman, does not have to peer through the rim to see the road. The wheel fits comfortably into the driver's hands and gives a sense of command over the road.

In addition, a slanted post has been added to the corner of the wraparound windshield, giving even more vision. And one of the most pleasant improvements have been made by relocating the front door locks. Formerly, these push buttons have been located at the rear of the door frame but now they are at the front, near the side vent window where they can be reached easily.

The hood latch also has been changed this year, and the hood itself opens like a sports car, from the rear instead of the front. The locking latch has been placed inside the car, as in models of a few years ago. The new system of opening the hood allows much more room for work on the engine, and

there is a safety latch on the side that prevents it from flying open, but the hood is difficult to close. We found that it was necessary to place both hands on the center of the hood, and then slam it down. Otherwise, the lock wouldn't catch properly. Service station operators, still unused to the new system, had difficulty getting the hood closed on our test car.

On the other hand, the trunk lid opened and closed with little effort, and I was greatly impressed by the lock hidden behind the sliding Ford emblem. It was both clever and attractive. The trunk itself afforded enough room for more than an average load of luggage.

Now for the part that seems to interest so many people the most. . . . Ford's new powerplant. Again, there are a variety of engines to choose from and, this year, any engine is available in any model, according to the buyer's desire. Engines include the 144 hp Mileage Maker Six; the 190 hp 272 cubic inch V-8; the 245 hp Thunderbird 312 Special V-8; the 212 hp Thunderbird 292 V-8. With any engine, Fordomatic, Overdrive or Conventional transmission is available.

Ford's new frame and suspension offer a variety of advantages, including more protection, which is in line with Ford's trend toward a safer automobile, more leg room, smoother riding and better handling. The frame itself has been changed drastically, but sensibly from the straight rail design to a new contoured frame that follows the outside body lines and puts the passengers inside the frame rails for more protection. In previous models, the outside body lines extended outward from the frame rails. The new contoured design allows a drop in the floor in both front and back, which gives more leg room. In addition, seats are now bolted directly to the frame for more security.

The new rear springs have been hung on the outside of the frame rails in front for a smoother, more even ride. The front end, featuring a great improved ball-joint suspension pioneered by Ford, has been lowered a great deal with swept back shock arms that iron out bumps better than ever.

Other improvements include an off-set hypoid rear axle, shorter on the left side for a smoother, more even take-off that minimizes wheel spin when full power is applied. Coupled with this is a straddle-mounted pinion in the rear end assembly, similar but greatly im-

proved to that used by Ford several years ago. It offers a quieter, longer life to the rear end assembly.

Improvements have been made on Ford's brakes this year, although there is a noticeable amount of fade under severe usage. In our tests for panic stops the car halted easily and quickly, but I did encounter some brake fade. At that, however, there was quick recovery.

A wide variety of models have been made available this year for the consumer to choose from, including the Fairlane series, Custom series, Custom 300 series and a variety of station wagons that include the Del Rio, Country Squire, Country Sedan and Ranch Wagon. They vary in style and price, but all compare basically with a long list of innovations that have made the '57 Ford an all new automobile.

Probably the first noticeable change in this year's Ford is the appearance of the car itself. It is bigger, longer and lower than previous models, so low in fact that a man of average height can peer over the roof without difficulty. It sports fourteen inch wheels, which helps give the car an overall lower look, and the body style has been changed completely from front to rear, giving it a sleek, fast appearance. Even the hood ornament has been changed to a "bulls eye" effect that acts as a guide to safe driving.

The front fenders are graceful and prominent, and easily visible from the driver's seat which helps, especially for women drivers who have difficulty viewing the right front fender in other models. Flared rear fins add to that racey look, and also are visible from the driver's seat, making for easier parking in tight squeezes.

Not too much chrome, cleverly placed, make the entire automobile most appealing. The wheelbase this year varies somewhat, according to models. For instance, the Custom series and station wagons have a 116-inch wheel base while the Fairlanes have been extended to 118. Overall width varies from 201.7 inches in the Custom series to 207.7 in the Fairlanes.

To sum it all up, I would say that the '57 Ford is undoubtedly the best car Ford has ever marketed and probably one of the best handling and best performing machines available today. It can go from road use to track use with hardly any pain at all and for everyday road driving Ford is, in my opinion, number one!

FORD

| | 1949-1953 | | | | 1954-1957 | | | |
| | V-8 | | 6 | | V-8 | | 6 | |
	LABOR	PARTS	LABOR	PARTS	LABOR	PARTS	LABOR	PARTS
ENGINE								
GENERAL TUNEUP	$13.50	EXTRA	$10.50	EXTRA	$26.00	EXTRA	$22.00	EXTRA
REMOVE & REPLACE REBUILT ENGINE	40.00	162.00	35.50	149.00	40.00	208.00	35.50	149.00
REPLACE RINGS	52.00	24.30	43.00	16.25	66.50	25.40	47.50	16.75
REPLACE BEARINGS (RODS & MAINS)	21.00	12.15	16.00	11.25	18.50	11.20	16.00	10.35
REPLACE CAMSHAFT	25.00	18.25	25.00	19.85	26.00	16.00	21.50	18.00
REPLACE LIFTERS	SOLID	SOLID	SOLID	SOLID	SOLID	SOLID	SOLID	SOLID
REPLACE CRANKSHAFT	52.00	78.50	51.00	75.80	46.00	70.00	41.00	80.00
VALVE OVERHAUL	42.00	EXTRA	30.00	EXTRA	47.50	EXTRA	29.00	EXTRA
VALVE ADJUSTMENT	NONE	NONE	3.00	.85	5.00	1.80	2.50	.65
REPLACE CYLINDER HEAD (ONE)	10.15	16.25	20.00	19.25	43.50	45.00	27.00	40.00
REPLACE PISTON (ONE)	35.00	5.15	30.00	5.85	36.00	5.85	31.00	5.85
OIL PUMP								
REMOVE & CLEAN OIL PAN	8.50	EXTRA	8.50	EXTRA	8.50	EXTRA	11.50	EXTRA
REPLACE OIL PUMP	8.50	12.25	10.50	12.75	8.50	13.75	10.50	13.75
REPLACE FILTER CARTRIDGE	1.00	2.10	2.00	2.15	2.00	2.15	2.00	2.15
CARBURETOR								
ADJUST CARBURETOR IDLE	1.00	NONE	1.00	NONE	1.50	NONE	1.00	NONE
OVERHAUL CARBURETOR	8.00	EXTRA	7.50	EXTRA	12.50	EXTRA	8.50	EXTRA
INSTALL REBUILT CARBURETOR	3.00	12.50	3.00	11.00	3.50	18.75	3.50	9.85
CLEAN & ADJUST AUTOMATIC CHOKE	1.50	NONE	1.50	NONE	2.50	NONE	2.50	NONE
CLEAN AIR FILTER (OIL BATH)	1.50	EXTRA	1.50	EXTRA	2.00	EXTRA	2.00	EXTRA
FUEL SYSTEM								
REPLACE FUEL & VACUUM PUMP	2.50	15.00	2.50	15.00	2.50	15.00	2.50	15.00
REPLACE GAS TANK	5.25	21.50	5.25	21.50	5.00	25.00	5.00	25.00
REPLACE GAS GAUGE (TANK UNIT)	2.00	3.85	2.00	3.85	2.00	3.75	2.00	3.75
REPLACE FLEXIBLE GAS LINE	1.00	2.85	1.00	2.85	1.00	1.25	1.00	1.25
EXHAUST SYSTEM								
REPLACE EXHAUST PIPES (LEAD & CROSSOVER)	10.00	8.00	5.00	6.00	12.50	8.00	4.00	8.00
REPLACE MUFFLER (ONE)	4.00	9.85	4.00	10.25	4.00	10.00	4.00	10.00
REPLACE TAILPIPE (ONE)	3.50	3.50	3.50	3.75	3.50	3.50	3.50	3.75
IGNITION								
SET TIMING	1.25	NONE	1.25	NONE	1.50	NONE	1.50	NONE
REPLACE POINTS & CONDENSER	3.50	3.00	3.00	3.00	4.50	3.25	4.50	3.25
CLEAN & ADJUST POINTS (INCL. SET TIMING)	2.50	NONE	2.50	NONE	3.50	NONE	3.50	NONE
CLEAN & ADJUST SPARK PLUGS	2.50	NONE	2.50	NONE	4.00	NONE	2.50	NONE
REPLACE COIL	1.50	5.75	1.50	5.75	1.50	5.50	1.50	5.50
OVERHAUL STARTER	8.50	EXTRA	8.25	EXTRA	7.50	EXTRA	7.25	EXTRA
REPLACE STARTER	2.50	23.80	2.50	23.80	2.75	25.00	2.50	25.00
GENERATOR & BATTERY								
CLEAN & ADJUST REGULATOR	2.75	NONE	2.75	NONE	2.75	NONE	2.75	NONE
REPLACE REGULATOR	1.75	9.00	1.75	9.00	1.75	9.00	1.75	9.00
OVERHAUL GENERATOR	8.00	EXTRA	7.50	EXTRA	7.50	EXTRA	7.50	EXTRA
REPLACE GENERATOR	4.00	27.00	3.00	27.50	3.00	28.00	3.00	28.00
COOLING SYSTEM								
REVERSE FLUSH RADIATOR & BLOCK	7.00	NONE	7.50	NONE	6.75	NONE	6.75	NONE
REPLACE RADIATOR	6.50	68.00	6.00	68.00	5.00	75.00	5.00	62.00
REPLACE WATER PUMP	6.00	9.25	7.50	13.50	6.50	12.75	4.75	12.75
REPLACE FAN BELT	2.00	2.25	1.50	2.00	1.50	2.25	1.50	2.00
REPLACE THERMOSTAT	1.50	2.50	2.00	2.50	2.00	2.50	2.00	2.50
REPLACE ALL HOSES (INCL. HEATER)	5.00	6.50	3.50	5.00	5.00	5.25	3.50	5.25
CLUTCH & TRANSMISSION								
ADJUST CLUTCH	1.50	NONE	1.50	NONE	1.50	NONE	1.50	NONE
REPLACE CLUTCH (COVER, DISC, & T.O. BEARING)	15.00	28.00	15.00	28.00	15.00	28.00	13.00	28.00
REPLACE TRANSMISSION (MANUAL)	12.50	123.80	12.50	132.00	10.00	123.00	10.00	123.00
OVERHAUL TRANSMISSION (AUTOMATIC)	58.00	EXTRA	58.00	EXTRA	50.00	EXTRA	50.00	EXTRA
ADJUST & SERVICE TRANSMISSION (AUTO.)	13.50	EXTRA	13.00	EXTRA	13.00	EXTRA	13.50	EXTRA
BRAKE SYSTEM								
ADJUST BRAKES	2.50	NONE	2.50	NONE	3.00	NONE	3.00	NONE
RELINE BRAKES (INSTALL EXCHANGE SHOES)	12.00	13.75	12.00	13.75	12.00	13.75	12.00	13.75
REPLACE MASTER CYLINDER	6.00	9.75	6.00	9.75	4.00	8.50	4.00	8.50
REPLACE WHEEL CYLINDER (ONE FRONT)	3.50	3.75	3.50	3.75	4.00	4.50	4.00	4.50
FLUSH & REFILL HYDRAULIC SYSTEM	5.00	1.00	5.00	1.00	5.00	1.00	5.00	1.00
CHASSIS								
REPLACE FRONT SPRING (ONE)	7.00	7.80	7.00	7.80	4.00	6.50	4.00	6.50
REPLACE REAR SPRING (ONE)	8.00	17.20	8.00	17.20	6.00	16.00	6.00	16.00
REPLACE FRONT SHOCK (ONE)	2.00	6.25	2.00	6.25	2.50	6.00	2.50	6.00
REPLACE REAR SHOCK (ONE)	1.80	6.25	1.80	6.25	3.00	6.00	3.00	6.00
OVERHAUL FRONT END COMPLETE	42.00	EXTRA	42.00	EXTRA	50.00	EXTRA	50.00	EXTRA
TIGHTEN CHASSIS	5.00	NONE	5.00	NONE	5.00	NONE	5.00	NONE
COMPLETE LUBRICATION & OIL CHANGE	2.50	EXTRA	2.50	EXTRA	2.50	EXTRA	2.50	EXTRA

ACCELERATION TESTS OF THE FORD STATION WAGON SHOWED IT TO BE QUICKER THAN THE SEDAN WITH SAME ENGINE.

Ford Wagon
ROAD TEST

IT HAS BEEN SUGGESTED that the best way to really test a car is to live with it for a couple of months, put at least 5000 miles on it under varying conditions and over all types of roads after taking delivery, and report on its every trait and characteristic, including its shortcomings, if any. Such is this report on a 1957 Ford Country Sedan, owned by one of the members of the road test crew for MOTOR LIFE magazine.

The six-passenger, four-door station wagon was purchased under normal conditions from an authorized Ford dealer. so its history might be compared to that of any new car which is serviced and prepared by factory-instructed mechanics of almost any dealership.

At the outset, inspection of the car on delivery day showed it to be excellent. Like most new car owners, the buyer operated everything that was operable, and looked at every part of the car to uncover any flaws or deficiencies in the manufacturing or preparation of the car for service. He checked the paint which was excellent throughout, free from any spots or scratches, orange peel, etc. He opened and closed the doors and checked their alignment with the body panels; these including the new tailgate with its two hinged support arms at the sides worked entirely satisfactory. The wrap-around liftgate with its wrap-around rear window glass automatically raises one-third open when the tailgate latch is released since new C-type hinges are used, concealing assist springs; this worked fine. It was noticed that knurled knobs lock the gate in any desired open position, an improvement over previous models.

With the tailgate down, the new owner inspected the spare tire compartment under the hinged floor. Jack and tools were securely fastened. He made a mental note that if this compartment were only slightly larger, it would have been an excellent storage area to keep valuable luggage out of sight of potential thieves. This, incidentally, has been one of the standing criticisms of station wagons by many would-be buyers—wagons do not have any lockable, out-of-sight compartments for the salesman or traveler who habitually carries small, valuable items. Some manufacturers other than Ford have already taken the lead in providing under-floor storage wells which can be locked.

Getting in behind the wheel, it was noted that the seating position seemed lower than in previous models though vision both forward and rearward was better, head and shoulder room about the same. The woven-plastic seatback inserts combined with the vinyl bolsters on well-padded cushions are neatly designed, practical for most station wagon users. The matching vinyls on the doors and panels and interior trim create an attractive. tastefully harmonizing effect. He checked out the controls: Lights, windshield wiper, left and right air vents. and the heating, ventilating, and defrosting controls operated easily and are positioned within easy reach of the driver. The power-operated windows worked perfectly, although he detected a very slight squeak in the left rear window, later corrected at the 1000-mile service. The transistor-powered, signal-seeking radio has a Town button for tuning in local stations and a Country button for picking up more stations. With its speaker mounted on top of the padded dash, this radio has excellent tone qualities. The glove compartment on the far right, although a long reach for the driver, is adequate in its storage capacity. The ashtray, however, he soon discovered, placed in the center of the dash panel, is difficult to "hit" by either driver or passenger, especially at night since it is unlighted. Perhaps a pull-out ashtray for each located closer to the user would be more convenient, safer.

Driving the wagon was a pleasant surprise; because of its bulk the buyer anticipated the feeling of trying to maneuver a truck through traffic. Such is not the case at all. Although the car definitely has a "big car" feel, it also is remarkably easy to drive. Power steering and Fordomatic transmission probably contributed their share of reducing the driving effort of the car. But beyond this, though, the car has a certain "feel" that makes the driver "at home" regardless of driving conditions or roads traversed. The engineering that has gone into these '57 models deserves credit for these improvements. The huskier and stiffer frame with its widely flared side rails

THE UNIQUE OWNER-TEST OF THIS CAR COVERED MORE THAN 5,000 MILES FROM THE TIME OF NORMAL DEALER DELIVERY

and the simplified, angle-poised four-way ball-joint front suspension and the ·outboard-mounted rear springs give the car a ride and roadability that is soft yet completely controllable and secure over bumps and curves.

Out on the open highway, the 312-cubic-inch engine responded effectively whenever the need arose for that extra surge of power to get around slower vehicles. Steep grades were smoothed out to no effort at all for the 245-hp Thunderbird Special overhead-valve V-8. There had been some warning that this power-packed engine was highly sensitive; that its low-silhouette four-barrel carburetor might act up under improper throttle operation in traffic. This is essentially true: You can "flood" and kill the engine should you "dig out" from a stoplight, then suddenly find it necessary to lift your foot off the accelerator for a slow down or quick stop. Never get panicky under these conditions, pumping the throttle to restart the engine; you'll only succeed in feeding raw fuel into the cylinders, prolonging the starting operation, and becoming a traffic hazard.

Get a group of new car owners together and you'll undoubtedly hear them discussing their particular car's good points or shortcomings, or the trouble they've had with minor defects. Perhaps you would like to compare notes with this owner-tester: During the first few weeks of ownership, he discovered (1) unusual consumption of oil, (2) backup lights inoperative, (3) a water leak inside car on passenger's side below dash, and (4) one power-operated window became inoperative. The oil leak was caused by an improperly installed grease seal between the engine and transmission; the backup lights were never hooked up; the water leak was caused by a loose seal; and a stop on the window was not tightened sufficiently on assembly causing it to come out and allowing the window to go beyond the catch. Of course, the dealer corrected all of these items at the 1000-mile service at no charge, but it suggests the need for better quality control—for greater care in new car assembly and inspection. On the good side of the ledger, the owner found that no further minor ailments have developed in over 3000 more miles of driving, even after giving the car some pretty stiff workouts during acceleration runs and roadability checking.

Remarkably outstanding is the acceleration performance of this particular Ford station wagon. From a standing start to 60 mph, it beat 10 seconds on two of the five runs taken, ending up with an overall average of 10.1 seconds. It is possible to spin the wheels on this Fordomatic-equipped car in either low or drive position of the lever, this despite the 3975-pounds curb weight of the vehicle. So, if this is any indication of what other 245-hp Fords will do, no driver should require anything any better for sheer acceleration performance. The figures also indicate that a wagon, with a better axle ratio, weight distribution and streamlining can match or beat a sedan.

Summing up, Ford wagons have already established a remarkable lead in sales. Disregarding factory-released press information, a check of station wagons on the road on a trip from Los Angeles to San Francisco showed Fords outnumbered other makes by a considerable margin, with a 3-to-1 count over its nearest competitor. Ford produces five wagons and have a wide choice of body colors with many excellent two-tone combinations. The sculptured split-level roof line, the canted tail fins, huge taillights, and low, wide appearance give the Ford station wagon styling that makes it highly desirable; power and engineering improvements are in keeping with the overall design—all combining to make it a car "worth owning." •

<hr>

FORD WAGON TEST DATA

Test Car: 1957 Ford Country Sedan four-door
Basic Price: $2549.50
Engine: 312-cubic-inch ohv V-8
Carburetion: One four-barrel
Compression Ratio: 9.7 to 1
Horsepower: 245 @ 4500 rpm
Torque: 332 @ 2600 rpm
Dimensions: Length 203.5 inches, width 77, height 58.9, tread 59 front 56.4 rear, wheelbase 116
Dry Weight: 3975 lbs.
Transmission: Three-speed Fordomatic torque converter
Acceleration: 0-30 mph 3.6 seconds, 0-45 mph 6.3, 0-60 mph 10.1 seconds
Gas Mileage: 13.3 mpg average
Speedometer Corrections: Indicated 30, 45, and 60 mph are actual 29, 42, and 56 mph, respectively

by William Carroll

TWO MONTHS AGO I drove the cars all America is talking about today: the uncompromising 1958 Thunderbird Hardtop Model 63-A. It seats four passengers, has 300 horsepower, a 113-inch wheelbase and a brand-new unitized body.

This is really a three-year-old story of dream cars come true, beginning in early 1955. Ford's Market Research Group has released answers to their survey: "What do 1955 Thunderbird owners want—that they don't already have?"

The answers: People want a car with room for four passengers. More luggage space. Larger doors. More passenger and driver comfort.

Following these suggestions Ford's Styling Section drew an entirely new Bird. By late 1955 the Thunderbird Engineering Department (as many as 2000 specialists) was in full cry after their target date. With a design and educated guesses as to what would sell, production was scheduled for 1958.

First efforts were along lines of the early Bird, *i.e.,* modified Ford frame, chopped, channeled and plated Ford body panels. But expanding the old body to a four-passenger unit proved nearly impossible. About this same time Lincoln drawing boards were hot with plans for the 1958 unitized body. And someone at Ford heard of it.

Picking up Lincoln's project like a found dollar, Ford engineers tossed aside compromise construction and began to design a unitized Bird from the inside out.

First, four passengers in *complete* comfort. Second, a low car with doors wide enough for the most awkward. Finally, an interior safer than any other car. Of course it had to "go," but this was up to the engine designers. With basic requirements in mind, engineers began noodling around the design load of four passengers, 300 pounds in front, 300 rear. Quite an improvement over the two-passenger 400-pound design load most hardtops are expected to handle.

The car's style proved ideal for unit spotweld construction. Engineers began with a flat floor pan using the driveline tunnel as a stiffening member of the platform. Next, six-inch-deep siderails were set along edges of the floor creating a step-down effect. The cowl area, and its built-in air intake became a massive stiffening member for the front, while the rear deck and quarter panels were stressed to further wiggle-proof the body. Finally a Continental-inspired top was spotwelded to the body and windshield frame, completing one of the strongest units Ford has ever built.

April snow was melting in 1957 before the Thunderbird (no longer Ford) group completed the first engineering prototype. Unlike cars displayed to the public a short time ago, this early design (of which several were built) had 1956 Ford rear fenders with a Continental flair aft of the doors. A molded belt line ran from front to rear as on the '57 Bird. Torpedo sculptures (now laid along the bottom of each

UNITIZED PROTOTYPE T-Bird is not

door) were in this original model laid only along the lower edge of the rear quarter panel. Nor was there any sculptured effect (like Lincoln) running from headlight brow to the door. Not the best-looking car, but a good start in a style-wise direction.

Engineering-wise the car was downright radical. In construction of the body engineers used what is called a "torque box." It's a reinforced area at each lower corner of the body where stub frame rails are attached. Not only does the torque box absorb road stresses from the suspension-carrying rails, but it provides the means by which a unitized body may be restyled year after year at minimum expense. Only

THE '58 THUNDERBIRD

An attempt to bridge the gap from "a personal sports car" to "a prestige automobile"

by William Carroll

identical to 1958 model. Note short torpedo across rear wheel opening and forward-leaning door frame.

front stub rails need be changed for improved engine mountings. Fender sheet metal and hood panels can be altered yearly and the rear stub frame can be lengthened for changes of wheelbase or trunk depth. Even the dash is bolted in place to make alterations easy.

Underneath, chassis engineers were having a field day. And a couple of headaches. A smooth underbody reduced wind resistance and noise, but left little room for mufflers and suspension members. Relief came when dual reverse-flow mufflers found a home behind the rear wheels. Then a crossover pipe was inserted in the system up front to reduce rumble and corrosion. Ford claims the lowest back pressure they've ever had.

Basic coil spring suspension is Ford, with differential, driveline and brakes borrowed also from the younger brother. Rear end stability is controlled by trailing arms (bushed to the housing by rubber "pucks" to control axle windup) and upper links of the system. Costs were cut by using the same link for both left and right sides of the suspension assembly. Because automatics are easier on rear ends, upper links are omitted from automatic-transmission-equipped cars. Optional air suspension appears to be a slightly modified Ford unit. Outboard mounting of front shocks (rears are inboard and tilted to the center) left plenty of room for installation of rubber and nylon air bags.

Contributing to the Bird comfort is a new function given the shock absorbers. Formerly, lowered cars suffered from an atrocious ride because there was little room left for suspension members to move up and down. A bright Ford engineer noticed that most systems used rubber rebound blocks two or three inches thick. Reasoned he: remove the blocks, design shocks to limit wheel travel (in place of the blocks) by means of hydraulic fluid and you could use space vacated by the rebound blocks to further lower the car. Result: the Bird has nearly as much spring action as other Ford products, but is lower than any.

Then came the tests to prove what had been built. One of the four engineering prototypes (completed April, 1957) was not to have a happy life. First stop: Kingman, Ariz., at Ford's rugged desert test track. A special five-mile course was prepared for the Bird's "run for the junkpile." The run: a mile of railroad ties planted to simulate chassis-busting curbs and four paved miles to let the driver rest. So rough, that even the most hardy test driver could hold out for no more than five trips after which a fresh crew took over to beat the Bird to death. Round and round they went (the frame of a competitive sedan broke at 150 miles) with frequent inspections made for failures and driver changes every 25 miles. At the end of 1500 miles the prototype and a 1957 Thunderbird running with it for direct comparison were taken to the garage. There, precise measurements by the staff disclosed the new unitized body structure had given way an almost unnoticeable 1/16-inch more than did the frame of the companion '57. Still

THUNDERBIRD released for production has Lincoln's sculptured fender, Ford's grille and the Continental's top. Careful analysis of Bird's design and engineering will disclose it to be a small edition of '58 Lincoln.

not satisfied though the 1/16-inch hurt nothing, engineers ordered the prototype Bird to Ford's test area at Romeo, Mich., where, with over 40,000 miles on the odometer, it was still bouncing around the durability track as this is written.

A lady's life was led by the prototype sent to Styling. It was finished and refinished, chromed and dechromed between showings at countless management meetings. From these meetings we heard rumors of a sample convertible, which was not approved for production, but which might be in the 1959 lineup.

The fourth prototype was belle of the Experimental Garage, alternately pampered, beaten, altered and nursed. It holds the record for performance on Ford's Dearborn Test Track, and this is the car most everyone drove. So did we.

But what a disappointment!

The test engine (some 350 horsepower but not scheduled for production) pulled the hardtop along at a rapid rate. Acceleration was good (0 to 60 in 8.9 seconds) with the quarter-mile being covered in 16.6 seconds at a solid 91 miles an hour. Passing times averaged 3.4 seconds from 35 to 50 and 5.2 seconds from 60 to 80 although the single four-throat was acting a bit rich. The ride was awful—somewhat like a farm cart. However, with super-stiff springs and shocks there was little one could do in the handling department (4.1 turns lock-to-lock) that caused control trouble. But my, it was a rough car.

Driving the worst didn't do much for my enthusiasm. After repeated requests Ford came up with something better, car number 5. The fifth *production* prototype —built on an assembly line—had only 26 miles on the odometer and inspection shortage tags all over the dash. But this was it. Here was the type of car Ford expects you to buy.

Behind the wheel my previous disappointment evaporated. The engine was quiet, muted by a successful combination of deadeners, Fiberglas plus aluminum sound barriers, and rubber, all of which pushes the noise level down to Lincoln quality. The Cruise-O-Matic (with 3.10 to 1 rear end ratio) functioned smoothly and brought us up to speed with the smooth shifts of a well-adjusted automatic. Zero to 60 ticked off at a nominal 13.5 seconds (10.5 if you shift from D1 to D2 at 50 mph) and the quarter-mile was tagged out at 81 miles an hour in 16.8 seconds. Passing speeds were clocked as follows: 30 to 50, 4.6 seconds; 45 to 60, 3.9; 60 to 80, 7.9.

Runs over the ride test road disclosed the usual "Fordy" solid ride. Cornering was established as above average with the bucket seats doing a wonderful job of keeping the fanny in position while trying to rip tires off around the track's even-radius curves. With four passengers (total

DREAM CAR design comes true with window controls, ashtrays and radio speaker in console between four genuine and comfortable bucket seats.

600 pounds) weight distribution is an even 50/50. Wheels and tires are factory balanced to insure safe performance from the first mile.

Technical specifications of the standard Bird include a 352-cubic-inch, 300-horsepower V8 with single four-throat carburetor pulling cold air through a hood scoop. It looks a great deal like the small Edsel engine and uses hydraulic lifters, although at first Ford was planning to use mechanical pushers. The aluminum coating on intake and exhaust valves has already demonstrated an astounding ability under the most severe tests.

In the brake department Ford has gone all-out. Their brakes require plenty of pedal pressure but function without argument or backtalk. Secret of the improvement is the rear brake-shoe in each wheel. There are three segments of lining on each rear shoe, two of which are lengths of standard lining. Between the two lengths is a ¾-inch-long piece of Cerame-

HOW THE '58 THUNDERBIRD COMPARES

	'58 T-Bird	'57 T-Bird	'58 300-D	'58 Cadillac 62
Wheelbase, in.	113	102	126	129.5
Length, in.	205.4	181.4	220.2	216.8
Width, in.	77	72.8	79.6	80
Height, in.	52.5	51.6	57.3	59.1
Max. bhp @ rpm	300 @ 4600	245 @ 4500	380 @ 5200	310 @ 4800
Max. torque @ rpm	395 @ 2800	332 @ 3200	435 @ 3600	405 @ 3100
Compression ratio	10.2:1	9.7:1	10.0:1	10.25:1
Front headroom	34.5	33.6	34.4	34.2
Rear headroom	33.3	——	33.7	34.0
Front legroom	43.4	44.9	45.5	44.6
Rear legroom	38.0	——	38.0	41.0
Weight	3869	3440	4390	4675
Minimum road clearance	5.8	7.1	5.6	6.4
Factory price	$3600 (Est.)	$3408	$5108	$4784

BROAD SHALLOW trunk holds spare tire and 20 cubic feet of space. Tilted tire well limits ground clearance to 5.8 inches. Quad tail lights all burn at once.

talix matching the standard lining in width and thickness. Ford engineers assured me there is no danger of drum scoring from the metal block and plenty of safety in heat-resisting properties of the insert. Effective brake area is a nominal 193 inches, more than a Ford but not up to Mercury's 223 square inches. But no one in the Ford family can match brilliance with the Bird's four 32-candlepower stoplights.

"Widest doors in the industry," says Ford, and I believe them. Seems almost like pulling a side (48.8 inches of it) off the car. Duck a little to get in, or better yet use the sports car technique of backing onto the front seats. This is where comfort begins. Each of the four seats (two separates in front and two-in-one for the rear) is an honest-to-goodness bucket job. Soft springs in the center and back allow your body to drop into (rather than sit on) the cushions. Then you become conscious of foam rubber cushion edges which ride up around your thighs and back to provide the most comforting support of all '58s. As one engineer said, "It's almost like riding with someone's arms around you." (How nice.)

The driving position is low and steering wheel high, a typical relationship of Ford productions. Vision is excellent in all directions, partially because front and rear glass is set into the body rather than on a rail as is common practice on production cars. An interesting cost reduction and safety feature is that only the driver's seat is movable. All others are screwed to the floor, unless you wish to buy seat tracks for the front passenger. The next thing I noticed was fully covered trim. All interior metal (except chrome styling strips) is covered with vinyl plastic which is glareless and easy to clean. The fully-padded dash (standard equipment) has two huge safety brows over the instruments and glove box. The driveshaft tunnel was at one time intended to carry all control switches and levers. But high cost ruled the idea out and now there is only a centrally located electric window lift control panel, two ashtrays and radio speaker grille.

Options are few. Other than the usual choice of overdrive or Cruise-O-Matic, there is a radio, heater, power brakes, steering, seats and windows, air suspension, heavy-duty shocks, shims to increase ground clearance, backup lights, heavy-duty battery and generator, electric clock, fender ornaments, non-glare mirrors, tinted glass and paint options.

Hatching the Birds is a novel project involving two separate plants. The bare body is constructed by the Budd Co., Philadelphia, Pa., and is shipped to the Lincoln assembly plant in Wixom, Mich. At Lincoln, Birds are dunked in primer, move down the same assembly line with Continentals and Premieres to be assembled and painted by Lincoln specialists. The only time a Bird separates from the line is when interiors are installed. For this operation a separate line is used, then back they go to the Lincoln line for completion, inspection and testing before shipment.

"Where are the Birds expected to roost?" was one question we threw at a Ford spokesman. In reply he let us see an office memo.

It read, "Ford management asked the stylists to design a car they'd like to own. Their 'dream car' is truly a unique automobile with no counterpart in design, wheelbase, maneuverability and performance. Its styling is in contours of the metal itself, not in trim, for there is practically none. It is the first prestige car designed for today's driving conditions."

We can't agree with everything in the statement. There are hotter engines, cars that handle better, look better and have the same wheelbase. But the 1958 Thunderbird is most certainly the "first *prestige* car designed for today's driving conditions."

Built in the Lincoln plant, priced in the upper medium bracket, with no monkey business about being a "personal car," the Bird has every feature that would appeal to a sophisticate. No matter what's in the garage now, I'll bet a lot of people are wondering if there's room for a new Thunderbird. **/MT**

SPOTWELDED unit body is one of strongest Ford has ever built. Floor pan, sills, driveline tunnel and eight crossmembers increase strength.

1958 FORD

FOLLOWING the complete model change made just a year ago Ford might have been expected to coast this year, be content with a mild facelift. Instead, $185 million was spent to design, style, engineer and tool 1958 models—just $24 million less than for the all-new 1957 cars.

It was possible to buy a lot of changes for that kind of money. New Fords have a lot of styling and engineering differences from 1957 models.

Front end appearance has been completely changed by new bumpers, new anodized aluminum grille, dual headlamps and a longer, lower hood line. Result of these changes is a visual illusion of greater lowness.

Bumper and grille appear to be an integral unit but they are separated by more than an inch. The new dual head lights are mounted side-by-side in the leading edge of each front fender. Directly below them are the combined parking/turn signal lights; these wrap around the corner of the fender so they are clearly visible from both front and side.

The scoop on the hood is non-functional in that it does not admit air to the engine compartment. This raised scoop section was necessary, however, to provide clearance for the engine with the hood line as low as it now is. (Mercury was forced to use a hood scoop for the same reason three or four years ago.)

Major restyling has changed the rear of 1958 Fords a great deal, too. Canted fins have been retained but bullseye tail lights—a trademark since 1952 —have been dropped. The new rear lighting setup has flattened oval lights mounted horizontally across the rear of the car. One light on each side is mounted in the fender. Two more are mounted in the deck lid.

The deck lid has an inverted Vee shape sculptured into its top surface, looks a lot like the Edsel deck lid.

Side body trim has been changed and each series now has its own identifying molding design.

The new roof for 1958 has seven grooves stamped in its surface. They run from front to rear and, in addition to adding styling interest, they add extra rigidity to the roof panel. They are used on all models except retractibles and convertibles. On station wagons the grooves start at the sculpture step line and run to the back edge of the roof.

Most important engineering new is that two new engines and air suspension have been introduced.

The new engines are basically the same design, differ only in displacement. The smaller one has a displacement of 332 cubic inches, with bore and stroke of 4.0 by 3.3 inches. The larger engine displaces 352 cubic inches and has the same bore size as its smaller twin. Stroke, however, is increased to 3.5 in.

The new engines have fully-machined combustion chamber located in the head (not in the block as in the largest of the new Ford engines used by Edsel, Mercury and Lincoln). Valve arrangement is such that no two exhaust valves are adjacent, minimizing the possibility of localized "hot spots" and warping.

Cylinder heads are smaller and intake manifolds much bigger than normal in the new engines. This has enabled engineers to make manifold passages all of nearly equal length to insure more even distribution of the fuel-air mixture. It also eliminates the need for a separate tappet chamber cover and adds to the rigidity of the engine assembly.

Ford is continuing the policy of mass

A lot of effort went into warming over the 1957 model for

the coming year, including air springing and a new engine.

It's a good car—but it might not be quite good enough

STAPLE TWO-DOOR SEDAN, of the middle-priced series, somehow has a Buickish touch about it, chiefly in the grille and the curved spear trim on the side. Dual lamps are also offered.

ROCKET LIGHTS, a Ford trademark in taillights since 1952, have vanished. The rear-end styling is better than the front.

balancing all V-8 engines electronically which it started in 1957. This is done while engines are running at operating speed and temperature under their own power. An important quality feature, this balancing minimizes vibration caused by imbalance—insuring quieter operation and reduced wear.

In addition to the two new engines, Ford continues to offer the 292-cubic-inch V-8 used for the past three years and the short-stroke ohv-6.

The ohv-6 is offered for all 1958 Fords except rectractible hardtops and convertibles. The 292-cubic-inch V-8 is standard in Custom and Custom 300 models. The 332-cubic-inch V-8 with two-barrel carburetion and single exhaust is standard for Fairlanes and station wagons. The same engine with a single four-barrel carburetor is standard on Fairlane 500 models. With four-barrel carburetor and dual exhausts, this engine is offered as an option for Custom and Custom 300 cars. The big 352-cubic-inch V-8, with four-barrel carburetor and dual exhausts, is optional for all except Custom and Custom 300 models. This engine has a 10.2-to-1 compression ratio. All 332-inch V-8's have a 9.25-to-1 ratio while the 292-inch V-8's have a 9.1-to-1 ratio. Compression of the ohv-6 is unchanged—8-6-to-1.

In addition to the regular Ford-O-Matic transmission, Ford now offers a new dual-range torque converter unit. It is a modification of the existing design, not an all-new transmission. It is available only in cars equipped with two new engines—and all models with one of the new engines and this transmission have 2.69 rear axle

gears as standard equipment!

Standard steel suspensions are basically the same as in 1957 except that the spring rate has been changed to give a softer ride.

New air suspension is optional for all Fairlane and station wagon models. Air springs are substituted for coils at front and are used with trailing arms and lateral track bar at the rear.

Changes in dimensions resulting from styling alterations are virtually unchanged. Wheelbase is still 116 inches for Customs and wagons, 118 inches for Fairlanes. Overall length and height are unchanged. Twenty different models are offered in the four car and one station wagon series again in 1958.

The sweeping changes made just a year after introduction of all-new designs are proof of Ford's determination to crack Chevrolet's hold on first place in sales. It has done that so far this year and has enough that is new to offer, both in styling and engineering, to put up a strong battle to stay in the top spot. •

FAIRLANE TRIM, shown at the top, below, is Ford's best in several years, if problems of matching at doors on four-door sedans can be solved.

STATION WAGONS increase in popularity each year, and Ford is aiming for its share of market again. 332 cubic inch engine is standard in wagons.

OPTIONAL AIR springing unit is most effective in snubbing rebound after hitting bumps. It does not reduce cornering lean.

CONVERTIBLE SERIES also includes the highly successful retractible hardtop for 1958. The current Ford body shell is in its second year now.

FORD

By JIM WHIPPLE

AFTER studying the specifications and physical changes on the '58 Ford we expected a car with evolutionary improvements all along the line plus some smooth and powerful new engines. However, nothing prepared us for the tremendous improvement in ride, handling and roadability due to the '58 Ford's optional air suspension.

Because Ford's air suspension is an extra cost option available only on Fairlane, Fairlane 500 and station wagons, it would be unfair to say that Ford is the best riding and handling automobile in its field. The standard Ford suspension system independent balljoint coil-sprung front and leaf-sprung Hotchkiss drive rear, is last year's set-up with minor improvements.

Rear springs have been made 5% softer and front suspension action has slightly increased damping action. The performance of Ford's standard '58 suspension would have been world-shaking had it been introduced in 1956. Compared to standard suspension systems of competing cars in its price class the '58 Ford rates average. This state of affairs is only due to the tremendous improvements made by Plymouth with its torsion bar system introduced last year and by the '58 Chevy with its new all coil suspension.

With air suspension, the ride of the '58 Ford is superior to the rest of its class by a clear margin. In roadability, the air sprung Ford is equal to the torsion bar Plymouth and a bit better than either the air sprung or all coil Chevy.

A standard sprung '58 Ford offers a noticeably less comfortable ride and has less "stickability" than the '58 Plymouth on curves and uneven road surfaces.

Compared to Chevy, the steel-spring Ford has a slightly less comfortable ride than either the air- or steel-suspended competition. In roadability the two cars are evenly matched until you compare cornering characteristics of the two cars on rough dirt or gravel roads.

In these circumstances, the rigidly-located rear axle of the coil-sprung Chevy does a great deal better job at eliminating skittering and sliding sidewise. If you start to spin off the road under these conditions you can get back more quickly and easily when you cut your wheels into the direction of the skid and tramp on it.

If you start to spin off the road under these conditions you can get back more quickly and easily when you cut your wheels into the direction of the skid and tramp on it.

All three cars, whether steel or air sprung, are, to a greater or lesser degree, more comfortable to ride in than either Studebaker or Rambler. However, the gap is not too wide, with the riding qualities of the Rambler Six coming very close to those of the Ford Custom 300.

Incidentally, Rambler will soon be in production with an air spring sys-

Ford silhouette for '58 includes
sloping hood, liberal use of "sculpture."
Fairlane models have contrasting color
panels extending back from front fenders.

FORD

is the car

for you

if... You need a sturdy, comfortable economy car—Custom Six with overdrive.

if... You want powerful performance, plus ride and handling unexcelled in Ford's price class in a car that's extremely easy to drive—Fairlane 352 cu. in. V-8 with Cruise-O-Matic and air suspension.

if... You're looking for a well-balanced family car with satisfactory performance—Custom 300 V-8 with Fordomatic.

FORD SPECIFICATIONS

ENGINES	SIX	V-8	V-8	V-8
Bore and stroke	3.62 in. x 3.60 in.	3.75 in. x 3.30 in.	4.00 in. x 3.30 in.	4.00 in. x 3.50 in.
Displacement	223 cu. in.	292 cu. in.	332 cu. in.	352 cu. in.
Compression ratio	8.6:1	9.1:1	9.5:1	10.2:1
Max. brake horsepower	145 @ 4200 rpm.	205 @ 4500 rpm.	240 @ 4600 rpm.	300 @ 4600 rpm.
Max. torque	212 @ 2100 rpm.	295 @ 2400 rpm.	340 @ 2400 rpm.	395 @ 2800 rpm.

DIMENSIONS	CUSTOM	FAIRLANE
Wheelbase	116 in.	118 in.
Overall length	202.2 in.	207.2 in.
Overall width	78 in.	78 in.
Overall height	57.1 in.	56.2 in.

TRANSMISSIONS

Synchromesh, overdrive. Fordomatic. Cruise-O-Matic

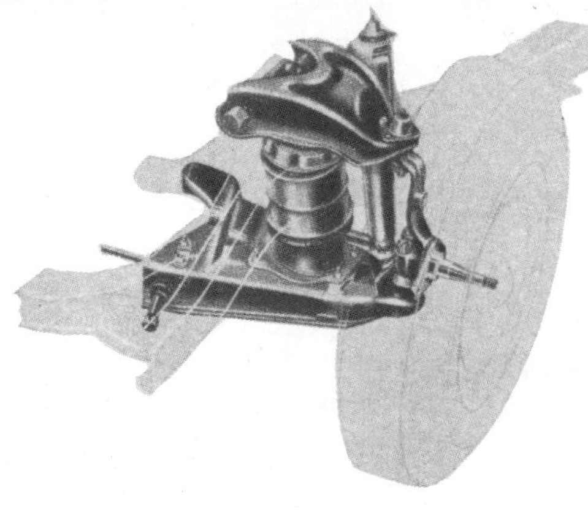

Custom 300 Tudor has anodized aluminum panel along side. Conservative Ford fins culminate in "double-jet" thrusting tail light treatment.

Air suspension ride, called "Ford-Aire," is option on Fairlanes and station wagons. "Ford-Aire" uses pressurized air bags.

Dual headlights and mock air-intake set off integrated bumper-grille on new Fords.

tem of its own which could give it a better ride than some of its competition.

It would be interesting to blindfold people and take them for their first ride in a '58 air-sprung Ford then let them guess the car's make before removing the blindfold. Ford's ride is an Olds 98 ride, a Lincoln ride, a Chrysler New Yorker ride. For once, wheelbase is not the criterion of superior riding comfort.

What's even more enjoyable is the combination of top riding comfort and roadability. After gradually warming up to the Ford-Aire Fairlane V-8 we took it over a rough stretch of Belgian block cobblestones at 70 mph and switched the wheel rapidly back and forth from left to right. This maneuver would have put you in the accident ward of the nearest hospital if tried in a car built just a few seasons back.

The '58 Ford leaned moderately, but never lost its footing.

Steering on all '58 Fords has been improved by adoption of a recirculating ball steering gear that has a very low friction co-efficient and velvet smooth action. The new gear has the same ratio (27 to 1) as last year with either manual or power steering.

In spite of its easy action the new steering gear is very precise, yet shock-free and has excellent road feel. When the linkage type power steering booster is added there is no loss of road sensitivity and the amount of boost is not so much that it tends to "take over" and rob the driver of his natural feel of the road.

Ford's engine and transmission lineup offers a wider choice of standard and extra-cost options than ever before with two brand new engines and a new transmission called Cruise-O-Matic heading the list.

The efficient and popular Six (145 bhp, 8.6 to 1 compression ratio) is available on all models except the convertible and retractable hardtop with either standard, overdrive, or Fordomatic. Last year's 292 cu. in. V-8 of 205 bhp is a "standard" (at extra cost) engine on Custom and Custom 300 models.

Standard V-8 choice on Fairlanes and station wagons is a brand new 332 cu. in. V-8 with 2-barrel carburetor. It develops 240 bhp.

This same engine with 4-barrel is used with the new Cruise-O-Matic transmission on Fairlane and Fairlane 500 and, with added dual exhaust, is

the optional "power pack" engine for Customs and Custom 300's. It develops 265 bhp. Power pack engine for station wagons and all Fairlane models is a new 352 cu. in. engine of 300 bhp with 4-barrel carburetor and dual exhausts as standard equipment.

Cruise-O-Matic is not just a gimmick name for an old transmission but a thoroughly redesigned version of Fordomatic with some very likeable qualities. First of all, there is the extremely low drive ratio of 2.69 to 1. With this ratio the new large displacement engines (Ford's largest in '57 was 312 cu. in.) will not use any more fuel under normal cruising conditions. Another feature we liked about Cruise-O-Matic is the elimination of the three-stage downshift when decelerating; the transmission downshifts directly to low gears at speeds of 7 to 10 mph.

On the upshifts in D1 range you start in low and a light throttle foot lets it shift to Intermediate at as low as 10 mph and into high at as low as 15 mph. If you're interested in full power acceleration, the shifts occur at 54 mph (to Intermediate) and at 81 mph (to high). For smooth operation in stop and go traffic D2 range locks the transmission out of Low gear en-

Custom Tudor, least expensive of Ford line, uses trim sparingly.

tirely. Low range is used for engine braking. A shift into Low range at any speed instantly drops the transmission into Intermediate gear and at 20 to 28 mph downshifts to Low and stays in that gear until shift lever is moved.

For all practical purposes, the styling changes on the '58 Ford have not altered the car in any way. Dimensions in the passenger compartments and trunks are virtually unchanged. Glass area, too, remains the same. For taller drivers, we feel that the headroom and height of windshield glass are somewhat shorter than they should be on Fairlane models. However, the lower-priced Custom and Custom 300 (and station wagon) models have greater headroom and a larger vision area (i.e. higher windshield and side windows).

Summing Up: The '58 Fords are very well-balanced cars with more good engines to choose from than any other low-priced car. With extra cost air suspension, premium Cruise-O-Matic transmission and 265 bhp V-8 engines, the Fairlane models assume the comfort and performance characteristics of medium-priced cars, while the Custom and Custom 300 models with six-cylinder engines and overdrive make very satisfactory economy cars. ●

FORD CHECK LIST

5 CHECKS MEAN TOP RATING IN ITS PRICE CLASS

PERFORMANCE	Ford's performance ranges from satisfactory to outstanding depending on the choice of model, engine and transmission.
STYLING	Basic lines are pleasing but some of the facelift changes such as quad tail lamps, dummy airscoop and out-thrust grille may take some getting used to.
RIDING COMFORT	All Fords with standard suspension are reasonably comfortable on all types of roads with the Fairlanes slightly better than the Customs and the Customs better than the station wagons. With air suspension, Ford has best ride in its class.
INTERIOR DESIGN	Generally well-balanced design although Ford doesn't make the most of its passenger space potential. Front headroom and vision is lacking on Fairlanes, and rear door openings on these models aren't large enough.
ROADABILITY	With optional air suspension, Ford is slightly better than its competition and that's very, very good. With standard steel springs, it doesn't have as good roadability as its important competition.
EASE OF CONTROL	New recirculating ball steering gear plus power steering and new Cruise-O-Matic transmission make Fords second to none of their competition in handling ease. Fairlanes are heavy steering without power assist.
ECONOMY	Here, as with performance, you have your choice. Custom models with six-cylinder engines will give 19 miles per gallon with Fordomatic, 20 to 21 with standard transmission and 23 to 25 with overdrive to average conservative drivers. Big V-8 station wagon models with automatic will get about 16 mpg.
SERVICEABILITY	The new V-8s have very accessible distributors, fuel pumps, spark plugs, etc., and, of course, the Six is one of the easiest to service of all U. S. cars.
WORKMANSHIP	In operation of mechanical items such as door locks, switches, windshield wipers, hood latch, etc., Fords are well above average. Upholstery and interior fittings are superior, too. Some cars have come through with less-than-perfect finish, but all in all, Ford is very close to the top in its field.
VALUE PER DOLLAR	Ford's durability is good, engineering is excellent and record of trade-in-value next to the highest in its class. Except for the intangible matter of public acceptance of styling, the '58 Ford should be a good buy.

FORD OVERALL RATING... 4.1 CHECKS

Top STATION WAGON in the Ford lineup of five wagons is the Country Squire, a high-style nine-passenger vehicle with features that keep it in the forefront of the station wagon popularity contests.

What has Ford done to maintain its lead in the station wagon field? For one thing, the wrap-around liftgate offers excellent rearward vision and a wide loading space. The tailgate can be opened with one hand, and the liftgate automatically swings upward since it features a "built-in" assist spring on each side. Telescopic-type support arms with a positive-locking mechanism hold the gate in the wide-open position. The inside cargo carrying capacity of the Ford Wagon is comparable to the Chevrolet and Plymouth wagons; actual interior dimensions, however, are somewhat smaller in the Ford than the other two. With the third passenger seat in position, there is still some space for carrying suitcases and other luggage behind it. This luggage, incidentally, is easier to get to than in the nine-passenger Plymouth wagon since the latter has a rearward-facing third seat and the cargo space is between the second and third seats. Access to this area would be awkward—with suitcases having to be lifted up and over the back of either the second or third seats regardless of whether it is being loaded from the rear or from the front.

Converting the entire area behind the front seat of the Ford wagon for cargo carrying or overnight sleeping on that weekend mountain trip is about the easiest of any wagon on the market. Pulling the backrest of the second seat forward and flipping the support legs around for holding the seat in its inverted position are operations that even a woman can do without too much effort.

Under the hood of all Ford wagons is a new 332-cubic-inch V8 engine with its fully machined combustion chambers designed to eliminate pre-ignition problems caused in ordinary cylinders by glowing carbon and lead deposits which have a tendency to cling to surfaces that aren't completely smooth. The test wagon was equipped with a single four-barrel carburetor which boosts the horsepower up to 265 @ 4600 rpm. With a compression ratio of 9.5-to-1 and torque of 360 pounds-feet @ 2800 rpm, there seems to be adequate power to give the wagon good acceleration performance despite its 3945-pound weight. Although not a bomb, as the saying goes, the Country Squire did a respectable 12.7 seconds in its 0-to-60 mph run.

The test car was equipped with the less costly two-speed Fordomatic transmission, found to be entirely adequate and practical for most driving conditions. The "Cruise-O-Matic," a three-speed automatic with reported "built-in" overdrive economy is the high-performance gearbox, costing about $20 additional over the Fordomatic, which shifts smoothly and gives good low-speed torque, but does not have any real advantage over the Fordomatic (see MOTOR LIFE, Feb. '58, "Ford 3000-Mile Road Test").

Test Car: 1958 Ford Country Squire
Body Type: 9-passenger 4-door station wagon
Basic Price: $2900.90
Engine: Overhead-valve V8
Carburetion: one 4-barrel
Displacement: 332 cubic inches
Bore & Stroke: 4.00 x 3.30
Compression Ratio: 9.5-to-1
Horsepower: 265 @ 4600 rpm
Horsepower per cubic inch: .79
Torque: 360 lb.-ft. @ 2800 rpm
Test Weight: 3945 lbs. without driver
Weight Distribution: 50 per cent on front wheels
Power-Weight Ratio: 14.8 lbs. per horsepower
Transmission: Two-speed Fordomatic automatic
Rear Axle Ratio: 2.91
Steering: 5 turns lock-to-lock
Dimensions: overall length 207 inches, width 78, height 56, wheelbase 118, tread 59
Springs: Coil front, leaf rear
Tires: 7.50 x 14 4-ply
Gas Mileage: 11.7 mpg average (city)
Speedometer Error: Indicated 30, 45 and 60 mph are actual 29, 42 and 56 mph, respectively
Acceleration: 0-30 mph in 4.9 seconds, 0-45 mph in 8.0 and 0-60 mph in 12.7 seconds

FORD WAGON TEST

THE COUNTRY SQUIRE STATION WAGON IS THE TOP ENTRY IN FORD'S WAGON PARADE. IT CARRIES NINE PASSENGERS EASILY.

Driving the Country Squire wagon is not much different than driving any one of the Ford passenger cars. Outside of the extra bulk that obviously is a part of the wagon, comparison in driving qualities is quite similar, except for one major difference. In traveling over a winding mountain road at faster than normally safe speeds on curves, the wagon definitely seems to handle better; this can be attributed to the 50/50 weight distribution giving the wagon better control on curves. Actually, the frame and suspension on both the Ford passenger cars and the wagons are the same, but because of the difference in weight distribution, the wagon has a slight advantage over the passenger cars as far as handling and roadability are concerned. The frame itself is a ladder type, with box section side members, and five crossmembers. Suspension is by four-way ball-joint front, and variable-rate, outboard-mounted rear leaf springs; double-acting shock absorbers are used all around.

The test car was equipped with considerable power-assist equipment and luxury accessories, making driving and riding in the car a pleasant undertaking. Power steering took the effort out of parking in tight spots, and power brakes made signal-stopping about as effortless as pushing the foot on the throttle. The car also had a six-way power-operated front seat—certainly a wonderful luxury item when more than one person of different height and build are driving the car regularly; it's also great for changing seat position on a long trip, thus providing the type of driving relaxation often recommended by safety people. Another item worth mentioning is the spotlight with its integral rear-view mirror which adjusts from inside the car.

Among the accessories that make station wagon owning even more advantageous—especially for the week-end camper, the small business man, or the suburbanite—is a bolt-on luggage rack; this unit installed on the multi-braced roof with its dimple-strengthened steel top will provide considerable additional cargo space for the traveler.

Although changes in engineering in the Ford wagon are minor, it still has a good chance of remaining in top position in sales because of its excellent reputation as a proven performer; it certainly has a lot of loyal owners according to recent sales figures. Styling, which follows the passenger car line, is still good although there are many who prefer the "bull's-eye" type taillights to the units now used; there seems to be little reason for the gunsight front fender ornaments. The Ford wagon is particularly quiet, free from rattles, indicating that insulation and quality of assembly are good. •

TEST CAR carried all of the power-assist and luxury accessories of the Ford line. Driving was easy and comfortable experience.

TAILGATE can be opened with one hand while liftgate swings upward automatically due to a spring assist located on each side.

WRAP-AROUND LIFTGATE OF THE FORD OFFERS DRIVER EXCELLENT REARWARD VISION

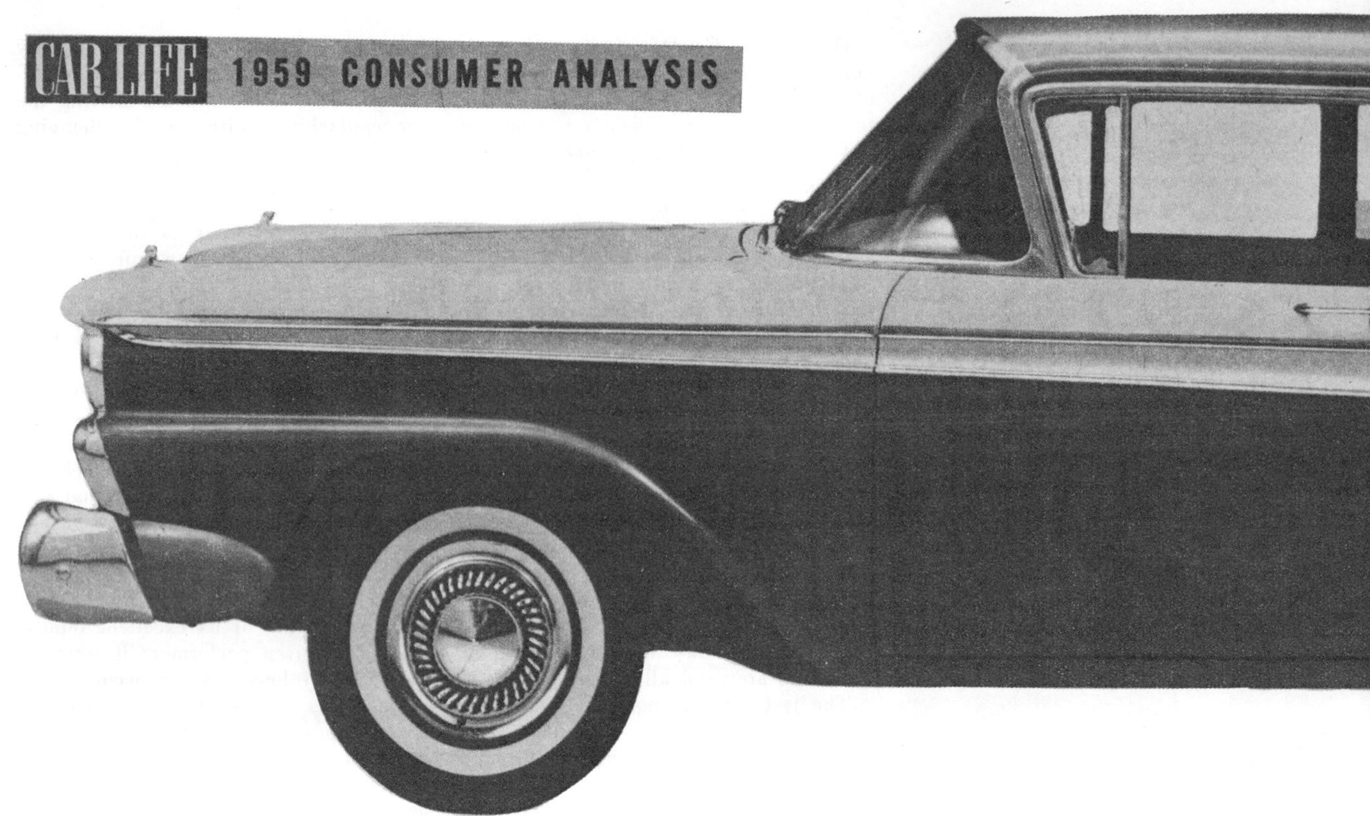

FORD

By JIM WHIPPLE

THE '59 Ford is a quietly impressive car. Although there's nothing wildly sensational about it in any given department, Ford delivers a very solid overall impression.

First of all, the styling is sharp, clean and well balanced. Ford looks sleek and fast, yet the designers haven't been swept away by what you could call the "Buck Rogers bit" — an attempt to make the car look like a TV set designer's conception of a space ship.

The point is that the '59 Ford's looks are in excellent taste and easy to live with. Even the purists who condemn Detroit chrome and praise the conservative styling of foreign cars will be hard pressed to find fault with the looks of the '59 Custom 300 or Fairlane done in a single color.

The '59 Ford styling has swung back, and happily so in my book, to the functional. Gone are the useless and irritating quadruple tail lamps, the dummy air scoop and the dirt-catching roof grooves of the '58 model.

But equally important, the brand-new body (and every panel is new

except the Skyliner's retractible hardtop) has brought with it practical items like increased windshield and window area, wider seats, slightly roomier trunk, and what I feel is an improved seating position. Although road-vision immediately ahead of the car is still not perfect, (the hood front is square and high instead of tapered between the fenders), I found that a collection of hard-to-pin-down qualities — placement of foot pedals, steerwheel location, rake of seat back, windshield size and shape, seat height, etc. — adds up to a very relaxed driving position.

If you think this isn't important, try 500 miles at the wheel of a badly designed car some day.

The new body replaces the two bodies used on '57 and '58 Custom-Custom 300, and Fairlane-Fairlane 500. No longer is there any 116-inch wheelbase 202-inch overall chassis. All models, including station wagons, share the same 118-inch wheelbase frame and all are 208 inches long from bumper to bumper.

Frankly, I'm sorry to see the shorter

Custom 300 chassis dropped. It was plenty big enough and its lower weight and more compact dimensions made it a nice combination with the 145 horsepower six-cylinder engine.

The new Fords weigh about 188 lbs. more (same models with equal trim) than last year's Custom 300. However the use of one body shell for the whole line makes '59 Fairlanes lighter than last year's comparable Fairlanes and "500's".

As soon as I got into the 59 Ford sedan I noted that it was roomier than the '58 Fairlanes, particularly in headroom and seat width both front and rear. I checked the figures and found that all interior dimensions had been increased, and this despite a reduction of one inch in overall height.

Out on the road, the '59 Ford is a really friendly car, one that grows on you as you roll up the miles. If early pilot production models are a good indication of what we may expect from the various Ford assembly plants this year, then the '59 Ford is going to be an outstandingly solid and rattle-free car. I did quite a bit of rough road

FORD SPECIFICATIONS

ENGINES	6	V-8 (292)	V-8 (332)	V-8 (352)
Bore and Stroke	3.62 in. x 3.6 in.	3.75 in. x 3.30 in.	4.0 in. x 3.3 in.	4.0 in. x 3.5 in.
Displacement	223 cu. in.	292 cu. in.	332 cu. in.	352 cu. in.
Compression Ratio	8.4:1	8.8:1	8.9:1	9.6:1
Max. Brake Horsepower	145 @ 4000 rpm	200 @ 4400 rpm	225 @ 4400 rpm	300 @ 4600 rpm
Max. Torque	206 @ 2200 rpm	285 @ 200 rpm	325 @ 2200 rpm	380 @ 2200 rpm

DIMENSIONS				
Wheelbase	118 in.			
Overall Length	208 in.			
Overall Width	76.6			
Overall Height	56.0 in.			

TRANSMISSIONS Synchromesh. Overdrive. Fordomatic. Cruise-O-Matic

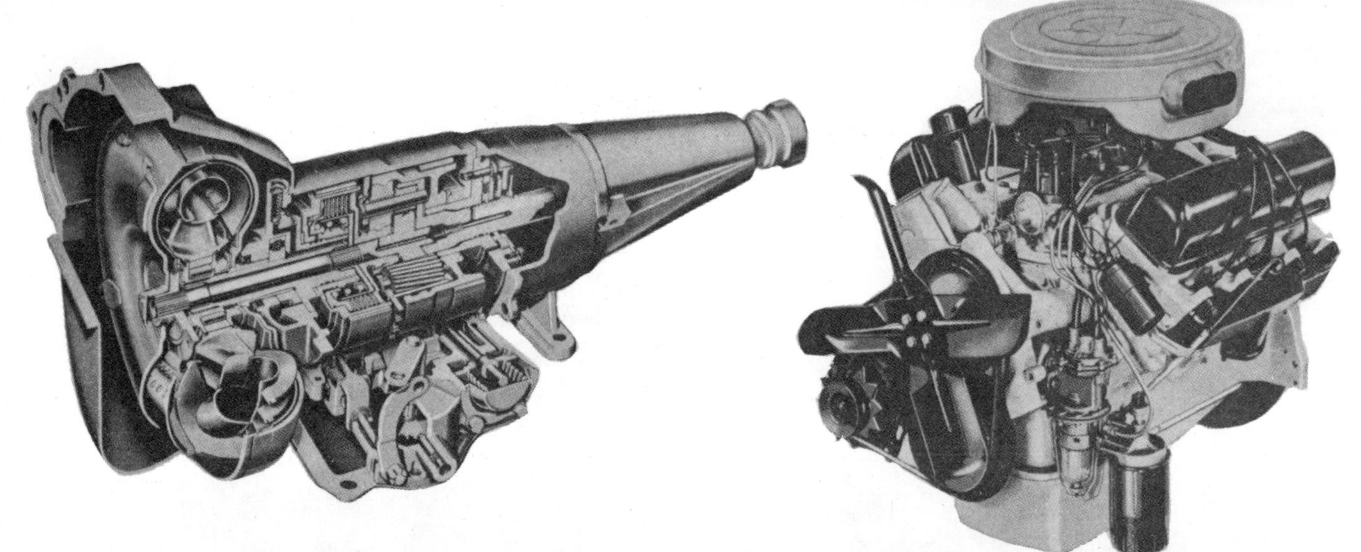

work on a two-door Ranch Wagon with the rear seats folded down. This model by all rights should be the rattlingest of all, but as I hurled it over the Belgian blocks at 30 mph the only noise was a slight squeak from the folded seats. Body shake, that rubbery shuddering that you feel in all cars with separate frames and bodies, is unusually low in the Ford — the least I found in any of the low-priced cars, except of course Rambler, which is a unit construction job.

Sound-proofing, too, is unusually good in the '59 Ford, with engine roar completely blanketed except under full throttle acceleration in low gear.

Although the suspension setup hasn't been changed much on the '59s, the ride seems a bit softer, yet at the same time better controlled on the bumps. I had to work hard to make the car toss and pitch, and it was pretty nearly impossible to bottom it on normal highways. Ford's ride isn't cushiony, but the riding qualities of the '59 are balanced up to give an extremely low overall total of disturbance to the passenger's nervous system, whether it be from bounce, sway, bumps, body shake or surface vibra-tion.

Air suspension, in an improved and simplified form, is again available on Fords, but the standard '59 coil and leaf suspension is good enough so that only the most tender and sensitive riders would find it a worthwhile extra cost.

Handling has been improved by the addition of a link-type front stabilizer, and it is very good indeed. Steering is precise, but the high overall ratio (number of turns of steering wheel from full right to full left) makes maneuvering slow.

The 292 cu. in. V-8 is available in all models in '59 with the same axle ratio (3.56) as in '58. This engine, which is the one that 95% of Ford V-8 buyers will be getting, has been reduced in compression ratio from 9.1 to 1 down to 8.8 to 1 — a sensible move, enabling use of almost all available "Regular" grade gasolines instead of premium. This means a sacrifice of only 5 horsepower, from 205 to 200, which hardly leaves a 3600-lb. sedan underpowered.

Ford has a new "standard" automatic transmission, which will be called Ford-O-Matic, but is almost completely different from last year's Ford-O-Matic in that it is a great deal lighter and that it has fewer parts and only two forward speeds instead of Ford-O-Matic's three.

This new transmission, which I'll call the "two-speed", weighs only 18 lbs. more than the manual transmissions (on the Six), thus eliminating one of the big objections to automatics. It will cost about $50 less than last year's Ford-O-Matic and about $79 less than Cruise-O-Matic, which still remains as '59's "Premium" automatic.

Ford Division brass evidently feels that the new "two-speed" will answer the needs of most drivers and offer an attractive cost savings for the strict economy buyer. I regret the passing of three-speed Ford-O-Matic as an automatic available with *all* engine options at $180.

The $200, three speed Cruise-O-Matic is available only with the extra-cost 332 and 352 cu. in. V-8's.

I tested the new transmission with a 292 V-8 in a station wagon with a 3.56 to 1 rear axle ratio. Acceleration was brisk, reaching 50 mph in 8.55 seconds with a 550-lb. payload. This run was made all the way in Low. There is an automatic upshift from this 1.75 to 1 ratio to a 1.0 to 1 High

New Fordomatic transmission (left) has been considerably simplified, eliminating 105 moving parts, which will mean fewer and simpler repairs. Transmission case and bell housing are aluminum. Ford's redesigned V-8 engines include the 352-cubic-inch pictured, a 292-cubic-inch, and a 332-cubic-inch. All have aluminum-alloy pistons with longer skirts for oil control.

Fairlane 500 convertible and hardtop head a line of 17 models. All '59 Fords share a 118-inch wheelbase and an overall length of 208 inches. The Custom 300 series is six inches longer than last year's models were.

at about 54 mph, which drops the engine speed abruptly and gets you to 60 mph in slightly over 12 seconds.

What this transmission lacks is the 1.47 to 1 Intermediate gear of old Ford-O-Matic, which, combined with a 2.40 to 1 Low and full throttle, kept your engine at peak output all the way up to 70 or so, when the final forced upshift to high came. Also the intermediate gear was ideal for maintaining a speed up fairly steep hills with a heavily loaded car without operating the engine at a noisy and fuel-consuming full throttle.

However, as I said before, most people will like the new transmission just as well, because it is more efficient than either of the older design two-speed automatics of Ford's chief competitors, and because it will sell at a very low price.

Summing Up: I found the '59 Ford a well-balanced and well-behaved car —one that was more relaxing to drive and live with than any in its class, and one which has no annoying faults to sour your driving and owning pleasure.

While its competition has gone in for way-out design and gadgety features, Ford has quietly come up with the well-rounded winner. ●

FORD CHECK LIST

5 CHECKS MEAN TOP RATING IN ITS PRICE CLASS

Category	Comment	Rating
PERFORMANCE	Ford acceleration, climbing and cruising are very good with both "standard" powerplants, the 145-hp six and the 200-hp, 292 cu. in. V-8. New, two-speed Ford-O-Matic is the best performer and the lowest-priced of the non-premium price automobiles.	✔✔ ✔✔
STYLING	The clean-cut, crisp, functional styling of the '59 Ford gets top rating in its class.	✔✔✔ ✔✔
RIDING COMFORT	The '59 Fords have a very high level of riding comfort. Ride is well-controlled yet not too firm, comes close to the best in its class.	✔✔ ✔✔
INTERIOR DESIGN	Ford's passenger compartment is a well-balanced design providing good seating width, headroom, driving position, vision, and the minimum of intereference from transmission housing and drive tunnel.	✔✔✔ ✔✔
ROADABILITY	Ford rates high in roadability, has a stable, steady bohavior in taking sharp curves or rough roads at high speeds. Car will lean in cornering but will not wallow or plunge.	✔✔ ✔✔
EASE OF CONTROL	Here again, Ford rates well up the scale. Steering is easy and precise, but like almost all other cars requires a lot of wheel turning. Brakes are smooth and steady in operation. Power steering is very good.	✔✔ ✔✔
ECONOMY	Ford Six with overdrive or manual transmission will give you the best mileage of the Big Three. The "standard" 292-cu. in. V-8 will equal or better equivalent V-8s.	✔✔✔ ✔✔
SERVICEABILITY	The Six and the two newer V-8s, "332" and "352," are fairly easy to service. The popular 292 V-8 presents more than average inaccessibility. Chassis is one of the easiest to service.	✔✔ ✔✔
WORKMANSHIP	Ford's standards of assembly, fit of trim and operation of mechanical items such as door locks, switches, windshield wipers etc., are above average, and exterior enamelling has improved so the overall "package" rates tops.	✔✔✔ ✔✔
VALUE PER DOLLAR	Ford's clean styling, good ride and handling, well-designed and well-built bodies, plus an excellent choice of engines and transmissions make it the top buy among the "big three".	✔✔✔ ✔✔

FORD OVERALL RATING... 4.5 CHECKS

FORD

For '59

...offers body modifications, an economy engine that runs on regular gas, a less complicated two-speed automatic transmission, and a heavier frame.

FORD FOR 1959 bears a striking resemblance to the '58 models, despite the claims of "all-new sheet metal." Wider bodies, thinner roofline, and more engine and luggage space have made new sheet metal necessary, but like Plymouth, only trim and tail light changes make the exterior body style different from last year. As its competitors, Ford is lower, wider, and heavier, and will probably cost more, although no suggested retail prices had been released as of presstime. Chevrolet and Plymouth are attempting to lower operating costs with more efficient engines and better reliability. Ford has taken a new tack by further detuning engines to operate on regular gas and attempting to hit a happy performance medium by juggling axle ratios. One new development is a low-cost optional automatic transmission.

One thing Ford stylists wanted to be sure of perpetuating were the tail lights. Large as they were in 1958, stylists went back to 1957 for next year's lights. They seem even bigger, set in bowl-shaped housings that look like fluted jello molds. Tail, stop and turn lights all in one unit probably solve a lot of lighting problems for the engineer, but following behind them at night can be very confusing—and often blinding.

FORD DEPENDS A GREAT DEAL on frame support for body strength, and with wider bodies, wider frames are necessary. Compared to the slender X-type Chevy frame, the Ford looks like a bass fiddle. Box section rails have been bowed out almost to the outer tire width and are naturally much heavier. A modified hat section rear crossmember absorbs twist loads and supports rear suspension stresses. Semi-elliptical rear springs, with the axle mounted forward of their center, do the entire job of suspension, alignment, and axle torque twist control, the latter being a difficult job without some sort of trailing arm.

Chevrolet with their rear coil springs have been forced into isolating springing from torque and alignment duties, but Ford is still depending on the springs for all these assignments and it shows up in excessive lean in the corners. The air bag load leveling option, which, unfortunately, has been withdrawn for 1959, probably does as good a job of preventing axle wind-up as it does leveling the car, due to the way it is mounted. One feature that impressed us was the aircraft-type nylon air lines in the air bag system. This is about the toughest stuff there is for holding pressures and providing long life. We may some day see them replacing our hydraulic lines.

A MAJOR CHANGE IN FRONT SUSPENSION is aimed at reducing wheel alignment costs. Slotted holes and serrated washers eliminate cams and shims for adjustment and cut labor time both in assembly and for future alignment checks. Chevy is sticking with their slotted and shim method but Plymouth has a new cam adjuster for front ends for 1959.

In keeping with Chevrolet's optional Posi-traction limited-slip differential, Ford has announced one of their own design as a '59 option. Unlike other competitive units, Ford's is interchangeable with production center sections and provides locking action at all times until slipping action is required, instead of locking only when one wheel is slipping excessively.

It is a shame that Ford has not solved their excessive body lean on sharp cornering because they have a steering system that is a real handler. The recirculating ball system with or without power assist, minimizes lost linkage motion without destroying the positive feel. There is a noticeable, but not objectionable, transmission of road shock in the standard unit. The power option eliminates this and still preserves the feeling that the steering wheel is connected to the front wheels. Chevrolet approaches this but Plymouth is so light one wonders if the wheel is connected to anything.

FORD HAS AN "ALL NEW" FEATURE for 1959 (if you don't look back too many years)—shades of the Model T, it's a two-speed transmission. Striving for economy in manufacture and consumer cost, the new transmission is a two-band, servo-operated automatic in an aluminum case, containing 105 fewer parts, and is 22.8 per cent lighter than a regular Fordomatic. The planetary gear train is composed of two bands, one for low and one for reverse. A multi-disc clutch is for high, which is direct drive. Under a feather-light throttle foot the low-to-high shift occurs at about 18 mph. Under full acceleration our test car was indicating 58 mph before it went into high. Acceleration is very good and standing starts (on a 17 per cent grade) were made without hesitation. Slightly lower rear axle ratios are necessary with the six-cylinder and the 292-cubic-inch V8 for best performance with the two-speed automatic, but engine revolutions in low did not seem excessively high nor did the car labor on steep grades from a standing start. A selector lever allows low-speed operation only and may be used to shift down for engine braking. This unit is a real step toward economy by

FAIRLANE 500 SKYLINER

FAIRLANE 4-DOOR SEDAN

FAIRLANE 500 CONVERTIBLE

FORD for '59

simplification that can be passed on to the consumer in lower initial and maintenance costs.

Ford engineers, like Plymouth, have been playing around with valving on their regular automatic transmissions in an attempt to produce a more lively shift. The Ford Cruise-O-Matic dual range has been adjusted to take better advantage of low-speed torque, and coupled with slightly higher rear-end ratios it performs well with the lower compression 1959 engines. One big advantage of dual range is the ability to use second gear for pulling out of mud, loose gravel or snow, without spinning the wheels, and it provides engine braking for downgrades.

THREE DIFFERENT BRAKE SHOE AREAS appear for the 1959 Fords. The 180.2 square inches, as last year, will be on the regular cars, with station wagons and the retractable hardtop going to 191.4 square inches, and the Thunderbird carrying a big 225.5 square inches. Increasing braking area according to weight is an effective way to solve braking problems, but the highest braking in this case is not on the heaviest vehicle. Almost a hundred pounds lighter and certainly without the space to carry the overload of the station wagon, the Thunderbird has the heaviest brakes. While the braking was adequate in the test cars, we would like to see the added safety of increased braking area on all models, especially the wagons.

A braking test that Ford, Chevy and Plymouth survived very well was one MOTOR TREND made up. Called the "freeway stop," the wheel is cut sharply at speeds between 45 and 55 and the brakes applied hard. A smooth quick stop without the sickening slide into another traffic lane surprised us as well as the proving ground engineers.

UNDER THE HOOD—and believe us, those big V8s with all the power accessories really fill up the space—Ford is offering four powerplants, including a Six. Despite the crowded conditions, the spark plugs are easy to change and the forward-mounted distributor delights mechanics. Lower hood lines have made air cleaners thinner and hastened the adoption of the highly efficient and re-usable paper filter. Ford continues a practice Chevrolet and Plymouth would do well to follow: a direct and positive cool air duct to the carburetor. Underhood temperatures are much the same as radiator temperatures and even higher on hot days. Cooler dense air provides much better mixtures for engines and an appreciable increase in power and gas mileage.

Speaking of mileage, Ford is attempting to achieve economy by setting up their engines to use regular gasoline, which in some states is five cents per gallon cheaper than premium fuels. Close to a dollar a tank in savings is just like more miles per gallon and Ford is going to try it without losing too much in performance. We tooled an engineering car around the Dearborn course and tried some quarter-mile acceleration tests after we found that the 352 engine, driving through a dual-range Cruise-O-Matic, was pulling a 2.91 to 1 rear axle ratio. This was slightly lower than the regular 2.69 to 1 and on regular gas turned the quarter-mile at 80 miles per hour in 17.5 seconds. This engine was driving no power accessories, but the speed and elapsed time are pretty respectable for a so-called de-tuned engine.

IT IS ALMOST IMPOSSIBLE to talk about wider bodies without mentioning frames again. Ford frames now extend out to nearly

COUNTRY SEDAN 4-DOOR STATION WAGON

THUNDERBIRD CONVERTIBLE

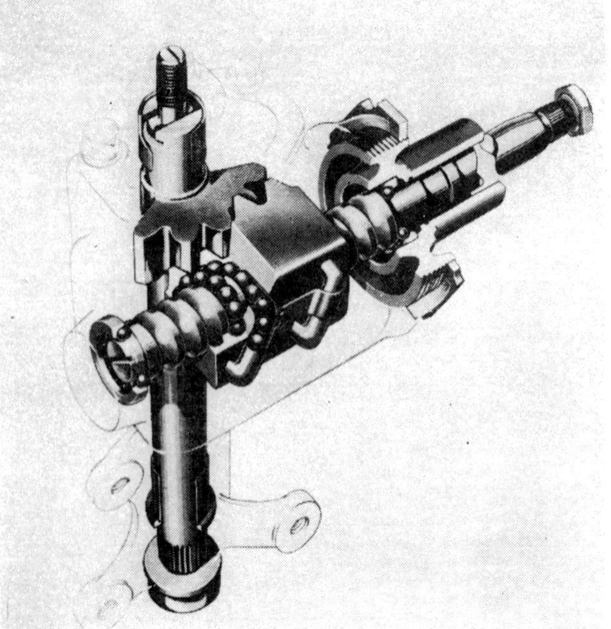

maximum body width. Passengers enjoy more room because they now sit between the frame rails. This allows deeper floorboards, more legroom, and lower center of gravity. The passengers are virtually surrounded by the box section frame and Ford is recalling some of their previous safety program by referring to it as a "guard rail."

Inside these wider bodies, Ford joins with Chevrolet and Plymouth in using more fabrics in combination with plastics in upholstering, producing a greater variety of colors and cooler seat coverings. Production and quality control will be very important to Ford interiors as metal trim strips used on door panels could well lead to ragged edges and sharp corners.

DRIVING COMFORT IS GOOD and increased glass area improves all-around visibility. Rear windows, creeping into rooflines, expose the rear passengers to some pretty uncomfortable sunshine, but Chevrolet and Plymouth are furnishing about equal amounts of excess vitamin A to the shoulders and necks of their passengers. Ford has finally come to the foot-operated parking brake Lower seats and chassis require a little more room when entering or leaving the front seats and the elimination of the brake handle will save a lot of bruised knees.

Soundproofing materials are thicker and are used on more surfaces than ever before, reducing engine and road noises to a mere whisper. However, the wind noise at speed is a howling banshee. Touring the outer speed course at the proving grounds in a Fairlane 500 at speeds from 60 to 85 miles per hour produced wind noises with the windows open, and sizzling whistles with them closed, making normal conversation impossible. Chevrolet and Plymouth body designs bring the side glass sur-

faces closer to the outer body surface, while Ford's recessed panes trap air into noisy turbulence.

Increased demand for air conditioning has the Big Three prepared very well for this option. Ford, in particular, has designed their heating and ventilating system so that much of the ducting can be retained with an air conditioning installation. Dealers can make that change and this package varies slightly from the factory-ordered unit.

INSTRUMENTATION is still more ornamental than functional, with lights for oil and generator and a sweeping speedometer dial with smaller versions of it indicating fuel and temperatures. Ashtray and radio are centered, and the glove compartment is generous. Cowl covering in all models is a low-reflection plastic over non-resilient padding, a nice safety feature followed by Chevrolet and the deluxe model Plymouths. Seating is good, driver visibility with lowered seats and wheel is excellent, and the mechanical seat adjustment works well with driver only but needs a little assist when carrying front seat passengers. Driveshaft tunnels, like all lower 1959 models, are more noticeable, but increased legroom makes them less objectionable.

Engine, power, and accessory items are still on the option list for 1959. You will be able to carry more passengers and more luggage in the new cars, so give yourself and the engineers a break when selecting options. To expect a car to ride as well with one passenger as with six, or to tow a trailer and fill up the luggage space with heavy gear, without taking advantage of load leveling or bigger engines, is just asking too much of engineering. Decide what you need and order it. Ford can supply it.

Handling characteristics smack more of the pickup truck. With only about 1615 lbs. of a total of 3870 (unladen) on the rear wheels, the Ranchero is definitely noseheavy and this shows up in its behavior on the road.

Rear wheels chatter and bounce on rough surfaces and the rear end thus tends to drift when cornering at even moderate speeds on poor roads. This is not so noticeable on smooth pavement but the light feeling of the rear end is still there. With enough weight in the bed to give better front-rear weight balance, the Ranchero is superior to most of the standard Ford passenger cars, however.

(It should be noted, too, that the Ranchero tested was equipped with the heaviest engine-transmission combination offered. With a lighter V-8 or the ohv-6 and manual or two-speed automatic transmission the forward weight bias would be less pronounced and handling correspondingly improved.)

Performance of the test Ranchero was surprisingly good; especially since it had a 2.69 rear axle and such a small percentage of total weight on the driving wheels. Standing starts were made by revving the engine to about 2000 rpm (more than that caused wheelspin) with brakes on and transmission in low range. Manual shifts to second permitted turning higher rpm in low than if the transmission was permitted to shift automatically and resulted in optimum acceleration.

Fuel economy was quite good considering the size of the engine and the weight of the vehicle, along with the

RANCHERO ROAD TEST

PIONEER of the plush pickups, Ford's Ranchero is now in its third year of existence and has established that there is a market—if a limited one—for this type of vehicle.

The Ranchero continues to be, as it has from the start, a combination of passenger car, station wagon and pickup truck. It is built on a station wagon chassis, has a sedan-like cab interior or passenger compartment and carries a long and roomy truck bed at rear.

Styling of Rancheros has been very pleasing since their introduction in the 1957 model year and the 1959 version is no exception. There is nothing cobbled or makeshift about the de luxe pickup's appearance; the design is well integrated and attractive—even more so than companion passenger cars, to some eyes!

These good looks and sedan-type comfort are obviously the two biggest assets the Ranchero has, aside from its utility value as a light hauler.

Ride is a bit firmer than that of Ford sedans, but much softer and smoother than in conventional pickups. In fact, with seating position and seat design so closely resembling standard passenger cars, it is possible to forget you are riding in a truck until you look back and see the pickup bed.

PERFORMANCE of the Ford Ranchero was surprisingly good. Fuel economy was quite satisfactory considering size of engine and weight of the vehicle.

sedan-type comfort are Ranchero's big assets

fact that it was driven rather hard with no particular attempt made to get maximum miles per gallon.

Quality was about on a par with standard 1959 Ford passenger cars. There were a few flaws—rough edges on the horn ring and mismatching of the stainless pickup bed trim molding with that of the tailgate molding, for example. In general, however, detail finish was substantially better than that of most conventional pickup trucks.

The interior was fully as attractive as that seen in most passenger cars.

The two-section seat back is hinged, like that in Ford's two-door station wagon, and folds forward to provide access to a storage compartment behind the seat. The spare tire is mounted at right and there is space for several suitcases in the left side. There are also small storage wells under the seats. The seats themselves and the seating positions are very close to those in two-door station wagons.

All-round vision is at least equal to 1959 Ford cars and the instrument panel is reasonably well laid out. It's easy to read all instruments without taking your eyes off the road for more than a split-second.

In judging the Ranchero as purely a utility vehicle, it is obvious that it is not capable of handling many of the more rugged hauling duties for which more prosaic half-ton pickups are used.

The Ranchero has much softer springs, for one thing—though this could be remedied to some extent by use of Air Lift inflatable rubber bags. Its six-inch minimum ground clearance is also a bit

RANCHERO is designed more for those who need or want a pickup-type vehicle for light hauling duty only, and want passenger car riding comfort and attractive styling, too.

on the low side for hauling on really rough surfaces.

Since the bed has rounded corners and uses a station wagon tailgate, the rear opening for loading material into the bed is not full-width. In addition, rear wheel housings extend into the bed quite a way so that the full width of the bed can't be utilized over its entire length.

Nor would the extremely low numerical rear axle ratio in the test Ranchero be the best choice for really heavy hauling, although the engine is powerful enough to compensate for that in most cases where this vehicle would be practical.

There is little doubt, however, that few buyers will choose a Ranchero primarily for utility purposes. Standard pickups will fill those needs for much less money.

The Ranchero is designed for those who need or want a pickup-type vehicle for light hauling duty only, and want passenger car riding comfort and attractive styling too.

It is the ideal solution for those who need a pickup in their work and can't afford a second family car. (The big advantage Rancheros have over station wagons in this respect is lower price—some $250 or more less than comparably equipped wagons in most cases.)

Rancheros also have great appeal for gentlemen farmers, outdoor hobbyists

and as tow cars for competition machines.

Limits of the market for plush pickups will be probed further this year because of introduction of Chevrolet's El Camino, but it looks very much like these vehicles are attractive to enough buyers to insure them a permanent future. ●

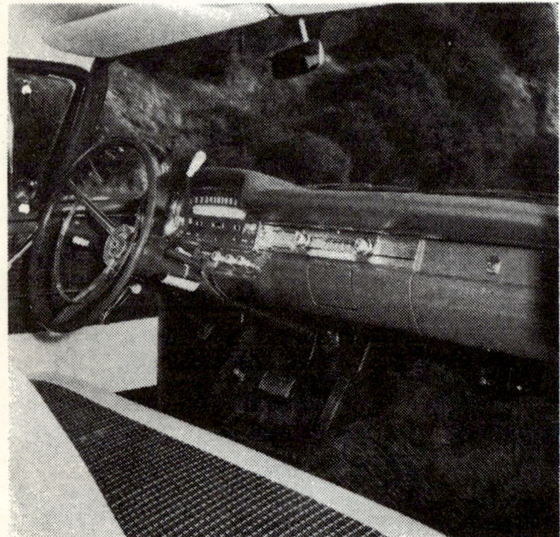

INSTRUMENT PANEL is well laid out and vision is equal to '59 Ford cars. Interior was as attractive as that of passenger cars.

Test Data

Test Car: 1959 Ford Ranchero
Body Type: pickup
Basic Price: $2287
Engine: ohv V-8
Carburetion: single four-barrel
Displacement: 352 cubic inches
Bore & Stroke: 4.0 x 3.5 inches
Compression Ratio: 9.6-to-1
Horsepower: 300 @ 4600 rpm
Horsepower per cubic inch: .85
Torque: 380 lbs.-ft @ 2800 rpm
Test Weight: 3780 lbs. without driver
Weight Distribution: 57% on front wheels
Power-Weight Ratio: 12.6 lbs. per hp
Transmission: Cruise-O-Matic three-speed automatic with torque converter
Rear Axle Ratio: 2.69-to-1
Steering: 5 turns lock-to-lock
Dimensions: overall length 208 inches, width 76.6, height 57.8, wheelbase 118, tread 59 front and 56.4 rear
Tires: 8.00x14
Gas Mileage: 13.2 city, 15.5 highway
Speedometer Error: Indicated 30, 45 and 60 mph are actual 27, 40 and 54 respectively
Acceleration: 0-30 mph in 4.4 seconds, 0-45 in 6.5 and 0-60 mph in 9.9 seconds